Postmodern Contentions

MAPPINGS: Society / Theory / Space

A Guilford Series

Editors

MICHAEL DEAR
University of Southern California

DEREK GREGORY
University of British Columbia

NIGEL THRIFT
University of Bristol

POSTMODERN CONTENTIONS
Epochs, Politics, Space
*John Paul Jones III, Wolfgang Natter,
and Theodore R. Schatzki*, Editors

THE POWER OF MAPS
Denis Wood (with John Fels)

APPROACHING HUMAN GEOGRAPHY
An Introduction to Contemporary Theoretical Debates
Paul Cloke, Chris Philo, and David Sadler

Postmodern Contentions

Epochs, Politics, Space

Edited by
JOHN PAUL JONES III
WOLFGANG NATTER
THEODORE R. SCHATZKI

Committee on Social Theory
University of Kentucky

THE GUILFORD PRESS
New York London

© 1993 The Guilford Press
A Division of Guilford Publications, Inc.
72 Spring Street, New York, NY 10012

Printed in the United States of America

This book is printed on acid-free paper.

Last digit is print number: 9 8 7 6 5 4 3 2 1

Library of Congress Cataloging-in-Publication Data

Postmodern contentions: epochs, politics, space / edited by John Paul
    Jones III, Wolfgang Natter, Theodore R. Schatzki.
        p.   cm. — (Mappings)
    Includes bibliographical references and index.
    ISBN 0-89862-494-0. — ISBN 0–89862–495–9 (pbk.)
    1. Social sciences—Philosophy.   2. Postmodernism—Social aspects.
    3. Postmodernism—Political aspects.   4. Civilization, Modern—20th
    century.   I. Jones, John Paul.   II. Natter, Wolfgang.
    III. Schatzki, Theodore R.   IV. Series.
    H61.P614   1993   92-30077
    300' .1—dc20   CIP

Contributors

RICHARD J. BERNSTEIN is Vera Luce Professor of Philosophy at the New School for Social Research, New York, New York.

FRED DALLMAYR is Professor of Government at Notre Dame University, Notre Dame, Indiana.

JOHN PAUL JONES III is Associate Professor of Geography and member of the Committee on Social Theory, University of Kentucky, Lexington, Kentucky.

CATHERINE LUTZ is Associate Professor of Anthropology, University of North Carolina, Chapel Hill.

WOLFGANG NATTER is Assistant Professor of Germanic Languages and Literatures and member of the Committee on Social Theory, University of Kentucky, Lexington, Kentucky.

THEODORE R. SCHATZKI is Associate Professor of Philosophy and member of the Committee on Social Theory, University of Kentucky, Lexington, Kentucky.

EDWARD W. SOJA is Professor of Urban Planning and Associate Dean, Graduate School of Architecture and Urban Planning, University of California, Los Angeles, California.

ERNEST J. YANARELLA is Professor of Political Science and member of the Committee on Social Theory, University of Kentucky, Lexington, Kentucky.

Preface

The impulse that led to the contributions assembled in this volume has its institutional origin in the attempt of a group of faculty members from the University of Kentucky to explore the multidisciplinary nature of social theory (general thought about social life and its comprehension). In the spring of 1989, a Committee on Social Theory was formed to develop a research and teaching program in this area. Its initial activity was a joint graduate seminar/public lecture series examining key issues in contemporary social thought. The success of this multidisciplinary exploration led the Committee to envision an annual spring semester graduate seminar/public lecture series combination which each year would focus on one problem area of broad critical import in contemporary social thought and result in the publication of a collection of essays combining the public lectures of visiting scholars with essays written by the University of Kentucky faculty who jointly taught the seminar. This volume represents the inaugural installment in the series.

The Committee invited scholars to Lexington to address what, from their disciplinary vantage points, appear as key aspects of the constellation suggested by the rubric "Reassessing Modernity and Postmodernity." Their contributions to this volume reflect interactions with the faculty and students participating in the graduate seminar. The essays of the faculty, on the other hand, were nourished by semester-long interactions on these debates with students, visiting scholars, and one another in a variety of formal and informal forums. This volume thus departs from other interdisciplinary collections, which either compile conference papers or commission special works.

As with any institutionally based effort, we have the pleasure of thanking a number of key persons without whose assistance and encouragement the project as a whole and this book would not have been possible. Initial financial support for the establishment of the Committee on

Social Theory came from the College of Arts and Sciences and the Graduate School. The Committee's more recent activities, including this year's volume, were supported through financial assistance provided by the University of Kentucky's Multidisciplinary Feasibility and Assessment Program (MFAP). We would like to thank the former Vice-Presidents for Research and Graduate Studies, Len Peters and Wimberly Royster, as well as Robert Hemenway, Chancellor of the Lexington Campus. We also bear a special debt to our MFAP liaison, Daniel R. Reedy, Dean of the Graduate School, for his support and advice.

A more general thanks is due to the twenty-four other members of the Committee on Social Theory and to the students participating in the seminars. Their enthusiasm for these efforts is gratefully acknowledged.

Contents

Postmodern Contentions

1

"Post"-ing Modernity

JOHN PAUL JONES III
WOLFGANG NATTER
THEODORE R. SCHATZKI

"Postmodernism," for all its multi-accentuality, has acquired undeniable force in contemporary theory (not to mention popular culture). It seems to summarize the diffuse senses of "afterness" that have arisen in many areas of academic endeavor. This convergence has taken place as scholars in the humanities and social sciences espy shifts in contemporary social life and in the procedures and concepts employed to comprehend it. In many eyes, these shifts add up not merely to a transformation, but to a disjuncture between the here and now and what preceded it. Some see this sea change as the advent of a new economic era marked by the globalization of capitalism. For others, it is the exhaustion and unmasking of Enlightenment concepts of self, progress, and rationality. For still others, it is the abandonment of various scientistic methodologies in social investigation. For scholars of these ilks, "post"-ing modernity indicates an essential break from modernist worlds, concepts, and methods.

Other accounts, however, see these shifts through the lens of continuity. Such changes then take on the character of developments which are linked to already existing concepts and states of affairs, or are versions thereof. Thus, the postmodern economy is but the most recent outcome of capitalism's historic annihilation of space; contemporary ethnic, feminist, and gay politics represent not the abandonment, but rather deeper appreciations of Enlightenment ideals of autonomy and equality; and most contemporary nonscientistic methodologies take up ideas first formulated in the late nineteenth century. For scholars of this persuasion, "post"-ing modernity means recognizing the new as the latest in an evolving series of modernities.

1

A common feature of the contributions in this collection is a stress on the "sameness within difference" characteristic of postmodern trends in relation to modern antecedents. Indeed, we believe that postmodernism is but the most recent chapter in the evolving historical identity of a general school of thought. The theses typically cited as characteristic of postmodernity are part of a wider cluster of ideas and emphases, different versions and subsets of which have been propounded by each of a line of prominent European thinkers stretching from the late eighteenth century to the present. In this introduction, we will combat the ahistoricism evident in much celebration of the postmodern by examining the anticipation of postmodern ideas in late-eighteenth- and early-nineteenth-century Germany, a "place" of study which for good reason has become a laboratory of social investigation. In particular, we will document similarities between postmodern themes and ideas that emerged at the origin of the school of thought alluded to above. In addition, we will show that similar socioeconomic forces led to the rise of both bodies of ideas. While our principle aim in juxtaposing the originary and current phases of a general school of thought is to unearth continuities, we will also attend to differences between the two.

There is no ready name for the school of thought that originated in the late eighteenth century and today takes the form of postmodernity. It embraces a range of thinkers too broad to capture with current isms. The contours of its identity were diagnosed, however, in a remarkable and still insufficiently appreciated article, "Conservative Thought," written by Karl Mannheim in 1927.[1] According to Mannheim, the rise of modern rationalism in the late eighteenth century, together with the ascending bureaucracy, bourgeoisie, and revolutionary fervor that accompanied it, forced a hitherto unreflective mode of experiencing and approaching the world (traditionalism) to become reflective and to articulate itself conceptually. The resulting systems of ideas Mannheim dubs "conservative thought" not only because their basic intention was preservation in the face of the aforementioned social forces animated by rationalism, but also because they represented the worldview and mode of thought of conservatism *qua* political force struggling against administrative bureaucracy and the bourgeoisie. Prominent conservative thinkers discussed by Mannheim include Edmund Burke, Adam H. Müller, Leopold von Ranke, F. C. von Savigny, Justus Möser, "Madam" J. Stahl, and, in certain regards, Georg Wilhelm Friedrich Hegel.

Mannheim contrasts rationalistic and conservative thought through a series of oppositions. Whereas rationalism stresses abstraction, generality, and universality, conservatism emphasizes concreteness, local particularity, and diversity. Whereas conservatism highlights holism as well as qualitative and/or "physiognomic" understanding, rationalism underscores atomism along with quantitative and/or "constructive" understanding. Moreover, while rationalism embodies a temporal understanding of history and seeks to grasp the actual via ahistorical norms, conservatism entertains a spatial understanding of history and seeks to understand norms via their embeddedness in actual history. Other oppositions characterizing conservatism versus rationalism include the irrationality versus rationality of human reality, the historical embeddedness versus autonomy of reason, varying local versus universal truths, and becoming versus being. The affinities between postmodern and conservative thought should be evident even from this brief list.

Mannheim distinguishes both a feudalistic and a romantic version of conservative thought. Unfortunately, he fails to explore fully the crucial contribution made by the German romantics, more specifically, early Jena romanticism, to this mode of thinking. Examining these romantics in greater detail will enable us to uncover precursors of postmodern themes in early-nineteenth-century German thought beyond those just mentioned, and to deepen thereby Mannheim's diagnosis of the origins of contemporary thought.

In the final three years of the eighteenth century and in the wake of the French Revolution, a remarkable group of thinkers known collectively as the Jena romantics combined their efforts to produce texts which thematized and staged a host of epistemological and political questions presaging issues familiar again in the "age of postmodernism." Equally attentive to the political convulsions associated with the French Revolution and its terror, as well as to the "eidaesthetic" challenge bequeathed by Kant's third *Critique*, the circle associated with the journal *Athenaeum* began to reconsider the relationship between aesthetics and philosophy. That the concepts of reason, unlike the concepts of understanding, do not lend themselves to presentation, had led Kant to the conception that "symbolic" approximation is the most adequate form of presentation to which these concepts may attain. In turn, this crisis of presentation, by effectively depriving the subject of its being-subject, reduced the subject to little more than a logical necessity, a purely regulatory idea of the unity of its representations.

The crisis of presentation provided an initial context for the development of idealism and romanticism alike. As formulated by Philippe Lacaoue-Labarthe and Jean-Luc Nancy, "this problematic of the subject unpresentable to itself, [and with it] this eradication of all substantialism"[2] becomes the most difficult and perhaps insoluble question of romanticism. This crisis of the subject, or in a more postmodern formulation, the "death of the subject," will resonate with myriad implications for art, philosophy, morality, and politics (the unity of which was designated by the romantics as "literature"). Such resonance permits Lacoue-Labarthe and Nancy the judgment that "we still belong to the era it opened up." So-called modernity, and we suggest by extension postmodernity, "has done little more than rehash romanticism's discoveries."[3]

Romanticism, however, proved even to its theoreticians to be as elusive and as polyphonous as the postmodern does to its chroniclers today. Dante, Cervantes, and Shakespeare were taken to be as fully "romantic" as the romantics' contemporary, Goethe. The term, moreover, connoted the novel (in both senses), the vulgar (the secular), love, the sentimental, Roman civilization, and medieval romances and ballads. It most pertinently came to mean the attempt to create a synthesis of ancient and modern in which the history of previous reflection was self-critically employed as an operating principle. Thus, although "romanticism" also centrally implied for Friedrich Schlegel and his circle the production of something entirely new, historical consciousness and reference became a fundamental element in the production of the new or modern. This impulse is already evidenced by the choice of key terms central to their thought; the romantics did not invent the terms "romantic" or "literature" but chose instead to infuse these already existing expressions with additional, synthetic meanings.

Jena romanticism's mixing of literary genres, fusing of poetry and prose, and attempt to syncretize criticism, philosophy, science, history, and art, along with its tendency toward the progressive and infinite, led to the production of varied forms of texts whose penultimate expression was the fragment. Even though the romantics viewed fragments as parts of wider systems, this form not only communicated but also represented the nature of language and communication as indirect, imperfect, and dialectical. In discussing incomprehensibility as a necessary element of all "literature," Novalis and Schlegel rejected easy, immediate comprehension as unproductive and delusive. Their fragments were designed neither to determine solutions nor to give final results, but instead to portray the "author's mind" in an activity which, in remaining inherently uncompleted, called for the active participation of the reader in the creation of that future which the fragment was meant to suggest. This recognition of the reader's role in generating meaning anticipates similar conceptions animating contemporary reader response theory. Contemporary theory will also recognize the questioning by the Jena romantics of assumptions about individual authorship and originality,[4] both through their practice of multiple or unidentified authorship of texts and through their reference to preceding genre traditions, which were understood as enabling writing.

The very postmodernlike stances of resistance against closure in the fragment and against totalization or the apparent unity and perfection of the closed, consistent system, are designed to represent (in the sense of *Darstellung*, not *Mitteilung*) the necessity of perpetual play and cancellation, which becomes nothing less (as romantic irony) than the capacity for self-consciousness and self-criticism. Irony invalidates any formulation or representation as an adequate expression of the infinity of nature or totality. "Irony," wrote Schlegel in his *Ideas*, "is the clear consciousness of eternal agility, of an infinitely teeming chaos."[5] The move from the "self-consuming artifact" such irony calls for to the pastiche identified by Fredric Jameson as constitutive of postmodernism's style is but one further indication supporting our judgment that we still belong to the era opened up with romanticism.

Mannheim, given his sociological interests in "Conservative Thought," does not consider these eidaesthetic impulses that ensue from romanticism's valorization of the aesthetic realm as the arena in which the sensible actualization of the Idea is thought possible. These impulses nonetheless foreshadow postmodernity's emphasis on the death of the subject, the crisis of representation, and the role of the reader in meaning. Mannheim does, however, supplement his analysis of the origins of the mode of thought which today appears as postmodernism by showing how a cadre of mid-nineteenth-century European thinkers advanced ideas of a "conservative" mold. Near the conclusion of his article, moreover, he speculates that, in his own day, life-philosophy is the school of thought carrying forward the banner of conservative thought. Three things will be evident to those conversant with the last century of German and French philosophy. First, Mannheim's comment about life-philosophy is dead on. Thinkers such as Nietzsche, Dilthey, Spengler, early Heidegger, even Simmel, Gadamer, and Wittgenstein, are conservative in the ontological-epistemological (but not necessarily political) sense Mannheim gives to this term. Second, although Mannheim does not focus on rationalism in his article, it is evident that, just as conservative thought has a legacy extending beyond its late-eighteenth- and early-nineteenth-century origins, so too does rationalistic thought. In the continental context, for instance, Marxist thought, including in this century Lukács, Gramsci, Horkheimer, and today Jürgen Habermas and Albrecht Wellmer, carry forward to varying degrees and in various combinations rationalist emphases upon abstraction, generality, universality, constructive understanding, the rationality of reality, the autonomy of reason, the temporal understanding of history, and the attempt to understand the actual via ahistorical norms.

Third, postmodernism maintains significant affinities with "conservative" thought. Although Mannheim's article was written more than sixty years ago, the categories of conservative thought he discusses often apply equally to postmodern thought. Like the ontologies and epistemologies of the life-philosophers, those of postmodern thinkers emphasize combinations of concreteness, particularity, diversity, holism, becoming, the irrationality of reality, embedded reason, and the like. Moreover, many of the other theses commonly taken as definitive of postmodernity, for instance, the death of the subject and an openness to alterity, are versions of one or more of the central ideas of conservative thought. Opposition to the metaphysical subject, for instance, results in part from the conservative stress on the historical embeddedness of human life along with its opposition to placing the origins and sources of human existence outside of history. Openness to alterity, meanwhile, can be understood in part as an instance of the conservative acknowledgment of particularity, diversity, and local truths. A wide range of "postmodern" thinkers, including Foucault, Lyotard, Derrida, Kristeva, and Castoriadis, can be profitably viewed as contemporary "conservative" writers in Mannheim's ontological-epistemological sense of that term.[6]

As we have seen, moreover, many postmodern theses are present in the work of romantic thinkers and writers. We suggest, therefore, that romanticism is an absent ghost haunting most contemporary accounts of postmodernism. Consider as an example the analysis of Frederic Jameson. The romantic effort to create a new mythology for a centerless era may be compared with his description of postmodernism as "an effort to take the temperature of the age without instruments and in a situation in which we are not even sure there is so coherent a thing as an 'age' or zeitgeist or 'system' or 'current situation' any longer." Parallel to romanticism's incorporation of the past in its creation of the new, moreover, Jameson emphasizes the survival of "residual modernist values into full postmodernism."[7] Jameson's neglect of romanticism in his genealogy of postmodernity is surprising given romanticism's aestheticization of cognition *and* Jameson's collapse of the cultural/aesthetic with the economic.

A further commonality between early conservative thought and contemporary postmodern thought concerns their dependence on contemporaneous social contexts. In a manner reminiscent of some commentators on postmodernity, Mannheim carefully situates the crystallization of conservative thought within economic (and political) upheavals taking place in the late eighteenth and early nineteenth centuries. In particular, he attributes the appearance of rationalism to the development of a new economic system centered on commodity production, which replaced traditional-feudal subsistence production. (It is also connected with the rise of bureaucratic organization.) Mannheim sees the onset of capitalist production and its attendant social relations as both leading to and signaling the emergence of quantitative as opposed to qualitative views of nature and of society. For instance, the supplantation of qualitatively based use value by quantitatively based exchange value gave rise to an abstract attitude that pervaded all human experience. The "other man," Mannheim asserts following Marx, was increasingly experienced only indirectly as all labor power was reduced to a commodity.

For Mannheim, the "mental climate of the age" was differentiated into styles of thought reflecting cleavages among socioeconomic groups. (Such styles are perpetuated and transformed in a manner analogous to the way artists conform to and redefine prevailing stylistic genres.) Thus, while the emerging bourgeoisie adopted a style of thought that analyzed the world rationally, systematically, and abstractly, the nobility, peasantry, and petite bourgeoisie generated, for largely defensive purposes, the intuitive, qualitative, and concrete forms of thought which rationalism repudiated. The proletariat, meanwhile, having no tradition outside of capitalism, aligned itself with rationalist thought (in the interests of overthrowing capitalism through the efficient bureaucratization of a social movement), although it also borrowed elements from conservative thinking. Finally, Mannheim describes how conservative thought ebbs and flows in the nineteenth century in response to the dynamics of politics, as the same ideas are deployed in different contexts to formulate different social programs. Thus, certain elements of "conservative" thought find their way at different times into left wing, anticapitalist political programs.

Some commentators today similarly situate postmodern currents within contemporary transformations of the capitalist economy. Just as postmodernity in the intellectual sphere is marked by fragmentation, discontinuity, alterity, locality, and difference, so too contemporary capitalism is described as entering a new phase variously characterized as "postindustrial," "post-Fordist," "late," "disorganized," or "flexible." These terms are employed to refer to an entirely new, but nonetheless capitalist, set of social and economic relations involving labor processes, firm organization, state relations, and geographic mobility. It is within the matrix of this economy that some authors choose to locate their explanations of postmodern thought and culture. In doing so, they, like Mannheim, assert an overarching sociological explanation, in this case in opposition to a particular postmodern picture of a world whose complexity and interconnectedness cannot be grasped in generalities.

For instance, David Harvey argues that a central feature of the contemporary economy is capital's success in overcoming time-space disjunctures in production and consumption.[8] Today's international capital has learned to produce at the lowest possible cost (using Third World labor), while at the same time shortening the time-space gap between production and consumption, by developing new systems of transportation (so efficient that even low-value commodities such as beer are now traded globally), global financial networks (operating twenty-four hours a day), and international telecommunications (which dispatch orders with such rapidity that response times to new designs and marketing arrangements are nearly instantaneous).

Harvey claims that these economic developments have given rise to postmodern thought and culture by transforming the experience of space and time. His analysis is most developed *vis-à-vis* postmodern culture. One indication that transformations of this sort lie at the heart of contemporary cultural shifts is the loss of historic continuity so often associated with the postmodern.[9] For instance, works of art are said to so juxtapose references to multiple earlier genres that they catapult themselves outside time and space. As a consequence, they parody any attempt at interpretation, offering instead only irony, schizophrenia, and indeterminacy. Meanwhile, postmodern architecture's appropriation of the past in neo-vernacular design is said to be not so much a resurrection of history, as a plundering of it via the incorporation of whatever elements are necessary to create an eclectic present. According to Harvey, temporal disengagements of these sorts act against interpretation and critical judgment, leaving postmodern cultural artifacts devoid of depth or meaning. Thus, postmodern invocations of fragmentation, diversity, and particularity are correlates in the realm of thought to the widespread appearance of pastiche, depthlessness, and, moreover, a disorganized urban morphology.

Both Mannheim and Harvey locate the link between the intellectual and socioeconomic spheres in experience. In Harvey's case, it is the experience of space and time, while in Mannheim's it is one of opportunities for or threats to socioeconomic well-being. In this way, we witness how the appearances of related bodies of thought at different moments in history are underlain by parallel socioeconomic transformations.

Of course, we do not mean to suggest that either contemporary postmodern and early conservative thought or their determinants are the same. The differences between capitalism in its early and contemporary stages are too obvious and numerous to enumerate. Moreover, "conservative" thinkers of all ilks are linked only by family resemblances. The central differences between postmodern and early strains of conservative thought are fivefold. First, contemporary versions have abandoned the themes of irrationality, subjectivity, and will characteristic of life-philosophical variants. Second, postmodern opposition to the metaphysical

subject not only arises from a general suspicion of all ahistorical postula-
tions, but also represents one entry among others in a widespread dismantling by twentieth-century Western thought of the Cartesian conception of the human subject. Third, postmodern openness to alterity, indeed its recognition of diversity, heterogeneity, and particularity, follow
in the wake of a range of twentieth-century liberation movements that
have sought to free women, racial and ethnic minorities, and Third
World peoples from oppression and exploitation. Had it not been for
these real-life struggles, theoretical acknowledgments of "otherness"
might not have advanced beyond the stark confrontations of Self and
Other portrayed in a spate of World War II–era existential tracts.[10]
Fourth, reflecting their valorization of diverse groups and viewpoints, the
form of politics most typically advocated by postmoderns is local struggle
against systemic and hegemonic domination. With its slogan, "Think
globally and act locally," the ecological movement in Europe and the
United States is a prime example. This form of politics resembles the
defense of traditional communities (*Gemeinschaften*) against centralized
and bureaucratized authority found scattered through the writings of the
original conservative think-ers. But not only are autonomy and equality,
instead of preservation, the basic values animating most postmodern politics, but the disassociation of groups from local communities and traditions, wrought by socio-economic developments during the intervening
period of time, means that local politics for virtually all postmoderns has
lost it organic rootedness.

A fifth difference between postmodernism and earlier conservative
schools lies in its entanglements with feminism.[11] Many of the ideas and
tendencies promulgated by feminism during the last three decades or so
are shared with postmodernism. Examples include challenges to prevailing notions of objectivity; exposure of the link between knowledge and
power; opposition to autonomous reason; abandonment of foundationalism; and sensitivity to difference, particularity, and plurality. At the same
time, many feminists have been wary of postmodernism, chiefly because
other postmodern tenets appear to undercut or at least to weaken the
specific political mission animating their work. For instance, some postmoderns are, or are taken to be, either skeptical about the possibility of
knowing the world or advocates of some form of relativism. Feminism
qua practical project must eschew such positions lest it lose one of its
chief weapons: the uncovering of actual oppression, exploitation, and
inequality. Similarly, postmodern challenges to the notion of the subject,
along with postmodern deconstructions of transcultural and transcommu-
nity categories such as gender, appear to many feminists to undermine
the supposition that there is something specific for feminism to liberate.

Whether these and other fears are warranted, feminism is nonetheless deeply entwined with the ways of thinking called postmodern. Its particular object and mission have led to important contemporary invocations of alterity, particularity, locality, difference, diversity, and sociohistorical embeddedness.

As we mentioned at the outset, "postmodernism" has come to signal in a multitude of ways. Rather than impose a unitary meaning upon the term, one strength of this volume is to display some of the occasionally overlapping, occasionally conflicting usages that "postmodernism" has acquired as it has entered the social sciences and humanities. Readers who have hitherto been puzzled to hear their discipline's postmodernism described in an unfamiliar way, may discover some of the reasons why. Despite differences partly attributable to disparate disciplinary vantage points, the chapters in this collection are conjoined by three features. First, their understandings and discussions of modernity and postmodernity proceed by reference to common reference points and texts. Second, each provides insights into the "sameness within difference" characteristic of postmodernity in relation to modernity. And third, the question of postmodern politics figures in each.

The first feature is of course not unique to this volume, but characterizes discussions of modernity/postmodernity generally. It has become impossible to write on this topic without referring to figures such as Foucault, Habermas, Lyotard, Heidegger, Derrida, Nietzsche, Freud, and Adorno. Perhaps these writers are cited and discussed so often because they have offered the most intriguing and far-reaching defenses and/or critiques of Enlightenment thought, the most significant context within which contemporary thought operates. However that may be, these authors' texts serve both as a common framework and as sources of possible convergence among the disciplines concerned with social life, thus opposing the tendency toward specialization so powerful in the twentieth century. Of course, varied horizons of expectation and significance perpetuated by disciplinary demarcations lead interpreters in different disciplines to interpret the above thinkers in disparate ways. This variance too is demonstrated in the present volume.

The second feature, discussed at length earlier in this introduction, is the theme of continuity between modernity and postmodernity. For Fred Dallmayr, postmodernity is primarily an internal critique of modernist ontological and epistemological concepts, an idea related to Ernest Yanarella's updating of Gramsci's modernist political concepts with Derridean postmodern ontology. While Catherine Lutz argues that men control canon formation in both modernity and postmodernity, Ted

Schatzki suggests that postmodern political thought is usually animated by Enlightenment values. Edward Soja sees in postmodernism the latest in a series of economic and conceptual transformations taking place in the interval between the Enlightenment and the present, each of which is a "postmodernity" in relation to a previously reigning "modernity." And Wolfgang Natter and John Paul Jones, in an historical analysis of literary theory and geography, demonstrate that, because disciplinary conventions constrain possibilities of authorized inquiry, it is impossible to construct a postmodern disciplinary knowledge absent of its modernist precursors. Together, these contributions reveal some of the varied dimensions in which postmodernity is an outgrowth of modernity. Richard Bernstein deepens this analysis by characterizing Derrida and Habermas as two irreducible and ineliminable sides of an intellectual climate widespread in the humanities and arts today, thereby implying that neither modernity nor postmodernity can exist without the other.

The third linking feature, the question of postmodern politics, has increasingly come into focus of late. What for many people is so unsettling about postmodern developments in thought and culture is the fear that, instead of preserving a liberating, perhaps utopian impulse, their fragmentation, pastiche, and particularity may disconnect the postmodern from any possibility of a meaningful political project (as suggested by the expression "the end of ideology"). Our contributors argue that this fear is unfounded. They examine political processes in two domains, the civic and the academic. Yanarella, Schatzki, Bernstein, and Dallmayr all suggest that postmodernity can lend support to Enlightenment projects in the public sphere, though they have different understandings of what these projects are and how postmodernity can contribute to them. Yanarella sees in Derrida's form of critique an important tool for vigilance in the face of forces which would foreclose the democratic process. Bernstein concurs, arguing that Derrida's emphasis upon openness to alterity not only alerts us to the ever-present danger of hegemonic political gestures and actions, but also complements Habermas's enthusiastic faith in reason and signals that democratic politics must do justice to both universality and particularity, sameness and difference. According to Schatzki, because postmodern theses imply that political ideals cannot be supported by argument or reason and do not intrinsically support any particular political program, postmodern thinkers such as Foucault and Lyotard can diverge in their allegiances to Enlightenment values. And Dallmayr concludes by suggesting that, despite appearances to the contrary, postmodernity is congruent with a democratic ethos, particularly that of radical democracy.

Lutz, Natter and Jones, and Soja deal most forcefully with the politics of the academy as it has impacted the disciplinary organization of knowledge. Lutz examines how political tensions within anthropology affect publishing practices, and how the demise of colonialism together with the rise of self-determination in the Third World helped bring about a crisis of representation, changes in anthropological self-conceptions, and the advent of postmodern anthropology. Natter and Jones critique geography's scientistic self-understanding through the theories of representation articulated by Foucault, Derrida, and Hayden White, which stress that the production of academic knowledge is a politicized process. Soja, finally, connects both forms of politics in a critique of overly historicized social theory which, in preventing the social disciplines from understanding the spatiality inherent in social life, limited theorists' capacity to identify effective paths of social transformation.

The organization of the volume reflects the above concerns. Dallmayr opens with an overview of the terrain implicated by the label, "modernity/postmodernity." Schatzki then discusses the work of two of the premier figures carving out this intellectual landscape: Foucault and Lyotard. Following this, Yanarella brings Derrida, a third such figure, to bear on democratic processes. Bernstein then concludes the volume's examination of civic politics by relating the tasks of democratic theory to the binary oppositions standardly employed in analyses of modernity/postmodernity. Soja's critique of historicism and its relation to material conditions serves as a transition to the contributions of Lutz and Natter and Jones, both of which consider the disciplinary organization of knowledge. More detailed descriptions of the individual chapters follow.

In the volume's opening chapter, Fred Dallmayr's ideal-typical overview carefully notes why the categories modernity and postmodernity can never be neatly segregated. There is room for multiple overlaps and reciprocal borrowings. In his view, the prefix *post-* in the term *postmodernism* does not simply designate a temporal annex or succession, but rather an internal happening, a critique from within. The prefix reveals, as does his chapter, "the inner complexity and ambiguity of modern consciousness and rationality." For Dallmayr, postmodernity is not the initiation of a general war of all against all, but rather a "radical relationism" in which no part can claim absolute primacy or supremacy.

Ted Schatzki begins by arguing that there is no distinct form or system of politics legitimately characterized as "postmodern." Nonetheless, he claims, one metaphysical-epistemological thesis commonly viewed as definitive of postmodern thought implies that a postmodern approach to politics consists in the denigration of theory in political-ethical matters. This aversion to theory is itself rooted in a deeper postmodern *Stimmung*, which abandons the need for cognitive defenses of political-ethical ideas. The bulk of his chapter analyzes parallels in the political views of two thinkers, Michel Foucault and Jean-François Lyotard, whose political ontologies and positions reflect this postmodern approach and *Stimmung*. He suggests that, because Foucault unlike Lyotard upholds Enlightenment values, Lyotard should be viewed as the "less politically modern" of the two.

Ernest Yanarella addresses the question of poststructuralism's political implications. Through his reading of recent works in political theory, he identifies in the concept of hegemony a way of examining the relevance of Derridian deconstruction for political theory and practice. He finds in Derridian thought a highly useful critique through which to rearticulate the Gramscian problematic in postmodern terms. Deconstruction, he argues, does have ethical intimations and political implications, particularly as a watchguard over the fallacies of the metaphysics of full presence and the excesses of ontological dualisms. Yet it is not itself an ethical system or a political philosophy, "for to do its work, it must not congeal into a reified system."

Richard Bernstein begins his contribution by summarizing the sense in which a juxtaposition of Habermas and Derrida taking the form of a "constellation" or "force-field" (in Adorno's and Benjamin's sense) treats their work not as an *either–or* but rather as a *both–and*, thereby providing an allegory for modernity/postmodernity. He then argues that not only would it be a mistake to associate differences between these two thinkers with traditional categorical oppositions, but that these differences identify complementary dimensions of the tasks facing democratic theory today. He continues by suggesting that the political mission underlying feminism would similarly be best served by a juxtaposition of and dialogue between critical theoretic and poststructuralist impulses. Bernstein's concluding remarks extend his reflections on dialogue and democracy by maintaining, first, that two conceptions of space of crucial importance in rethinking contemporary democracy are public space and dialogical ethical space, and second, that the absence of dialogue is the central form of intellectual barbarism.

Edward Soja argues that post-Enlightenment thought has been characterized by a series of modernities affecting both theory and the culture of space and time. Each has been overturned by its own version of the postmodern, and the current period is but one such transformation. The contemporary is characterized by a Baudrillardian *episteme* of the simulacra, by rapid restructuring of the worldwide space economy, and, he hopes, by the reinsertion of space into critical social theory. Soja describes how historicism became equated with emancipatory projects, and how this trenchant perspective has blinded social theory to the critical insight that space offers. His attempt to reassert a dialectical view of space draws upon Lefebvre and Foucault. The resulting sociospatial dialectic, he argues, provides proper ground from which to launch a postmodernism of the left. Such a project is necessary for understanding the contemporary capitalist economy as well as the material conditions giving rise to simulacra.

In her contribution, Catherine Lutz examines the increasing invocation of and debate over postmodernism in anthropology. She begins by surveying the form postmodernism has taken in this discipline, concentrating on the postmodern anthropologist's concern to make clear to herself and her audience both the perspective from which she is doing ethnography and the disciplinary institutions and practices in which this occurs. She then explores three social contexts responsible for postmodern anthropology: (1) changes in the political economy of capitalism, (2) the discipline's institutional framework, and (3) altered relations between North and South. Following this, she highlights problems with postmodernism from a feminist perspective and describes the dance of attraction and opposition that has embraced these two movements. She also shows, most revealingly, that pairs of concepts used (largely, by men) to differentiate postmodernity from modernity line up with ideologically conceived gender differences. Postmodernism, she concludes, is "a man in women's clothing."

In the final chapter, Wolfgang Natter and John Paul Jones take as their starting observation the modernist separation of disciplines which have thought about space from those which have thought about representation. Social life is messier than our theories of it, they argue, precisely because both space and representation create differences not yet captured by contemporary social theory. Their historical sketch of these separate domains provides an opportunity for the discovery of heretofore submerged affinities. Following Derrida, they argue the importance of conceptualizing the "incessant recontextualization" of social life and the necessity of questioning the capacity of any theory to make universalizing pronouncements irrespective of differentiations of space or contexts of reception. By moving beyond the one-sided perspectival account provided by either discipline, they lay the groundwork for a poststructuralist geography and a spatialized poststructuralist critique of representation. The implications of permeating the boundary between literary theory and geography are suggested through their critique of geographic narration, and in their reconceptualization of the duality of the "material" and the "representational."

Notes

1. Karl Mannheim, "Conservative Thought," in *From Karl Mannheim*, ed. Kurt H. Wolff (New York: Oxford University Press, 1971), 132–222.
2. Philippe Lacoue-Labarthe and Jean-Luc Nancy, *The Literary Absolute*, trans. Phillip Barnard and Cheryl Lester (Albany, N.Y.: State University of New York Press, 1988), 30.
3. Ibid., 15.
4. See, for example, Michel Foucault, "What Is an Author?" in *The Foucault Reader*, ed. Paul Rabinow, trans. Josué V. Harari (New York: Pantheon, 1984), 101–120, and Roland Barthes, "From Work to Text" and "The Death of the Author," in *Image-Music-Text*, trans. Stephen Heath (London: Fontana, 1977), 142–48, 155–64.
5. Friedrich Schlegel, "Ideas," in *German Aesthetic and Literary Criticism: The Romantic Ironists and Goethe*, ed. Kathleen Wheeler (Cambridge: Cambridge University Press, 1984), 56.
6. See Richard Bernstein's spirited criticisms of this claim in his contribution to this volume. He maintains that, when rationalism and "conservatism" are characterized in terms of the earlier mentioned oppositions, associating Habermas with rationalism and Derrida with "conservatism" distorts their thought. We stress that our claim is that significant *affinities* link "conservative" and contemporary postmodern thinking, not that one simply continues the other. No postmodern thinker can be straightfowardly lined up with the "conservative" side of the oppositions Mannheim lists. In fact, none of the thinkers Mannheim discusses can be either. Our point is simply that these oppositions work in changing combinations to establish a large-scale, perpetually shifting, *ontological-epistemological* front between two camps of continental theorists. We endorse Bernstein's request that one should "ask precisely how each side (and there are more than two) conceives of rationality, universality, concreteness, particularity" and so on. We claim, however, that, in their analyses of social reality, though not necessarily in their normative preferences, Habermas *emphasizes* rationality, systemicity, generality, and understanding the actual via ahistorical norms, while Derrida *emphasizes* a-rationality, fragmentation, particularity, and understanding norms via their embededness in actual history. We would even suggest that the urgency and propriety of Bernstein's juxtaposition of these two thinkers in a "forcefield" or "constellation" arises from the large-scale historical dichotomy we discuss.
7. Fredric Jameson, *Postmodernism, or the Cultural Logic of Late Capitalism* (Durham, N.C.: Duke University Press, 1991), xi, 427.
8. David Harvey, *The Condition of Postmodernity* (Oxford, England: Blackwell, 1989).
9. See Jameson, "Introduction," *Postmodernism*, and Harvey, *Condition of Postmodernity*, ch. 3.
10. See Michael Theunissen, *The Other: Studies in the Social Ontology of Husserl, Heidegger, Sartre, and Buber*, trans. Christopher Macann (Cambridge: MIT Press, 1984).
11. On these entanglements, see *Feminism/Postmodernism*, ed. Linda Nicholson (New York: Routledge, 1990).

2

Modernity in the Crossfire: Comments on the Postmodern Turn

FRED DALLMAYR

Something curious is happening in the midst of our modern (Western) civilization: "modernity" is under siege today. To speak with Gallie, Alasdair MacIntyre, and others, modernity has become a "contested concept."[1] This, of course, is not an entirely new development. From its inception, the direction and achievements of modernity have been surrounded by uneasiness and doubt—but such doubt was typically directed at specific features and only rarely at modernity as an epoch or paradigmatic framework. Before I proceed further, let me suggest a rough sense of the term: by "modernity" or "modern culture," I mean a culture or way of life that is the product of the Western Enlightenment and that has undergone the Weberian process of "rationalization" in every domain, including intellectual secularization, disenchantment from nature, political reorganization in the direction of rational-administrative efficiency, and economic industrialization. The problematic regard of this way of life, in the form of a pervasive malaise, emerged first in *fin-de-siècle* Europe (prototypically in Vienna and Berlin). The malaise gathered momentum during the interbellum period, particularly in Weimar Germany, which was characterized by a progressive polarization of intellectual life. During World War II the unease found expression in a major document written by two intellectuals in exile: Horkheimer and Adorno's *Dialectic of Enlightenment*, which is still one of the most gripping and penetrating texts on the glory and pitfalls of Western modernity.[2]

17

After the war, cultural and intellectual issues were at first overshadowed by the emerging East-West confrontation, that is, by the conflict between the superpowers—which in essence was a dispute over which side represented or embodied more genuinely the aspirations of modernity. Only after the cold war settled into a conventional routine did the issue of modernity itself resurface again—now on a broad front and with almost unprecedented intensity. It was only then that the controversy surrounding modernity gathered into a genuine philosophical and intellectual debate. Under such rubrics as the "modern project," the "age of technology," or the "age of the worldview," the strengths and weaknesses of modern (Western) culture were placed under the limelight of public scrutiny. It was also now that modernity was specifically defended by philosophers against its detractors, for example, by Hans Blumenberg in his *The Legitimacy of the Modern Age*.[3] It was during the same period that the terms "postmodernity" and "postmodernism" began to come into vogue, first in architecture and art, and then in philosophy, literature, and cultural analyses in general.

One should probably not forget that these intellectual discussions were and are silhouetted against a changing global background: specifically, the emergence of non-Western societies and cultures in Africa and Asia—societies whose presence on the world stage for the first time calls into question the primacy or preeminence of Western culture and modernity. Not surprisingly, the notion of postmodernity has been seized upon by many thirdworld intellectuals as a handy category to employ in the struggle for emancipation and as a virtual synonym for postcolonialism.[4]

My presentation in this chapter proceeds in three steps. First, I give an overview of the contemporary dispute surrounding modernity and postmodernity. Second, I highlight some particularly prominent features of this dispute, by drawing attention especially to the contested status of "tradition," the role of Nietzsche, and the continued relevance of the Enlightenment legacy. Third, I indicate possible directions or meanings of postmodernity and particularly the meaning that seems most plausible to me. Finaly, I differentiate my conception from competing perspectives, especially the notion of postmodernity advanced by Lyotard.

A Three-Cornered Debate

If one surveys the debate surrounding modernity, one can sort out three major avenues or positions: one that critiques modernity from the vantage point of a way of life and mode of rationality that preceded modern culture (and from which that culture departed to its detriment);

another that, while acknowledging historical irreversibility, attempts an internal or immanent (postmodern) critique of key features of modern life; and finally, a third that seeks to vindicate modernity against both its premodern and its postmodern detractors. To be sure, in concrete arguments, these postures are never neatly segregated, and there is room for multiple overlapping and reciprocal borrowing. Nevertheless, there may be an advantage to surveying the terrain along broad, ideal-typical lines.

The first alternative was prominently articulated (if not inaugurated) by Leo Strauss in his critical assessment of the "modern project." According to Strauss, this modern prospect involved a basic shift from reason to will and desire, and thus a lowering of the standards of rationality established by the ancients (see below). As he wrote in 1964,

> According to that modern project, philosophy or science was no longer understood as essentially contemplative, but as active. It was to be in the service of the relief of man's estate, to use Bacon's beautiful phrase. It was to be cultivated for the sake of human power. . . . Philosophy or science, which was originally the same thing, should make possible progress toward an ever greater prosperity.

In one of his earlier works, Strauss claimed that the instigator of the modern project was Thomas Hobbes, but he later modified this claim and located the rupture with the past in Machiavelli. Basically, Strauss's critique of modernity was a deliberate attempt to renew the "battle of the books," that is, the *querelle des anciens et des modernes*. In this battle, he resolutely sided with the ancients. To quote him again: "The inadequacy of the modern project, which has now become a matter of general knowledge and of general concern, compels us to entertain the thought that this new kind of society, our society, must be animated by a spirit other than that which has animated it from the beginning." We have to think, he added, of the "restoration of (classical) political-philosophy. . . . Such a return to classical political philosophy is both necessary and tentative or experimental. Not in spite, but because it is tentative, it must be carried out seriously; that is to say, without squinting at our present-day predicament."[5]

From a slightly different perspective (though one not incompatible with that of Strauss), Stanley Rosen has formulated the modern predicament in terms of a rift between formal reason and will—a rift deriving from the abandonment of classical substantive or holistic rationality. As he writes in one of his recent books, *Hermeneutics as Politics*, "Kant is the paradigm of the internal incoherence of the Enlightenment," namely, of the "conflict between mathematics and Newtonian science on the one hand and the desire for individual and political freedom on the other." In

Rosen's view, Kant's paradigm illustrates both the incoherence of the Enlightenment and the collapse of reason into unreason (or arbitrary choice). In his words, "Reason is itself constituted, or let us say constitutes itself, in accordance with the will to freedom. The upshot is that freedom both grounds, and is grounded by, reason. . . . Judged by the canons of traditional logic, which Kant accepts, his argument is invalid." Since Kant's time, rationality has been further eroded by the steadily intensified stress on the value of imagination and spontaneity. The entire development, according to Rosen, highlights the two chief trouble spots of modern Enlightenment: "the self-destruction of an exclusively or predominantly formalist rationalism, and the celebration of freedom as spontaneity." The emphasis on spontaneity, in particular, makes reason "unreasonable because arbitrary"—which leads to the consequence that reason is seen as "an artifact of history," which is the reverse of the earlier view that "history is an artifact of reason."[6]

As presented in *Hermeneutics as Politics*, the path of modernity reaches its culmination in Nietzsche and his deliberate abandonment of objective-rational standards in favor of the will to power: "We thus come directly to the late-modern view, made dominant by Nietzsche and today accepted among postmodernist thinkers without prominent exception: to reason is to interpret, because reason is itself an interpretation." Translated into political terms, the infatuation with interpretation (or hermeneutics) is said to lead ultimately to Maoism or anarchism, and in any case to some type of nihilism. An example would be Michel Foucault, on whom Rosen lavishes some of his most eloquent polemical passages:

> As a decadent product of the Enlightenment, Foucault's "value-free" commitment to a suitably modified scientism and his complicity in the attempt to tear down "rationalist" or "bourgeois" power structures do not constitute a serious political position but rather amount to, or serve, a romantic identification with the outcasts and the oppressed. Archaeological science is replaced by a genealogical transvaluation of values, or a paradoxical, but today almost obligatory, left-wing Nietzscheanism.

The same proclivities are exacerbated in Derrida's work, and especially in his celebration of *"différance."* Derrida, Rosen notes, "radicalizes Kantian spontaneity and entirely detaches it from concepts or rules. Spontaneity qua *différance* is not the transcendental ego but the primordial writer that produces signifiers rather than rules. The spontaneous Derridean signifiers themselves signify *other* signifiers—exactly as in the case of Jacques Lacan." Like Strauss, Rosen does not place much hope in any internal or immanent critique of the Enlightenment and of modern liberalism. For him, there is no liberal solution to the *aporia* of the

Enlightenment, because—he states—"liberalism (and a fortiori social-ism) is itself the crystallization of that aporia."[7]

Rosen's comments are addressed both to advocates of modernity and to their postmodern critics. Regarding the former, the leading and most articulate spokesman in our time is undeniably Jürgen Habermas. From Habermas's perspective, modernity is a condition that can neither be ret-rogressively undone nor radically transcended. As he insisted in 1980 when receiving the Adorno Prize, modernity is far from exhausted but rather an ongoing and inexhaustible enterprise, indeed an "incomplete project" awaiting further development. Appealing specifically to the *querelle des anciens et des modernes*, he argued that the term "modern" in earlier times was always linked with the model of antiquity. However, the spell cast by the ancient world was "dissolved with the ideals of the French Enlightenment." What emerged at that time was a notion of modernity wedded to a belief, inspired by modern science, in the "infi-nite progress of knowledge and in the infinite advance towards social and moral betterment." What Habermas calls "the project of modernity" or "the project of Enlightenment" is basically a three-pronged departure from tradition and a movement toward emancipation. Formulated first by the philosophers of the Enlightenment, the project—he writes—consist-ed in the effort "to develop objective science, universal morality and law, and autonomous art according to their inner logic." At the same time, Enlightenment philosophers sought to utilize or unleash the cognitive potential of these cultural spheres for the enrichment of everyday life— that is to say, "for the rational organization of everyday social life."[8]

More recently, in his *The Philosophical Discourse of Modernity* (1985), Habermas has provided greater detail to flesh out his picture of the intel-lectual scenario of the modern age. Going beyond broad synoptic assess-ments, the study presents the Enlightenment and its aftermath as a series of philosophical discourses (or modes of argument) and corre-sponding counterdiscourses and antidiscourses. A central trademark of modernity is again located in the differentiation of "autonomous" cultur-al spheres—science, morality, and art, and their respective validity claims —together with the resulting rationalization of the domains of everyday life or the "life-world." In Habermas's words, "The specific dignity of cultural modernity consists in what Max Weber called the relentless dif-ferentiation of 'value spheres.' . . . For now questions of truth, of justice and of taste can be treated and unfolded in accord with their own types of inner logic." Regarding the life-world, *The Theory of Communicative Action* (1981) has pinpointed its role as a background reservoir of cultural meanings, while simultaneously outlining its transformation under the impact of progressive rationalization and differentiation (of value spheres).[9]

The Weberian-Habermasian division of value spheres into three units is a derivation from and quasi-canonization of Kant's three Critiques (whose division was precisely pinpointed by Rosen as the dilemma of modernity). In the meantime, the canonical schema of modernity has been challenged by many writers and thinkers as an intellectual straitjacket whose "foundations" have become dubious. If it is granted that the schema does involve basically three types of subject-centered relations—subject-object (science), ego-alter ego (morality and law), and subject to itself (art)—then its structure can be traced to the modern paradigm of "subjectivity" (or the philosophy of consciousness) whose grounds have been eroded by the combined impact of language philosophy and poststructuralism. This erosion provides the occasion for an internal or immanent critique or "deconstruction" of modernity that is the hallmark of postmodern thought; as is well known, the leading philosophical figures in this deconstructive enterprise are Heidegger, Derrida, and Foucault (and, to some extent, Benjamin and Adorno). For present purposes I want to highlight the approach of immanent critique by turning to a political theorist: William Connolly, and particularly to his recent book entitled *Political Theory and Modernity*.

In Connolly's presentation, modernity or the modern project is rooted in human subjectivity and revolves around the Baconian equation of knowledge and power. With modernity, he claims, the insistence upon "taking charge of the world" comes into its own. Nature, he writes, becomes "a set of laws susceptible to human knowledge, a deposit of resources for potential use or a set of vistas for aesthetic appreciation. . . . Human and non-human nature become material to work on." And, he adds, modernity involves a relentless process of modernization—which has its own inner momentum and its own dialectic: "The drive to mastery entails or intensifies the subordination of non-masters, and recurrent encounters with the limits to mastery make even masters feel constrained and confined." These experiences, in turn, "accelerate drives to change, control, free, organize, produce, correct, order, empower, rationalize, liberate, improve and revolutionize selves and institutions."[10]

While linked to perpetual modernization, however, modernity for Connolly is not a completely open-ended enterprise or an unfinished project; instead, it is a paradigm or a discursive framework whose contours can be more-or-less clearly discerned and hence critically assessed. Looking back over the period running roughly from Hobbes to Nietzsche, he perceives a distinctive though not monolithic *gestalt*. "Modernity, then," he writes, is an epoch in which a set of contending understandings of self, responsi-bil-ity, knowledge, rationality, nature, freedom and legitimacy have estab-lished sufficient presence to shuffle other possible perspectives out of consideration. The room to maneuver allotted to each of the terms in this lexicon helps to demarcate the space within which the others may vary.

Mapping this lexicon or discursive *gestalt*, however, is already a first step toward transcending it or at least toward bending some of its consti-tutive ingredients out of shape—a move bound to be resented and resist-ed by champions of canonical modernity. Thus, Connolly continues, "if one seeks to rethink radically dominant theories of the self, one is called into court for failing to live up to established theories of freedom or responsibility; if one seeks to rethink dominant understandings of na-ture, those thoughts are jeopardized by the effects they engender for established understandings of the modern self as subject." Small wonder, then, that postmodern thinkers have been treated as outcasts not only by defenders of the "great tradition" (of classical thought) but also by devout modernists concerned about the erosion of pillars of modern Western society. The latter are bound to "condemn efforts to extend thought in this way as 'unthinkable,' 'self-contradictory,' 'self-defeating,' 'perverse' or 'mad'"—accusations which occasionally (he says) may indi-cate "the limits of the thinkable as such" but in other respects may also "disclose, darkly and imperfectly, boundaries within which modern dis-course is contained." Undaunted by such accusations, Connolly takes up the cause of the outcasts, that is, of critical-experimental thought, partic-ularly as an antidote to the disciplinary conformism of our age. "In trou-bled times," he states, "it may be imperative to try to push thought to the edge of these boundaries that give it its form. It may be important, however unlikely it is that the attempt will meet with complete success, to try to rethink the conceptions of self, truth, nature and freedom which bound modern discourse."[11]

Some Litmus Tests

Before I proceed, I think it may be desirable to glance back briefly over the terrain of the discussion so far. The issue of modernity coalesces today into a multifaceted debate, into a kind of second-order discourse about the discursive structure of modernity. All the participants in the debate assume such a second-order stance—since to thematize the "dis-course of modernity" is to stand at an angle to it, someplace outside its meshes. As one will also note, despite strong contrasts, disagreement among the contestants is not complete. Connolly agrees with Rosen at least regarding the paradoxical or dilemmatic character of modernity. Rosen in turn concurs with Habermas in his defense of "rationality" and in his strong distaste for all forms of postmodernism. Connolly finally agrees with Habermas at least on the point that modernity is irreversible and cannot be canceled *post hoc.*

These concordances, of course, are only the reverse side of their conflicts. Rosen wishes the "pox" on both modernism and postmodernism; he goes so far as to claim that both are the same: "the distinction between postmodernism and modernism is absurd." His strongest invectives are reserved for postmodern thinkers such as Foucault and Derrida, but he is not particularly mellow on modernists either. He writes:

> The doctrines of Habermas, like those of his colleague K.-O. Apel are a fashionable and well-meaning attempt to circumvent the exhaustion of modern philosophies of subjectivity and thereby to continue with the goals of the Enlightenment in a coherent, self-consistent manner. Their method is a friendly eclecticism that sacrifices nothing. Unfortunately, this amiability leads to the loss of everything.

Habermas pronounces a similarly acerbic verdict on both Straussian "premodernists" and deconstructive postmodernists, occasionally subsuming both (and other critics of modernity) under the summary label of "young conservatives." Connolly on his part silhouettes both modernity and postmodernity (or late modernity) against the backdrop of premodern visions of "order" that cannot be retrieved. In a statement that resembles Rosen's view, he sees a continuity between modernity and postmodernity: "The aspiration to become postmodern is one of the paradigmatic ways to be modern." However, the continuity here is also marked by rupture and internal contestation.[12]

In the following discussion I want to lift up for closer inspection some prominent issues dividing the contestants in the debate I have sketched. My focus will be chiefly on three points: their assessment of Nietzsche, their attitude toward the Enlightenment, and their view of tradition. One telling gauge of the controversy—a kind of litmus test or *experimentum crucis*—is the status assigned to Nietzsche (and post-Nietzscheans such as Foucault and Derrida). For Rosen, Nietzsche is the harbinger of nihilism and anarchism; he is the first to cross the bridge from rational knowledge to the chaos of interpretation. As I previously indicated, Foucault is presented as a "decadent product of the Enlightenment"—though not nearly as decadent as Derrida. "As he comes closer to Nietzsche," Rosen states, "Foucault also moves closer to the romantic and largely negative version of Maoism. . . . But at no stage of his career does Foucault illustrate the speculative madness of Nietzsche, whereas this is perhaps Derrida's outstanding feature." In this assessment Rosen joins ranks with Habermas, for whom Nietzsche is basically the pacemaker of archaic regression and primitivism. In *The Philosophical Discourse of Modernity*, Nietzsche occupies the position of a "turntable" (*Drehscheibe*) separating the Enlightenment discourse of Kant and Hegel from the headlong plunge into the abyss of irrationalism and irresponsibility. In his function as turntable, Nietzsche represents the "dark writer" (or *bête noire*) of the bourgeois age, opening the gates to a host of equally dark or sinister figures (such as Heidegger, Derrida and Foucault).[13]

A very different outlook pervades Connolly's work. Nietzsche there emerges as a *Grenzgänger* or "marginalist" of modernity who, for this very reason, can address probing and unsettling questions to the modern project. "Friedrich Nietzsche," he writes (and the statement can be extended to post-Nietzscheans), "sought to interrogate modernity from the perspective of imaginary points in the future, and he developed a set of rhetorical strategies designed to loosen the aura of necessity and sanctity surrounding categories of the present." In Connolly's presentation, Nietzsche aspired to call modernity into question without either lapsing into nostalgia for past modes of life *or* postulating a future utopia where we could finally reach a "home in the world." As he adds, Nietzsche "fosters thinking, for those who do not ward him off before thought can proceed."[14]

Another, closely related litmus test has to do with the status assigned to the Enlightenment tradition. In Strauss's view, Enlightenment is a deeply problematical and ultimately misguided endeavor—because it means the indiscriminate spreading of light where the latter cannot really penetrate, that is, the erasure of the divide separating Plato's cave from the sunlight of truth. Harshly put, Enlightenment signifies the artificial electrification of the cave. For Rosen, Enlightenment is no less problematical. As I have indicated, he finds the Enlightenment project basically incoherent, or at least rent by an internal rift: the rift between mathematical or scientific reason and political emancipation (guided by human will). As a result of this rift, modern Enlightenment is said to "self-destruct" in the end, for it is crushed between the millstones of an "exclusively or predominantly formalist rationalism" and the "celebration of freedom as spontaneity."[15]

This view is entirely at odds with that held by Habermas who regards Enlightenment as an inexhausted and basically inexhaustible enterprise, as an "incomplete project" calling for further expansion. From this vantage point, there cannot be an end to the spreading of light, a light cast by human inquiry and rationality; eventually all corners of the cave of this world are to be illuminated or spotlighted—in Weber's terms, they are destined to be "rationalized" (or "disenchanted"). Modernity for Habermas is wedded to the belief in the "infinite progress of knowledge and the infinite advance towards social and moral betterment." As presented in *The Philosophical Discourse of Modernity*, the Enlightenment project was inaugurated by French thinkers from Descartes to Voltaire and then crystallized in German idealism from Kant to Hegel. In Kantian thought, Enlightenment signaled the emergence of mankind from a condition of self-induced tutelage. For both Kant and Hegel, modernization or the achievement of modernity meant the progressive refinement of consciousness and subjectivity, specifically in the domains of science, ethical freedom, and aesthetic judgment. During the nineteenth century, the Enlightenment project was further developed by Hegel's heirs, especially by the Left-Hegelians whose perspective—in Habermas's view—is still the dominant guidepost in our time.[16]

Habermas's belief in the continuity of the Enlightenment project is not shared by poststructuralist (or postmodern) thinkers—at least not along the same unidirectional lines. Shortly before his death in 1984, Foucault wrote an essay entitled "What Is Enlightenment?" which was meant as a tribute to Kant (who had written an essay with the same title two hundred years earlier). The tribute, however, was complex and multifaceted. In the opening section of the essay, Foucault accepted Kant's definition of Enlightenment as the effort to awaken mankind from a self-induced state of tutelage or immaturity—where immaturity means "a certain state of our will that makes us accept someone else's authority to lead us in areas where the use of reason is called for." In reflecting on what was happening in his own age—the eve of the French Revolution—Kant included a historical dimension in his own critical enterprise; by considering the import of "today" for philosophical thought, he adopted the "attitude of modernity." For Foucault, however, paying homage to Kant was by no means a matter of simply celebrating the accomplishments of "*the* Enlightenment" or of imitating the Kantian outlook or style of inquiry. Rather, Enlightenment as critique of immaturity and authority had also to be turned into a critique of the authority of "Enlightenment" (thus making room for a double gesture of critique). He wrote that the ethos of modernity "implies, first of all, the refusal of what I like to call the 'blackmail' of the Enlightenment." Recognition of the achievements of the classical Enlightenment, and of Kant's philosophy in particular, should not lead to a simple submissiveness to the past: such recognition, he observed, does not mean that one has to be "for" or "against" the Enlightenment. It even means precisely that one has to refuse everything that might present itself in the form of a simplistic and authoritarian alternative: you either accept the Enlightenment and remain within the tradition of its rationalism . . . ; or else you criticize the Enlightenment and then try to escape from its principles of rationality.[17]

For Foucault, it was particularly important to free or extricate the continuing relevance of Enlightenment as critique from the historical accretion of "humanism" and anthropocentrism (that is, the focus on modern subjectivity); in his view, Enlightenment and such humanism were far from synonymous but rather in a state of tension. In our own time, it was important to relegate this humanist accretion to the past: "Just as we must free ourselves from the intellectual blackmail of 'being for or against the Enlightenment,' we must escape from the historical and moral confusionism that mixes the theme of humanism with the question of the Enlightenment." According to Foucault, the Enlightenment ushered in an attitude of critique—but this critique has now to be concretized and sharpened into a critique of all preconceptions, including those bequeathed by the Enlightenment itself. The required philosophical ethos, he wrote, "may be characterized as a limit-attitude. . . . We have to move beyond the outside-inside alternative; we have to be at the frontiers. Criticism indeed consists of analyzing and reflecting upon limits." In exemplary fashion, Kant reflected on the rational limits of knowledge or the knowable; but this was no longer enough:

> The critical question today has to be turned back into a positive one: in what is given to us as universal, necessary, obligatory, what place is occupied by whatever is singular, contingent, and the product of arbitrary constraints? The point, in brief, is to transform the critique conducted in the form of necessary limitation into a practical critique that takes the form of a possible transgression.

For Foucault, this point entailed as a consequence the idea that criticism is "no longer going to be practiced in the search for formal structures with universal value, but rather as a historical investigation into the events that have led us to constitute ourselves and to recognize ourselves as subjects of what we are doing, thinking, saying." In that sense, and in contrast to Kant, contemporary criticism is "not transcendental, and its goal is not that of making a metaphysics possible: it is genealogical in its design, and archaeological in its method."[18]

Commenting on Foucault's essay, Habermas (in a memorial paper written after the former's death) mistook its tenor as simply a tribute to

Kant and Enlightenment philosophy, thereby ignoring the complexity of
the text. Seen as a tribute to, and endorsement of, the Enlightenment,
the essay for Habermas was in conflict with the rest of Foucault's opus:
"Up to now [until 1984], Foucault traced this [critical] will-to-knowledge
in modern power-formations only to denounce it. Now, however, he presents it in a completely different light, as the critical impulse worthy of
preservation and in need of renewal. This connects his own thinking to
the beginnings of modernity." In his earlier work, Foucault allegedly
contrasted the critique of power with the rational "analysis of truth" in
such a fashion "that the former became deprived of the normative yard-
sticks that it would have to borrow from the latter. Perhaps the force of
this contradiction caught up with Foucault in this last of his texts."
Habermas's reading or misreading can readily be challenged—indeed,
has been challenged by numerous writers, including Hubert Dreyfus and
Paul Rabinow. Focusing on the escape from immaturity promoted by
Enlightenment, Dreyfus and Rabinow compare and contrast the Kantian,
Habermasian, and Foucauldian conceptions of maturity. According to
Habermas, they write, Kant's maturity consisted "in showing us how to
save the critical and transcendental power of reason and thus the triumph
of reason over superstition, custom, and despotism—the great achievement of the Enlightenment." From Habermas's own vantage point, maturity is the discovery of the "quasi-transcendental basis of community as
all we have and all we need, for philosophy and human dignity." For
Foucault, however, our critical task today is different: "On Foucault's
reading, Kant was modern but not (fully) mature. He heroically faced the
loss of the grounding of human action in a metaphysical reality, but he
sought to reground it in epistemology." Habermas, in turn, seeks to find
this grounding in a transcendental language community. Foucault resist-
ed both of these universalizing positions. Instead of relying on abstract
principles, he counseled an experimental testing of limits, a "limit-attitude" always ready to transgress "universal" categories or "necessary limitations." His work thus fostered a practical ethos that respects difference
and otherness without subduing them to a universal formula. [19]

The final test or gauge I want to mention here is in a way the counterpart to Enlightenment: namely, tradition. This issue is perhaps the
most complex and most difficult to disentangle; yet it is also quite central
and perhaps not unmanageable. For my present purposes, a brief ideal-
typical differentiation must suffice: that is, a distinction between traditionalism (as a return to the past); modernization theory; and a retrieval
of, or reconciliation with, tradition or the past beyond traditionalism and
its antipode.[20] As I indicated before, Strauss deliberately revived the
querelle des anciens et des modernes and took his stand squarely with the

ancients, by advocating a "restoration" of classical political thought. This does *not* mean that he envisaged the possibility of a return to the Greek *polis*; he fully realized that modern conditions of life—including industrialization and the territorial nation-state —rendered such a return impossible in practice. Yet, on a theoretical plane, the classical model appeared to him superior and therefore worthy of imitation (to whatever extent feasible). As he wrote in a letter to Karl Löwith:

> I really believe . . . that the perfect political order, as Plato and Aristotle have sketched it, is the perfect political order. . . . I know very well that *today* it cannot be restored; but . . . the contemporary solution, that is, the completely modern solution, is *contra naturam*. . . . Details can be disputed, although I myself might actually agree with everything that Plato and Aristotle demand (but that I tell only you).

In a subsequent letter, Strauss further elaborated his point: "I assert that the *polis*—as it has been interpreted by Plato and Aristotle, a surveyable, urban, morally serious (*spoudaia*) society, based on an agricultural economy, in which the gentry rule—is morally-politically the most reasonable and most pleasing."[21]

In a more subdued fashion, this preference for the classical or premodern tradition also animates Rosen's writings. In the meantime, the notion of "tradition" has been powerfully valorized on a much broader scale by philosophers outside the Straussian frame of discourse. A prominent example is Alasdair MacIntyre's insistence that philosophical arguments generally are plausible or intelligible only *within* the confines of a tradition, and not in the abstract no-man's-land of universal principles or ideas. To this extent, modernity itself—or modern liberalism—can be seen as one tradition among others, albeit as a tradition beset with grave handicaps or deficiencies when compared with older and more cohesive structures of thought. As MacIntyre writes, while discussing the "liberal project" as a derivative of the modern Enlightenment:

> The most cogent reasons that we have for believing that the hope of a tradition-independent rational universality is an illusion derived from the history of that project. For in the course of that history liberalism, which began as an appeal to alleged principles of shared rationality against what was felt to be the tyranny of tradition, has itself been transformed into a tradition whose continuities are partly defined by the interminability of the debate over such principles.[22]

The counterpoint to a traditionalist or tradition-oriented outlook is modernization theory, a perspective that, following the Enlightenment example, regards modernity basically as an exodus from tradition. The philosophical doctrine of "progress" and sociological theories of evolution all pay tribute to this notion of an exodus—as is evident in developmental formulas like "from status to contract," from *Gemeinschaft* to *Gesellschaft*, or from "traditional" to "modern" society. In his *Legitimation Crisis*, Habermas largely subscribed to such developmental or "neoevolutionary" schemes. Thus, the development of class-based societies (following a "primitive" kinship-based stage) was traced in that study from "traditional" over early modern or "liberal-capitalist" to late-modern or "late-capitalist" modes of social organization. In a modified and more elaborate form, a similar scheme continued to be operative in *Communication and the Evolution of Society* and also in *The Theory of Communicative Action* (with its focus on processes of societal rationalization and differentiation). In his controversy with Hans-Georg Gadamer, one of Habermas's chief accusations concerned Gadamer's presumed recuperation of tradition and authority in deviation from the liberating thrust of Enlightenment thought. In particular, Gadamer's emphasis on prejudgment and his attack on the Enlightenment's "prejudice against prejudice" were seen as evidence of a basic hostility to critical rationality and to modern processes of rationalization and emancipation (from tradition).[23]

The third alternative—which I associate with postmodernity—involves not only or not chiefly an opposition to traditionalism and modernization, but a move away from this contrast, that is, from history as a reservoir or else as a steady unfolding or accumulation of meaning. The alternative was intimated by Nietzsche in his denunciation of both rationalist progressivism and historical antiquarianism (in his *Untimely Meditations*). With starkly anti-progressivist accents, the move was recaptured by Walter Benjamin in one of his "Theses on the Philosophy of History" (Thesis XII) that explicitly recalled Nietzsche's statement: "We need history, but not the way a spoiled loafer in the garden of knowledge needs it." For Benjamin, the task of historiography was recollection of the past—not for its own sake but in order to remember the victims of history and to retrieve the redemptive sparks buried in the past. Hope for the future, in his view, could not be garnered through social engineering or rationalist designs, but only through retrieval of untapped potentials or promises. As he wrote (in Thesis VI), the task of historiography is "to seize hold of a memory as it flashes up at a moment of danger" and thus to continue "fanning the spark of hope in the past."[24] Commenting on the "Theses," Adorno observed in *Minima Moralia*: "What transcends the ruling society is not only the potentiality it develops but also all that which did not fit properly into the laws of historical development. Theory must needs deal with cross-grained, opaque, unassimilated material, which as such has from the start an anachronistic quality, but is not wholly obsolete since it has outwitted the historical dynamic." In their introduction to *Dialectic of Enlightenment*, Horkheimer and Adorno struck a similar theme. Countering antiquarian nostalgia, they stated, "The point is rather that the Enlightenment must reflect upon itself, if men are not to be wholly betrayed. The task to be accomplished is not the conservation of the past, but the redemption of the hopes of the past. Today, however, the past is preserved only in the form of a destruction of the past."[25]

Seen in this light, postmodernity heralds neither a "brave new world" nor a regressive primitivism, but rather a peculiar meshing of the temporalities of past and future; the intersection of these temporalities marks the terrain of the present—though not in the sense of a transparent culmination of meaning. This is one way, I believe, that one can interpret Foucault's attempt to write a "history of the present," via a Nietzschean or post-Nietzschean genealogical inquiry. The meshing of temporalities also characterizes, in my view, Heidegger's turn to pre-Socratic thought, the beginnings of Western philosophy. Contrary to frequent allegations of a nostalgic classicism or archaism, Heidegger's study of the pre-Socratics was explicitly guided by the hope to find resources for a new or "other beginning" (*anderer Anfang*). Thus, his *Contributions to Philosophy* describe the "destruction" of Western metaphysics (as inaugurated in *Being and Time*) as the necessary bridge or gateway to the "other beginning"— blending transgression and retrieval.[26]

Whither Postmodernity?

At this point it may be time—perhaps high time—for me to drop the mask of *rapporteur* or bystander and disclose my own leanings. This can readily be done. In the debate as sketched (and without intimating a complete consensus) my own sympathies are basically with Foucault's, Adorno's, and Connolly's position, that is, with a conception of postmodernity as an internal critique of modernity. In my own view, the prefix *post-* in the term *postmodernity* does not simply designate a temporal annex or succession but rather an internal happening; differently phrased, the prefix has the significance more of a dash or incision, revealing the inner complexity and ambiguity of modern consciousness and rationality.[27] As an incision, the prefix also has the connotation of a wound or an affliction undergone by contemporary experience; in Hegelian language one might say that postmodernism is a marker along the "highway of despair" of modern consciousness. This notion of incision or internal critique undergirded some of my earlier writings in which I attempted a subdued deconstruction of many key categories of modern thought (though without ever exiting completely from the Hegelian confines of "determinate negation" and "sublation" or *Aufhebung*).[28]

As forays into *terra incognita*, these writings—like those of other postmodern explorers—cannot possibly claim conclusiveness or pretend to settle the course and significance of postmodernity. In fact, contrary to the summary condemnations pronounced by Habermas and Rosen, its adepts are far from constituting a uniform phalanx; congruent with the acceptance of ambiguity, the postmodern terrain is itself a field characterized by many contests. To highlight this last point I want to turn briefly to one of the most prominent advocates of postmodernism whose work actually gave broad currency to the term itself: Jean-François Lyotard. By way of conclusion I then want to indicate my disagreement with his approach (which will be seen to revolve again around the issue of determinate negation).

In his *The Postmodern Condition* Lyotard portrayed postmodernity as the disintegration or dismantling of the great "metanarratives" of the past, that is, of the stories assigning a holistic meaning or purpose to Western culture and its evolution. In Lyotard's usage, metanarrative or metadiscourse refers to "some grand narrative such as the dialectics of spirit, the hermeneutics of meaning, the emancipation of the rational and working subject, or the creation of wealth." These grand stories, in his view, are in progress of being dispersed into heterogeneous language games, into "clouds of narrative language elements." In lieu of comprehensive unifying schemes, postmodernism is said to tolerate only a "pragmatics of language particles" and socially or politically only an institutionalization "in patches—local determinism." Critiquing totalizing models of social life, including Habermas's model of communicative consensus, Lyotard insists that "Such consensus does violence to the heterogeneity of language games. And invention is always born of dissension." Employing Nietzschean imagery concerning a perpetual struggle for power, he presents speech acts and actions in general as "moves" within a game—where "move" signifies a combative strategy or challenge. This, he writes, "brings us to the first principle underlying our method as a whole: to speak is to fight, in the sense of playing, and speech acts fall within the domain of a *general agonistics*."[29]

Lyotard's perspective on speech acts and language games is amplified into a broader theory of social and political life—always with an edge against integrative or harmonizing visions or frameworks. The chief target of his deconstructive effort is the view—shared by idealists and functionalists alike—that society is "a unified totality, a 'unicity'" (a view that

Lyotard in a more recent work calls "totalitarism"). Departing from such unifying schemes, our age (our postmodern age) is said to witness the "'atomization' of the social into flexible networks of language games"— with each speaker or participant being located at particular "nodal points" of competing communication circuits. Instead of being submerged in social harmony, the "atoms" of society are perceived as operating at the crossroads of pragmatic relationships and involved in perpetual "moves" and "countermoves." "What is needed," Lyotard asserts, "if we are to understand social relations in this manner, on whatever scale we choose, is not only a theory of communication but a theory of games which accepts agonistics as a founding principle." According to a more recent work, entitled *Le Différend*, postmodernity denotes the radical "decline of universalistic discourses," a process giving rise instead to "thought in dispersal" (or thinking in the mode of diaspora).[30]

I do not wish to prolong unduly this discussion of Lyotard; the general strategy of his argument seems fairly evident. In his presentation, modernity relates to postmodernity much as homogeneity relates to heterogeneity, unity to multiplicity, universalism to particularism, and harmony to dissension or contestation. While I share his apprehensions regarding unity and uniformity, I cannot entirely concur with his emphases. My reservations extend to several dimensions of his argument. First of all, I distrust radical reversals or substitutions, especially if they are meant to offer an exit route from the metanarratives of modernity or "foundational" metaphysics. In my view, the move from metaphysics to postmetaphysics is more difficult to accomplish than is often assumed (by postmodernists). Generally speaking, metaphysics can scarcely be "overcome" by inverting its premises or priorities: particularly by turning from holism to dispersal, from consensus to dissensus, from "paradigm" to "paralogy," or from harmony to agonal contests. What these reversals neglect is the complex interlacing of the paired opposites and the ambivalent status of their meaning; they also tend to cloud or obscure the continuing import of metaphysical teachings—and the hazards involved in their abandonment without replacement.[31]

More importantly, Lyotard's reversals (I am afraid) restore "foundationalism" in a new guise: namely, the foundational status of particulars, of language-particles, of separated agonal contestants or contending antagonists. In the absence of mutual bonds or constitutive relationships, the contending parties are liable to lapse into self-centeredness and unrelated fixity, that is, into the very kind of self-enclosure (or egocentrism) that deconstruction is supposed to undermine. This point does not necessarily vindicate traditional holism or "totalitarism"—to the extent that such holism involves a restrictive enclosure and a barrier against "otherness" (or difference). After the experiences with totalitarianism in our century, there can be no intellectually viable road leading back to this kind of holism. In this sense, postmodernism excludes a restorative path or the path of a simple "homecoming"—a fact that does not transform it into nihilism or a "cultural deathwish" (except insofar as death, of sorts, is always part of a genuine renewal and transformation). In my own view, postmodernity signifies indeed a farewell to the grand "metanarratives" of metaphysics. But the abandonment of all fixed foundations does not lead to chaos or a general "war of all against all," but rather to a radical relationism in which no part can claim absolute primacy or supremacy. In this respect, I believe, postmetaphysics seems congruent with the outlook and requirements of a democratic ethos (or of "radical democracy" as formulated by Chantal Mouffe). In more philosophical (Hegelian) terms, one might say that the "absolute" is relational or relationship, or that relationship is what "being" in the end is all about.[32]

Notes

1. See W. B. Gallie, "Essentially Contested Concepts," in *The Importance of Language*, ed. Max Black (Englewood Cliffs, NJ: Prentice-Hall, 1962), 121–146; Alasdair MacIntyre, "Social Science Methodology as the Ideology of Bureaucratic Authority," in *Through the Looking-Glass: Epistemology and the Conduct of Inquiry*, ed. Maria J. Falco (Washington, D.C.: University Press of America, 1979), 42–58; and William E. Connolly, *The Terms of Political Discourse*, 2d ed. (Princeton: Princeton University Press, 1983), 9–44. For some recent literature on modernity and postmodernity, compare Agnes Heller, *Can Modernity Survive?* (Oxford, England: Blackwell, 1990); Albrecht Wellmer, *In Defense of Modernity* (Cambridge, MIT Press, 1990); David Harvey, *The Condition of Postmodernity* (Oxford, England: Blackwell, 1990); John F. Rundell, *The Origins of Modernity* (Madison: University of Wisconsin Press, 1989); Anthony Giddens, *The Consequences of Modernity* (Stanford, Calif.: Stanford University Press, 1989); Henry Kariel, *The Desparate Politics of Postmodernism* (Amherst: University of Massachusetts Press, 1989); Alex Callinicos, *Against Post-Modernism: A Marxist Critique* (Cambridge, England: Polity Press, 1989); Lawrence E. Cahoone, *The Dilemma of Modernity* (Albany, N.Y.: State University of New York Press, 1988); Gianni Vattimo, *The End of Modernity*, trans. Jon R. Snyder (Baltimore: Johns Hopkins University Press, 1988); and David Kolb, *The Critique of Pure Modernity* (Chicago: University of Chicago Press, 1986).

2. Max Horkheimer and Theodor W. Adorno, *Dialectic of Enlightenment*, trans. John Cumming (New York: Seabury, 1972). Regarding fin-de-siècle and antebellum Europe, compare Allan Janik and Stephen Toulmin, *Wittgenstein's Vienna* (New York: Simon and Schuster, 1973); also David Frisby, *Fragments of Modernity* (Cambridge, England: Polity Press, 1985). Using familiar social-scientific vocabu-

lary, the emergence of Western modernity may be characterized as a shift from "status" to "contract," from *Gemeinschaft* to *Gesellschaft*, from substantive to formal-procedural rationality, from integral holism to social-cultural differentiation. See Eva Etzioni-Halevy, *Social Change: The Advent and Maturation of Modern Society* (London: Routledge and Kegan Paul, 1981).

3. Hans Blumenberg, *The Legitimacy of the Modern Age*, trans. Robert M. Wallace (Cambridge: MIT Press, 1983).

4. Compare Ian Adam and Helen Tiffin, eds., *Past the Last Post: Theorizing Post-Colonialism and Post-Modernism* (Calgary, Canada: University of Calgary Press, 1990).

5. Leo Strauss, "The Crisis of Our Time," in *The Predicament of Modern Politics*, ed. Harold J. Spaeth (Detroit, Mich.: University of Detroit Press, 1964), 41, 44, 54. In fairness one should also cite these lines (54): "The relative success of modern political philosophy has brought into being a kind of society wholly unknown to the classics, a kind of society in which the classical principles as stated and elaborated by the classics are not immediately applicable. Only we living today can possibly find a solution to the problems of today." See also Strauss, *The Political Philosophy of Hobbes: Its Basis and Its Genesis* (Oxford: Claredon Press, 1936) and *Thoughts on Machiavelli* (Glencoe, Ill.: Free Press, 1958); compare in addition Joseph Cropsey, ed., *Ancients and Moderns* (New York: Basic Books, 1964).

6. Stanley Rosen, *Hermeneutics as Politics* (New York: Oxford University Press, 1987), 3–5.

7. Rosen, *Hermeneutics as Politics*, 5–7, 15.

8. Jürgen Habermas, "Die Moderne—ein unvollendetes Projekt," in *Kleine Politische Schriften 1–4* (Frankfurt, Germany: Suhrkamp, 1981), 445, 452–53; trans. by Seyla Benhabib as "Modernity—An Incomplete Project," in *The Anti-Aesthetic*, ed. Hal Foster (Port Townsend, Wash.: Bay Press, 1983), 3–15.

9. Habermas, *The Theory of Communicative Action*, vol. 1, *Reason and the Rationalization of Society*, ch. 2, and vol. 2, *Lifeworld and System: A Critique of Functionalist Reason*, ch. 6, trans. Thomas McCarthy (Boston: Beacon Press, 1984, 1987); and *The Philosophical Discourse of Modernity: Twelve Lectures*, trans. Frederick Lawrence (Cambridge: MIT Press, 1987), 112–13.

10. William E. Connolly, *Political Theory and Modernity* (Oxford, England: Blackwell, 1988), 2.

11. Connolly, *Political Theory and Modernity*, 4. Connolly prefers to characterize his position as "late modern" rather than postmodern—which, however, is a nuance. For a detailed discussion of his study, see my "Connolly's Deconstruction of Modern Political Theory," *Strategies*, 4–5 (1991): 45–58.

12. See Rosen, *Hermeneutics as Politics*, 15, 17; Connolly, *Political Theory and Modernity*, 2–3; Habermas, "Modernity versus Postmodernity," *New German Critique*, 22 (1981): 3–22, and "Die Utopic des guten Herrschers," in *Kleine Politische Schriften 1–4*, 318–27.

13. Rosen, *Hermeneutics as Politics*, 6; Habermas, *Philosophical Discourse of Modernity*, 83, 106.

14. Connolly, *Political Theory and Modernity*, 6, 15.

15. Rosen, *Hermeneutics as Politics*, 5.

16. Habermas, *Philosophical Discourse of Modernity*, 16–44, 51–69.

17. Michel Foucault, "What Is Enlightenment?," in *The Foucault Reader*, ed. Paul Rabinow (New York: Pantheon Books, 1984), 34, 38, 42–43.

18. Foucault, "What Is Enlightenment?," 44–46. Elaborating on this passage, the essay continued (46) that the criticism is "archaeological—and not transcendental—in the sense that it will not seek to identify the universal structures of all knowledge or of all possible moral action, but will seek to treat the instances of discourse that articulate what we think, say, and do as so many historical events. And this critique will be genealogical in the sense that it will not deduce from the form of what we are what it is impossible for us to do and to know; but it will separate out, from the contingency that has made us what we are, the possibility of no longer being, doing, or thinking what we are, do, or think." Stressing the practical-experimental aspect of critique, Foucault added in a Nietzschean vein (47): "I shall thus characterize the philosophical ethos appropriate to the critical ontology of ourselves as a historico-practical test of the limits that we may go beyond, and thus as work carried out by ourselves upon ourselves as free beings."

19. See Habermas, "Taking Aim at the Heart of the Present," and Hubert Dreyfus and Paul Rabinow, "What Is Maturity? Habermas and Foucault on 'What Is Enlightenment?'" in *Foucault: A Critical Reader*, ed. David C. Hoy (Oxford, England: Blackwell, 1986), 107–8, 110–11, 118–21. (In the above I move somewhat beyond the Dreyfus-Rabinow essay.)

20. In her essay on "Radical Democracy" Chantal Mouffe distinguishes in a similar way between traditionalism and tradition. Tradition, she writes, "allows us to think of our own insertion into historicity, the fact that we are constructed as subjects through a series of already existing discourses, and that it is through this tradition which forms us that the world is given to us and all political action is made possible." As she adds, however: "To be able to think about the politics of radical democracy through the notion of tradition, it is important to emphasize the composite, heterogeneous, open, and ultimately indeterminate character of the democratic tradition"; see Mouffe, "Radical Democracy: Modern or Postmodern?," in *Universal Abandon? The Politics of Postmodernism*, ed. Andrew Ross (Minneapolis: University of Minnesota Press, 1988), 39, 41.

21. See Karl Löwith and Leo Strauss, "Correspondence Concerning Modernity," *Independent Journal of Philosophy*, 4 (1983); 107–8, 113. (I am indebted to Ronald Beiner for alerting me to this correspondence.)

22. Alasdair MacIntyre, *Whose Justice? Which Rationality?* (Notre Dame, Ind.: University of Notre Dame Press, 1988), 335. On the revalorization of tradition, see also Edward Shils, *Tradition* (Chicago: University of Chicago Press, 1981).

23. See Habermas, *Legitimation Crisis*, trans. Thomas McCarthy (Boston: Beacon Press, 1975), esp. 17–24; *Communication and the Evolution of Society*, trans. Thomas McCarthy (Boston: Beacon Press, 1979); *The Theory of Communicative Action*, 2 vols., trans. Thomas McCarthy (Boston: Beacon Press, 1984, 1987); and "A Review of Gadamer's *Truth and Method*," in *Understanding and Social Inquiry*, ed. Fred Dallmayr and Thomas McCarthy (Notre Dame, Ind.: University of Notre Dame Press, 1977), 335–363.

24. For an English translation of the "Theses" (by Harry Zohn), see Hannah Arendt, ed., *Illuminations* (New York: Harcourt, Brace and World, 1968), 255–66. Compare also Peter Szondi, "Hope in the Past: On Walter Benjamin," *Critical Inquiry*, 4 (1978): 491–506; and Ronald Beiner, "Walter Benjamin's Philosophy of History," *Political Theory*, 12 (1984): 423–34.

25. Theodor W. Adorno, *Minima Moralia* (London: New Left Books, 1974), 151; Horkheimer and Adorno, *Dialectic of Enlightenment*, xv.

26. Martin Heidegger, *Beiträge zur Philosophie (Vom Ereignis)*, ed. Friedrich-Wilhelm von Herrmann (*Gesamtausgabe*, vol. 65; Frankfurt, Germany: Klostermann, 1989), 176–9. With Martin Bernal we may have to go back still further beyond the pre-Socratics, namely, to the "Afroasiatic roots" of Western civilization; see his *Black Athena*, vol. 1 (New Brunswick, N.J.: Rutgers University Press, 1987). According to Andreas Huyssen, postmodernism operates in "a field of tension between tradition and innovation, conservation and renewal, mass culture and high art, in which the second terms are no longer automatically privileged over the first"; see his *After the Great Divide: Modernism, Mass Culture, Postmodernism* (Bloomington, Ind.: Indiana University Press, 1986), 216. Com-pare also Jon R. Snyder's comments, in his Introduction to Vattimo's work: "What is it, though, that has distanced contemporary thought from modernity, and pushed it towards the post-modern era? Not surprisingly, what is responsible for this change is precisely the dissolution of progress and of the value of the new . . . . The philosophy of post-modernity seeks to shake off the 'logic of overcoming, development and innovation' that has been elaborated and sustained by modernity"; see Vattimo, *End of Modernity*, xxxvi.

27. In Huyssen's view, postmodernism represents "a new type of crisis of that modernist culture itself"; see *After the Great Divide*, 217. The notion of an affliction undergone closely resonates with Heidegger's notion of *Verwindung*. To quote Snyder again: "The notion of *Verwindung* contains the essence of the postmodern in philosophy, and is indeed 'the sole possible form of metaphysical thought' available today, because it is, paradoxically, opposed to metaphysics. Perhaps, however, it would be more accurate to say instead that the notion of *Verwindung* is the sole *legitimate* form of metaphysical thought that survives today"; see Vattimo, *End of Modernity*, xlvii.

28. Thus, my *Twilight of Subjectivity* (Amherst:University of Massachusetts Press, 1981) probed the implications of an imaginary decentering of modern "subjectivity" in a number of domains, specifically the domains of intersubjectivity, man-nature relations, social development and ethics. Building on this exploration, *Polis and Praxis* (Cambridge: MIT Press, 1984) pursued the same kind of decentering or eclipse into more overtly political terrain: by focusing on the notions of political agency (or *praxis*), of political "power" and human "freedom," and finally on the enterprise of political theory or philosophy itself. A companion volume, entitled *Language and Politics* (Notre Dame, Ind.: University of Notre Dame Press, 1984), linked the eclipse of the *cogito* with the contemporary "linguistic turn," tracing the repercussions of the latter on the conception of humans as "languaging creatures" (*zoon logon ekhon*) and as "political animals" (*zoon politikon*). More recently, my concern has been with the meaning of modernity, with

the prospect of global politics (between development and underdevelopment), and with the status of democracy. See *Margins of Political Discourse* (Albany, N.Y.: State University of New York Press, 1989); *Life-World, Modernity, and Critique* (Cambridge, England: Polity Press, 1991); compare also *Critical Encounters: Between Philosophy and Politics* (Notre Dame, Ind.: University of Notre Dame Press, 1987).

29. Jean-François Lyotard, *The Postmodern Condition: Report on Knowledge*, trans. Geoff Bennington and Brian Massumi (Minneapolis: University of Minnesota Press, 1984), xxiii–xxv, 10.

30. Lyotard, *Postmodern Condition*, 12, 15–17; see also *Le Différend* (Paris: Editions de Minuit, 1983), 10–11.

31. Arguments akin to those above have been expressed by Albrecht Wellmer in *Zur Dialektik von Moderne und Postmoderne: Vernunftkritik nach Adorno* (Frankfurt, Germany: Suhrkamp, 1985), 48–114—a study which by no means counsels a simple acceptance of modernity.

32. In addition to Mouffe's essay cited above (note 20) compare Ernesto Laclau and Chantal Mouffe, *Hegemony and Socialist Strategy: Towards a Radical Democratic Politics* (London: Verso, 1985); also my "Rethinking the Hegelian State," in *Margins of Political Discourse*, 137–57.

3

Theory at Bay: Foucault Lyotard, and Politics of the Local

THEODORE R. SCHATZKI

Is there any distinct form or system of politics that can justifiably claim the label "postmodern"? Or is postmodernity primarily a nonpolitical phenomenon that lends support to or is compatible with a range of political visions? To resolve this issue, we must first of course determine what postmodernity is. Unfortunately, the expression "postmodernity" covers poorly defined terrain. In different eyes, it is a style, an epoch, a condition, a state of mind, or a school of thought. It is true that what this epoch, condition, or whatever consists in or stands for is customarily thematized as a combination of theses, emphases, and stances. The most important of these are the destruction of the metaphysical subject; an accent on fragmentation, heterogeneity, and particularity; openness to alterity; skepticism about universal truths; and opposition to totalizing metanarratives and theories. However, which theses are most central to postmodernity is a contested issue. Furthermore, not only are most of these ideas essential ingredients in a variety of recent strands of thought, for example, poststructuralism, deconstruction, and feminism, but a line of thinkers in the nineteenth and twentieth centuries has espoused varying combinations of them. Even literary and artistic modernism, under many interpretations,[1] adopts a number of these stances. It seems, consequently, that "postmodernity" stands at best for a ill-defined contemporary juxtaposition of theses shared by various movements of thought.

The vagaries of the concept mean that there is not going to be a single widely recognized postmodern politics. It also means, however, that there is not going to be a single widely recognized range of political visions supported by or compatible with postmodernity. Even if we could agree, furthermore, about which theses and emphases are central to postmodernity, we would scarcely be in a better position to discern postmodern politics. These theses might be thought to have specific political implications. For instance, skepticism regarding the metaphysical subject sometimes underlies disdain of Marxist politics, especially in its traditional articulations. But not all forms of Marxist politics presuppose such a subject. An accent on heterogeneity and particularity in combination with openness to alterity, moreover, is sometimes thought to implicate some form of democratic politics. But this is disputable. In short, it seems that there is little point in talking about postmodern politics.

Among these theses and emphases, however, lies the denigration of theory, especially in political and ethical matters. This attitude unites many contemporary writers commonly characterized as postmodern. This unity suggests that, even if there is no particular postmodern politics, there might be a postmodern way of approaching political-ethical matters, one that eschews abstract, systematic political-ethical thinking regardless of a thinker's stances on particular political issues. I believe that there is indeed such an approach and that what makes the abandonment of political-ethical theory by certain thinkers postmodern is its rootedness in a shared *Stimmung*,[2] which itself has its roots in Nietzsche.

This *Stimmung* arises in the context of a contemporary cultural situation to which most twentieth-century thinkers have reacted in one way or another. This situation consists in a loss of faith in the groundedness of political-ethical values combined with a recognition of their diversity. For many thinkers, this situation poses the challenge of navigating between foundationalism and relativity, between belief in standards guaranteed to be valid for all and the specter of an unrectifiably agonistic dispersion of values among cultures, communities, and individuals. These thinkers believe that, although values have no certain foundation, they can be cognitively defended, for example, by theory. Ultimately underlying this belief, and thus all attempts to steer between the shoals of foundationalism and relativity, is apprehension: apprehension (1) that if values cannot be cognitively defended, it is dishonest and illegitimate to base judgments and actions upon them, so that (2) if "we" lose faith in the cognitive integrity of our values, "we" will be reduced to moral confusion and some combination of recklessness, frivolity, and paralysis. Such thinkers have faith that theory and argument will steer us clear of the abyss lurking beneath the fragmentation and ungroundedness of values.

Maybe, however, it is only intellectuals in need of assurance who believe that advocating and working for what one believes requires cognitive defense and that the lack thereof will lead to political-ethical chaos. A postmodern response to fragmentation and ungroundedness is to bid farewell to this need and to the capacity of theory and reason to satisfy it. This response counsels intellectuals, first, to take leave of theory and simply get on with acting and judging on the basis of what they accept, and second, to see the folly in believing that fealty to values requires rational defense. One postmodern *Stimmung*, in other words, is believing in and acting upon the values one accepts in the face of the fragmentation and ungroundedness of values, without need of assurance or illusions of theoretical armature. This *Stimmung*, it should be added, does not exclude questioning values and acknowledging their possible duplicities, antinomies, and perils. Indeed, it can welcome such investigation.

This chapter examines two exemplars of this *Stimmung*, Michel Foucault and Jean-François Lyotard. I will focus on motifs that appear in their thought in the early and late seventies, respectively. In particular, I want to consider their visions of politics and what room the above postmodern *Stimmung* allows for theory in the political arena. By "theory" I shall mean systems of abstract, general ideas. I choose Foucault and Lyotard for two reasons. First, they exemplify as well as anyone the theses for which "postmodernity" is a label; and second, their visions of political activity and theory are remarkably alike. After examining their views on these topics, I will conclude this chapter by first considering whether Foucault and Lyotard are postmodern in a sense more rigorous than the one discussed so far and by then offering some general criticisms of their ideas.

Ontology

Social ontology is the theoretical study of the basic constituents of social reality. Although neither Foucault nor Lyotard devotes much space to this topic, it occupies a key position in their thought. Like social theorists generally, in fact, they are bound to the view that theory *qua* ontology is a necessary component of social-political investigation. This remains true regardless of whatever pronouncements they make about the status of theory in political activity (or social investigation.) Indeed, some of their claims about theory in politics reflect their ontologies.

Foucault's and Lyotard's ontologies emphasize the complexity, heterogeneity, and diversity in social life. They, along with Wittgenstein, are three of the contemporary writers who take this complexity and heterogeneity most seriously. Of course, they do not agree about what there is a complex, heterogeneous, and diverse stock *of*. Foucault pictures history as a maze of events formed by myriad forces, a tangle of historical phenomena having numerous beginnings and complex descents (e.g., *NGH*, 81, 89; *TP*, 114).[3] Historical events and phenomena emerge out of elaborate webs of shifting, aggregating, and segregating "force relations" between individuals. (Force relations are relations of control, domination, determination, formation, subjection, constraint, empowerment, and so on.) In Lyotard, on the other hand, social life is "atomized" into "flexible networks of language-games," at the nodal points of which live individuals (*PMC*, xxiv, 15–17). As these language games join, fall apart, and evolve, social life passes through states of order, free play, and transformation. Institutions, consequently, exist only in patches (*PMC*, xxiv). Both history and "the people" are swarms of narratives (*LP*, 134; *DGR*, 57). When Lyotard, in The *Differend*, focuses on phrases instead of individuals, he continues to picture phrases, like individuals before them, as embedded in moving webs of language games.[4]

Lyotard's and Foucault's ontologies also highlight contingency. For Lyotard, the fundamental category of reality is the event (*Ereignis*). Reality happens. Between a state of affairs that happens and what succeeds it, however, there is a metaphysical gap of nothingness. No state of affairs can determine or render necessary what follows it (*TD*, 100, 102). Something must follow, but the possibilities are manifold, and whatever does happen is absolutely contingent. In Foucault this idea appears at a less metaphysical level in his recognition of the fundamental role played in history by accidents, contingencies, and discontinuities. The only necessities Foucault recognizes in social reality are temporary inertias and coagulations (see *CTIH*, 37). In a sense, everything in history is contingent (*NGH*, 88; cf. 81).

It is obvious that the main target of both these ontologies is the existence of totalities in history. Foucault's and Lyotard's opposition to the notion of totality is not only, as sometimes thought, political, a retreat from leftist thinking in the face of the gulag (e.g., *RA*, 233), but also ontological: the nature of social reality does not admit totalities. In particular, it does not admit completeness and reconciliation in history (*NGH*, 86–87; *TD*, "Result"). History is a multistranded spectacle whose future is undetermined and whose movement never ceases. A final totalizing utopia is incompatible with its complexity. The idea that it inexorably progresses toward that whole is equally contrary to the intricacy and heterogeneity of forces operative in it.

Political Ontology

Foucault's and Lyotard's ontologies give rise to a conception of politics that emphasizes local struggle. Although I do not want to pursue biographical matters, I should mention that this emphasis probably also reflects a disillusionment with large-scale, systematic politics born of a series of events during and after World War II. For example, as disproof of all the great "metanarratives" which motivated political action in the nineteenth and twentieth centuries, Lyotard cites singular occurrences: Auschwitz, Budapest 1956, May 1968, the economic crisis of 1929, the 1974–79 crisis of overcapitalization (*TD*, 257; *SH*, 393). Be that as it may, it is clear that their ontologies and conceptions of politics closely intertwine.

Foucault conceives of social reality atomistically as a network of individuals connected by force relations of which they are both the targets and the transmitters. Similarly, for Lyotard social reality is composed of individuals or phrases connected to one another by language games (genres of discourse). In either case, reality is a multiplicity of elements that are caught and interconnected within a web of some sort.

Politics, consequently, concerns the state and management of these connections. Since its object pervades the social arena, it is an omnipresent affair. Inverting Clausewitz's dictum that war is politics continued by other means, Foucault writes that politics involves "sanctioning and upholding the equilibrium of forces that was displayed in war . . . conflicts waged over power, with power, for power, the alterations in the relations of forces, the favouring of certain tendencies, the reinforcements etc., etc." (*2L*, 90–91). That politics concerns the disposition and management of force relations is reflected in Foucault's resurrection of the definition of government as "the way in which the conduct of individuals or of groups might be directed; the government of children, of souls, of communities, of families, of the sick" (*SP*, 221). In Lyotard, since what follows a given state of affairs or phrase[5] is contingent, and since states of affairs or phrases from a plurality of genres can link onto any given state of affairs or phrase, linkages are forever contentious (*TD*, xiii, 190, 199). Politics concerns the contest waged over linkage. Everything, consequently, is politics (*TD*, 192). What politicians do is an instance of politics in this broader sense since what concerns them when, for example, they are negotiating or deciding how to intervene in financial markets is linkages between certain phrases or states of affairs.

Foucault, furthermore, analyzes the domain of politics with concepts borrowed from the arena of war and struggle, for example, battle, strategy, tactic, and resistance (see *TP*, 114; *2L*, 90ff.) Likewise, although

Lyotard does not employ such concepts in his analysis, he thinks of the domain of politics as a contest (*agon*). In *The Postmodern Condition*, for example, he claims that a theory of agonistics is as central to social analysis as a theory of communication—if not more so (*PMC*, 16). Thus both thinkers see languages of contention as singularly appropriate for analyzing the shaping and subjection or competition and jousting that characterize the connections among the elements of social reality. One wonders if Nietzsche stands behind their portrayal of social life.

    This notion of politics in turn yields a conception of political activity which promotes local struggle and recognizes the pluralization of modes of oppression and of oppressed groups in the contemporary Western world. Examples of local struggles are those directed against the power of men over women, of parents over children, of psychiatry over the mentally ill, of medicine over the population, and of administration over the ways people live (*SP*, 211). Local struggles are not geographically restricted. What makes them "local" is their immediacy, the way people focus on the instances of a particular form of power or oppression closest to them and expect a solution today rather than in a promised future.

    It is probably obvious that Foucault's account of developments in modern Western society makes local struggle especially pertinent in the contemporary era. Since force relations link individuals in every age, local struggles have always been and will always remain possible. During the last two centuries, however, the net of relations has thickened through the evolution of disciplinary- and bio-power. Force relations belonging to earlier forms of power remain (cf. *SP*, 213). But the development of new forms, by multiplying the ways and targets of power, has augmented the possibilities while enhancing the urgency of local struggles.

    Of course, Foucault does not think that local struggle is the only possible form of political activity. Although he is skeptical that society as a whole can be transformed, he acknowledges that governments can be overthrown. A serious problem with overthrowing governments today, however, is that, because government control relies on disciplinary- and bio-power force relations, doing so is more likely to result in the "recodification" than in the neutralization of these relations (*TP*, 122; cf. *RA*, 230, 233). If they are to be overturned, they must be directly challenged on their own ground of deployment. At the same time, meaningful victories against the government might be won through local struggles. Precisely because governments today rely upon disciplinary- and bio-power force relations, a multiplicity of successful struggles against these relations, even though they do not directly target government oppression, might undermine the state's (and also capitalism's [*RA*, 230]) capacity to operate. So local struggles are all the more urgent today.

Needless controversy has surrounded Foucault's notion of resistance and struggle. Some critics have argued that, since power forms the individuals upon which it is exercised (is "productive," in Foucault's language), all possible points of resistance are the products of power and hence incapable of resisting it. This argument succeeds only if the totality of power relations is in question (and all power relations are productive). For, in this situation, the issue is whether there are points of resistance outside of and opposed to *all* power relations, and the answer is no. Resistance, however, is always offered against particular relations of power. And the entity that can resist a particular relation is the individual (or group). An individual always has features and capacities beyond those formed by any given relation and is able, on the basis of these, to confront and oppose that relation and its effects.[6] Of course, different parts of an individual can be the target of different kinds of power and thus a possible source of inflammation and resistance. As examples Foucault mentions the mind, pleasures, the body, behaviors, and moments of life. Note that although, for Foucault, the biological is constantly present in human life (*HS1*, 152), his position does not require that there be something natural or biological about minds, bodies, and so on. The features and capabilities on the basis of which an individual can oppose a given power relation and the effects it has on her may themselves be products of other force relations.

Finally, the expansion of force relations in modern life has multiplied the number of subjugated groups, each composed of individuals subjected to a particular form of power: women, welfare-dependent women, pregnant women, and housewives, for example; or children, tested children, schoolchildren, and latchkey children; or prisoners, death-row inmates, juvenile delinquents, white collar criminals; and so on. There are as many types of local struggle as there are force relations and subjugated groups. The dissemination of new forms of power also means that traditional "we's" may be partly antiquated and future "we's" still inchoate. Traditional "we's" include We the people (citizens), the people (*Volk*), the proletariat, the aristocracy, royalty, and Jews. The proliferation of power relations means that much of the oppression that individuals experience does not reflect their membership in these groups. This membership, as a result, is incidental in the struggle against those relations. Targets of a particular power relation might be unaware, moreover, that they form a subjugated group. This situation is increasingly the case in the modern world, and local struggle is thus a means to the formation of future "we's" (*PPP*, 385).

Lyotard's defense of local struggles is best understood through his concept of a differend. A differend is a conflict "that cannot be equitably resolved for lack of a rule of judgment" admissible to one or more of the sides (*TD*, xi). A wrong occurs when such a conflict is settled by a rule which one side does not admit. The existence of wrongs is signaled by suffering, silences, and feelings (of anguish, sorrow, anger, etc.) that cannot be articulated in terms of the rules of adjudication. These are signs that "something which must be able to be put into phrases cannot yet be." (*TD*, 22; cf. 93, 236). Now, differends threaten to occur with every phrase or state of affairs since what follows a phrase or state of affairs is open to contestation by a multiplicity of incommensurable language games. Wrongs too threaten to occur with every phrase or state of affairs since linkages that induce wrongs and deny victims the capacity to express them can always take place. When linkages are systematically regulated with this result, hegemony exists. For instance, at work workers feel anger, alienation, and frustration. These feelings signal that they suffer a wrong. According to Lyotard, what it is that they cannot put into phrases is labor. Workers must exchange their labor for wages. They have no choice but to submit to the rules of the economic genre which, in mediating everything as a matter of exchange, conceives of labor as an exchangeable commodity. Labor can, however, be phrased in other genres as self-expression, or as something else. Subjugated to the economic genre, however, laborers are unable to perform this alternative phrasing and to link onto their production accordingly. Their feelings indicate that this subjugation induces a wrong.

Politics, then, is a matter of watching for differends, preventing wrongs from occurring, uncovering wrongs where they exist, and finding idioms in which they can be expressed (*TD*, 22). Political struggle, accordingly, is the effort to thwart oppression and to enable individuals and groups to express something about their lives that the reigning discourses are unable or unwilling to articulate.[7] Local struggles "consequently" aim at the prevention or articulation of particular wrongs. Since every wrong is unique and requires a unique articulation, each local struggle is unto itself. Campaigns conducted in the name of metanarratives might enable certain groups to phrase the wrongs they suffer, but the generality of metanarratives renders them inadequate to the singularity of most wrongs. The extirpation and prevention of wrongs, consequently, must be prosecuted case by case. Of course, since some wrongs are the hegemonic results of the systematic control of certain linkages, some local struggles will target governments and economic systems. Even these struggles, however, require flurries of small-scale actions (*LP*, 152).

Now, according to Lyotard, politics is usually conducted as a genre. This means that a particular language game (e.g., myth, deliberative consensus, divine right, economics) possesses authority to regulate conflict, and does so with an eye to achieving a particular end, for example, con-sensus, self-perpetuation, freedom, or maximum performance (*TD*, 200–201). Each of the resulting forms of politics (Greek *polis*, traditional community, democracy, and capitalism) is a hegemonic project dictating what is to succeed certain states of affairs or phrases. Consequently, since for Lyotard political action aspires to prevent and to counter all oppres-sion and hegemony, these genres of politics are appropriate targets for local struggle.

An oppressed group, furthermore, is the bearer of a particular wrong. The large number of ways in which the indefinite plurality of incom-mensurable language games can induce wrongs means that Lyotard's politics, like Foucault's, recognizes oppressed groups beyond those tradi-tionally discussed in social theory. His favorite examples are workers and Jews, but prisoners, women, the insane, children, and the other groups Foucault mentions presumably are also examples. The existence of oppressed groups which are unaware of themselves as such, moreover, is signaled by community in feelings and suffering.

Since hegemony and oppression always exist, local struggle is always an appropriate form of political activity. It is especially incumbent in the present age, however, because today we are more keenly aware than ever before of the existence of plurality and differends. According to Lyotard, political (and scientific) activity in the nineteenth and twentieth cen-turies was dominated by metanarratives of emancipation which provided legitimacy for governmental arrangements. Today, however, "we" in-creasingly find these metanarratives unbelievable. In the wake of and concurrently with this loss of faith, two developments have occurred: capitalism, a system which has no need for legitimation because it pre-scribes no obligations (*NOL*, 118), has expanded its hegemony; and there has been a resurgence of particularistic communities maintaining "local legitimacy" (*UHCD*, 322) through narratives of historical identity. Hence, at the same time that plurality becomes especially apparent, so too has the threat of hegemony. Contemporary politics, as a result, faces the urgent task of struggling against hegemony—not, however, by resurrect-ing metanarratives or encouraging these particularistic communities, but by recognizing the heterogeneity of language games and the plurality of oppressed groups and by abetting both the evolution of language games and the thwarting of oppression (*TD*, 262–63; *RPS*, 213–14).

Finally, it is important to realize that local politics is an infinite task. For Lyotard, this is so because the threat of oppression and hegemony occurs with every phrase or state of affairs, and each new arrangement with its rules for governing linkages is bound to create new oppressions even while dissolving others (*TD*, 201). Any group that has successfully articulated the wrong from which it suffers, for example, will inevitably experience new wrongs stemming from oppressions and hegemonic projects other than the one which it has overcome. In Foucault, similarly, power is inescapable. An individual is always ensnared in power relations of various types, and all arrangements and institutions, while ameliorating some such relations, introduce new ones. A touch of pessimism, consequently, grips both writers. All that is possible is endlessly to continue the struggle. Lyotard formulates his pessimism with the thesis that the goal of politicians must be the lesser evil, meaning the system that produces the least oppression (*TD*, 197). At the same time, historical contingency is grounds for optimism. Change is always possible. Every state of affairs or phrase, in awaiting a linkage, offers a new opportunity to prevent or to articulate oppression (*PC*, 156; cf. *TD*, 263–64).

Theoryless Politics

What role does theory play in the above enterprise? Practically none.

In his discussion with Foucault, Gilles Deleuze characterizes theory as a "box of tools." For Foucault, this means that theory should *be* practice; it should be pursued only in ways and only so far as is required to fulfill the ends and needs of practice. Theory, in other words, should take up existing local struggles (*SP*, 211) and assist them. It accomplishes this, first, by gathering concrete knowledge of the historical constitution and development of the particular form of power opposed in a specific local struggle. This "strategic knowledge" identifies "in what is given to us as universal, necessary, obligatory, what place is occupied by whatever is singular, contingent and the product of arbitrary constraints" (*WiE*, 45) In thereby uncovering possibilities of no longer "being, doing, or thinking what we are, do, or think," it contributes to both the formulation of specific strategies by which local struggles can oppose power relations and the determination of what sorts of specific changes are possible and desirable. Theory assists struggles, second, by questioning the assumptions upon which practices rest, showing that things are not as self-evident as believed. It therewith galvanizes the thought that "exists independently of systems and structures of discourse" (*PC*, 155). Most of Foucault's own writings are devoted to carrying out these two tasks.

Is the accumulation of strategic knowledge and the critique of assumptions a theoretical enterprise? Although it is informed by the analytic grid of Foucault's ontology of power, historical investigation that gathers strategic knowledge is not a theoretical undertaking. It is critical history, not theory or doctrine (*WiE*, 50). Remember, however, that by "theory" I mean systems of abstract, general ideas. Under a different definition of "theory," Foucault's critical histories might count as such and be interpreted as having abandoned one distinction between theory and practice. The existence and fundamental role of his political ontology, however, show that he has not abandoned all such distinctions. In any case, he is clear that totalizing theories of, say, the Marxist or Freudian sorts are more of a hindrance than a help in abetting local struggles. For only bits and pieces of such theories when removed from their place in the theoretic wholes can help illuminate the historical constitution of the situation confronted by local struggles (*2L*, 81). Similarly, while the act of questioning preconceptions can in principle be a theoretical enterprise, this is not how Foucault pursues it. He challenges assumptions by reflecting upon the constitution and development of power relations. His reflections, however, are not carried out in the terms of some theory. They are simply thoughtful probings of the sort often offered by observers of the current scene. So theory has little or no role to play in Foucauldian politics.

Lyotard leaves a bit more room for theory in politics. It is not part of politics to advocate political-ethical theories and to seek to implement them. For such theories, in claiming to possess the correct system of right and wrong or the ideal state of social-political affairs, prescribe systematic ways of linking onto states of affairs or phrases and are thus inevitably hegemonic. Of course, it might be objected that even the ideal of opposing oppression and hegemony is hegemonic with respect to some people, for example, fascists. Lyotard cannot defend this ideal by claiming that it is "the lesser evil" because the latter standard presupposes it. He can point out, however, that the objection upholds the ideal by employing it to criticize itself. It only demonstrates, in other words, that the ideal paradoxically fails to live up to itself.

In any case, politics calls for "critical watchmen" (*TD*, 135; Kant, 3.3), vigilant observers and listeners sensitized to both the situations in which wrongs can occur and the signs that reveal them. Apprehending these situations and the feelings, suffering, silences, and damages (such as loss of kin) that signal wrongs requires no theory beyond the one (Lyotard's) that describes the nature of this brand of politics (and identifies some of the central hegemonies at work in the modern world). Formulating wrongs, on the other hand, can make use of theory. Victims might turn to existing theories or even themselves theorize when striving to phrase the wrongs signaled by their feelings and so on. Consequently, theories of many sorts (political, ethical, economic) can contribute to local struggles, though not in all cases (see *RPS*, 214). Lyotard seems to say as much when he writes that Marx had tried to find the idiom "which the suffering due to capital clamors for" (*TD*, 237). As in Foucault, therefore, theory is practice in the sense that it enters politics solely as a means to eliminate wrongs.

Judgment, Values, and Theory

Although Lyotard acknowledges that theories might prove useful for the purpose of articulating wrongs, the only theory politics demands is political ontology. To complete our understanding of Foucault's and Lyotard's views on theory, we need to consider what drives their advocacy of local struggle.

How is the intellectual to know where and on what occasion to become political, to gather strategic knowledge and criticize assumptions or to watch for wrongs and counter hegemony? Foucault would have the intellectual begin from extant struggles. His own work, he remarks, was always carried out in response to struggles he observed to be occurring about him (*PC*, 156). So the political activity of the intellectual is somewhat haphazard. One just comes across or learns about particular struggles, including those at one's place of work (e.g., the university), decides which ones oppose the power relations posing the greatest dangers (*OGE*, 232), and begins to gather strategic knowledge. In Lyotard, similarly, there is no formula to guide vigilance. The watcher knows what to look for, but encountering it depends on myriad contingencies over which he or she has no control. The choice of which victims to assist, moreover, is criterionless.

Some commentators have criticized Foucault for not specifying a criterion for distinguishing between right and wrong forms of power and resistance. I believe Foucault doubted that there is any such criterion. He would probably have said that each intellectual must judge for him- or herself which power relations should be opposed and which permitted, which resistances should be fostered and which hindered. Presumably there is room for thoughtful discussion on the matter, and critical intellectuals surely can profit from these discussions. But dialogue cannot produce criteria of judgment—it simply hones the capacity to judge. For Lyotard, all ethical judgments are criterionless because criteria are appropriate only in the descriptive, cognitive, or theoretical language games (*JG*, 98) and ethics, the prescriptive language game, must not be made beholden to any of the latter. Ethical judgments are based on feelings (*TD*, 41; *JG*, 69) and are anarchistic as a result (*LL*, 286). Ethical communities, accordingly, are haphazard and unstable, and the specter of irresolvable disagreement looms forever. Lyotard would reject the criticism made of Foucault by denying the appropriateness of criteria in ethical judgments and continuing: My judgments are based on my feeling, your judgments on yours. If we disagree, it means war (*JG*, 67–69). Of course, one of the main tasks of ethical and political theory is to articulate criteria, that is, values, concepts, and images that guide the making of judgments. Hence, because judging which power relations should be opposed and which struggles fostered is without criteria, theory is unable to assist it.

Lyotard would also deny the necessity to defend one's judgments. There is no obligation to defend or persuade, and attempting to do so is probably pointless. What is incumbent is upholding one's individual responsibility before the event: to watch for differends and wrongs and to seize opportunities for defending or righting them. We should also free our ethical judgments from any discourse that claims that right and wrong, good and bad *is* such and such. Foucault seems to agree that there is no obligation to defend judgments. He nowhere tries to defend or persuade us of what he judges to be the main dangers today. He simply passes judgment and gets on with his political task. As Thomas Flynn writes, he "neither offers nor seeks foundations beyond the presumed commitment of his audience to" certain values.[8] I assume that, although Foucault believes it is pointless to defend basic political-ethical values, he thinks that there can sometimes be reason to defend and persuade others of one's judgments. Theory, however, has no role to play here. Plain speaking is all that is required.

Hence, Lyotard and Foucault epitomize the postmodern *Stimmung* described in the introduction. Unintimidated by the diversity and ungroundedness of values, they are unafraid to judge and to work for what they believe, and feel no need or obligation to justify or defend these beliefs through argument and theory.

It should be clear from my discussion thus far that, although Foucault's and Lyotard's judgments do not rely on criteria, their endorsement of local struggle reflects particular values. Neither is an anarchist, maintaining that no system is as good as any system, nor a "nihilist," regarding any system as good as any other. Indeed, both are in a straightforward sense liberationists.

The value animating Foucault's advocacy of local struggles is individuality: the liberty, autonomy, and growth of the individual or group. Earlier difficulties in identifying Foucault's normative framework stem from the fact that, until the early 1980s, he did not clearly commit himself. In, for instance, "What Is Enlightenment?" however, he states that "critical ontology" aims "to give new impetus, as far and wide as possible, to the undefined work of freedom" (46; cf. 48, 50). Liberty means negative freedom: freedom from specific—but not all—power relations. The space of freedom *vis-à-vis* a particular form of power is the space of possible transformations relative to that form (*CTIH*, 36). Autonomy, meanwhile, means self-determination: individuals and groups crafting their own lives, including their identities, uncoerced by the scientific and administrative forms of individualization forced on them by disciplinary- and bio-power:[9]

> [T]he political, ethical, social, philosophical problem of our days is not to try to liberate the individual from the state, and from the state's institutions, but to liberate us from the state and from the type of individualization which is linked to the state. We have to promote new forms of subjectivity through the refusal of this kind of individuality which has been imposed on us for several centuries. (*SP*, 216; cf. 212)

Growth, furthermore, is the acquisition of capabilities (*WiE*, 47–48), presumably capacities to make choices, to take stands, to mold oneself, to perform actions, in short, the capacities required for self-determination. In sum, Foucault aims to make possible the growth of forms of individuality that are not forms of subjection either to others or to interiorized scientific and administrative models of selfhood (*SP*, 212; cf. *RA*, 222).[10]

Foucault is even willing to call upon the language of rights in defense of individuality. As he notes, a historically important weapon against disciplinary- and bio-power has been the invocation of rights unrecognized by the classical juridical system: "the right to life, to one's body, to health, to happiness, to the satisfaction of needs . . . . , to rediscover what one is and all that one can be" (*HS1*, 145). Some commentators take Foucault's discussion at the end of "Two Lectures" as evidence that he banishes the discourse of rights from the struggle against power. A careful reading of these pages reveals, however, that what Foucault charges with complicity with the disciplinary power regime is the notion of sovereign political right: the ideas of popular sovereignty, of the delegative status of the individual, and of other essentially political rights. He concludes his discussion not by calling for a new ethics, but for "a form of *right*, one which must indeed be anti-disciplinarian, but at the same time liberated from the principle of sovereignty" (108; my emphasis).

Recall in passing that what it is that can become free, autonomous, and mature is unmysterious. It is not, as some writers think it must be, some metaphysical or biological entity that stands outside all power relations. It is simply human beings *qua* socially formed biological creatures who live, as individuals or as members of groups, in fields of possibilities exceeding the actualities of their existence; and who, by virtue of their socially formed capabilities, are able to oppose specific power relations (even those responsible for these capabilities) and to realize alternative possibilities of existence.

These values are admittedly vague, and Foucault does not essay to make them more precise. There is no need for him to do so, however, since local politics does not require it. All Foucault needs in order to commit his work to the advancement of local struggles is a vague notion of a "commonly valued human freedom-autonomy"[11] combined with perceptions of concrete danger to those values.

It is important to point out, moreover, that what concretely freedom is freedom *from*, autonomy self-determination *to*, and growth a becoming *into* is a contingent matter varying from circumstance to circumstance. Exactly which power relations are to be resisted, which changes are possible and desirable, which capacities people acquire and utilize, and what they make of themselves depends on the circumstances and individuals concerned. In no case, furthermore, is the intellectual to prescribe what is to be done. Endorsing individuality means that the intellectual must relinquish all claims to legislate for others (*PaS*, 124; *CT*, 215; *IP*, 206-209; *TP*, 120) and allow oppressed groups to speak for and determine themselves.

So, Foucault does not reject "liberal" values. Indeed, he is an advocate of good ol' "emancipation politics" who calls for freedom from power and space for self-determination and growth. Nor does he seek a new normative vocabulary or rhetoric as opposed to a new normative theory.[12] He seems perfectly content with at least some existing normative concepts, and he can hardly be said to use innovative political-ethical rhetoric. What he does clearly reject is any role for theory in political activity. Theory is not required either to make more precise or to defend, let alone to justify, the values in the name of which local struggles are abetted. Nor should it legislate either what is to be done to realize these values or what people should do subsequent to their realization. It cannot even provide a criterion with which intellectuals can know which struggles to foster.

The animating value in Lyotard, on the other hand, is the Idea of Justice. Lyotard uses "Idea" in the sense of Kant's Ideas of Reason, which in his language are representations whose reality cannot be established on the rules of the cognitive language game. As the content of the Idea of Justice Lyotard proposes diversity, or multiplicity (*JG*, 94). The only explication he offers for this proposal is that this is the content we need today to make decisions in political matters. What he means, I believe, is that this content formulates the unnamed "sublime" feeling experienced by individuals advanced in "the culture of skill and will" when witnessing the "fission" of metanarratives wrought in the contemporary world by the singular events earlier mentioned (see *SH*, 409).[13] In any case, Lyotard maintains that what justice is cannot be determined by any sort of theoretical discourse. There is no learned discussion or knowledge of what justice is because justice lies in the realm of opinions and not that of truth (*JG*, 25–27). Part of what Lyotard means is that there isn't anything that justice, that is, diversity, is in general. All there is is what different people judge it to be in particular circumstances. So what justice-diversity is awaits specification by concrete judgment, which determines from case to case and from person to person exactly what diversity amounts to. Lyotard also says that the Idea of Justice "regulates" judgment without furnishing it a criterion. Again, he means that there is no stable, univocal formula for what diversity is with which it can be determined whether *X* is just. Resolving whether *X* is just is ascertaining whether it is commensurate with what one judges diversity specifically to amount to in the circumstances involved.

Lyotard offers some examples of what justice amounts to more specifically. In social life, diversity consists in no group having domination over others (*JG*, 95). Phrased in terms of language games, this means that no language game exerts hegemony over another and that the purity of language games is upheld (*JG*, 96). In the realm of knowledge, meanwhile, diversity amounts to legitimation through paralogy (see *PMC*, 61). And from all this it clearly follows that when differends exist, justice consists in preventing their adjudication by rules inadmissible to any of the parties, and that when wrongs occur, it amounts to enabling the victims to articulate them. Justice even means that people must be free to phrase their own senses of right and wrong on the basis of their feelings. One must hope that if the Idea of Justice were ever nearly realized there would be significant commonality in feelings.

Hence justice for Lyotard, like individuality for Foucault, requires that the particular be allowed to speak for and be itself. Granting particulars the right to freedom and self-determination coincides with the demand for diverse particulars. Lyotard and Foucault advocate a liberation politics, consequently, that aims both to free people from power or hegemony and to grant them the space to determine and be themselves. For both writers, "Postmodernity can refer simultaneously to the most disparate projects" (*UHCD*, 319).

Postmodern Politics and Theory?

The main contribution of theory in the politics of Foucault and Lyotard is an ontological analysis, a picture of the complex, atomistic constitution of social reality. While this picture generates a conception of politics as the management of the connections among the elements of this reality, theoretical analysis cannot legislate how or to what end these connections should be managed. Underlying Lyotard's and Foucault's ideas on these matters is a noncognitively based commitment to the values of diversity or freedom/autonomy which neither thinker believes can be justified or defended theoretically. These values champion struggle against power relations or oppression/hegemony. In obligating Foucault and Lyotard to allow others to speak for themselves, these values also oblige them to deny the propriety of theories and intellectuals legislating for others. They even help prevail upon Lyotard and Foucault to refrain from prescribing to other *intellectuals* either the political activity they believe in or the values upon which that activity rests. We have also seen, lastly, that theories about how society as a whole should be organized are useless for the purpose of local struggle. Such theories are counterproductive, moreover, if they help motivate changes in governmental and economic organization that leave many of the power relations and hegemonies oppressing people unchanged.

Foucault is silent, however, about another possible role for theory: the creation of new political-ethical concepts and of new meanings for existing ones. He nowhere indicates whether systematic abstract general thinking can invent new values or give more flesh to his vague notions of freedom, autonomy, and growth. He does write that, "the traditional question of political philosophy . . . [is] how is the discourse of truth . . . able to fix limits to the rights of power? That is the traditional question. The one I would prefer to pose is rather different" (*2L*, 93). This statement suggests that he might accept these activities as legitimate tasks for theory so long as it does not stray into the construction of entire systems of society. The politics most urgent in the contemporary world, however, need not await the results of this endeavor.

Lyotard, on the other hand, admits that theorizing can put at the disposal of oppressed individuals and groups concepts and discourses with which they might be able to phrase the wrongs they suffer. By implication, therefore, he acknowledges that theory can invent, elaborate, and redefine political-ethical concepts. Another reason for thinking he believes this is that he himself theoretically elaborates the Idea of Justice by specifying in what diversity consists in certain general contexts. (This is not excluded by the claim that case by case judgment determines what justice is since theoretical judgment as much as practical judgment can work case to case.) Lyotard's explicit position is that theory should be banished from the ethics language game. He conceives of theory, however, as a cognitive language game that aims to copy faithfully that to which it refers (*TA*, 75). He means, therefore, that judgments of right and wrong cannot be held responsible to any discourse that claims to represent what right and wrong truly are. So he does not deny that systematic abstract general thought can or should work on political-ethical concepts.

Is anything gained by calling Foucault's and Lyotard's conception of local politics and the role of theory therein "postmodern"? I suggested earlier that postmodernity might be understood as a name for an ill-defined collection of theses. I have now outlined a conception of politics that "articulates" these five theses. So if these theses capture the content of postmodernity, this conception warrants the appellation. The admitted contentiousness of my characterization of postmodernity, however, nullifies whatever benefit could result from this fact.[14]

I also suggested, however, that there is a postmodern approach to political matters that eschews theory in the political arena. I indicated that this approach is rooted in a particular *Stimmung* which, in leaving behind the need for assurance, no longer requires theory to provide cognitive guarantees for values. We have seen how Lyotard and Foucault exemplify this *Stimmung* and forsake theory in political-ethical matters. On this criterion, therefore, their approach to politics counts as postmodern. What at first sight might seem to undercut this claim is the uncanny resemblance of their views on theory to those of Hans-Georg Gadamer. Gadamer maintains that values cannot be justified; that theory should not legislate what people are to do; that the utopias outlined in theories are not aims of action (but critiques of the present); that it is the business not of theory but of practice to make the meanings of universals, norms, and utopias concrete; and even that theory does not invent values but only articulates those unthematically developed in practice. For Gadamer, the main role of theory in the political-ethical realm is to analyze the nature of that realm.[15] However, although Gadamer sees as restricted a role for theory in political-ethical matters as do Foucault and Lyotard, his position is not born of their postmodern *Stimmung*. He has not abandoned the need for assurance, which he fulfills by stressing the positive, founding virtues of community, unity, and tradition. Thus, although their perspectives on theory converge, the classical, neo-Aristotelian basis of Gadamer's views differentiates them from the postmodern, Nietzschean views of Foucault and Lyotard.

The different historical and *Stimmungsgemassig* sources of these parallel views of theory point, moreover, toward a more rigorous way of defining postmodernity. This definition takes the composition of the expression seriously. Postmodernity, if it is anything in particular, is something that comes after, takes leave of, or leaves modernity behind.[16] What, then, is modernity?

Since our concern here is primarily with philosophical postmodernity, we can set aside modernity conceived of as an epoch of Western social history. Philosophically speaking, modernity is constituted by two projects, one epistemological, the other political. The epistemological project is the search for the foundations of knowledge or values. These foundations were usually thought to be connected somehow to a metaphysical subject. The political project is the realization of autonomy, freedom, individual rights, and democracy. Together, these two projects form a single quest, that of humanity's self-determination or self-assertion.[17] It is important, however, to emphasize the distinction between them since many commentators on the modernity-postmodernity scene either assume that the two projects stand and fall together or overlook the second entirely.

In taking leave of foundationalism, most thinkers today are epistemologically postmodern, though foundationalism has resurfaced, significantly enough, in contemporary ethics. Relatively few writers, however, are politically postmodern. Here Foucault and Lyotard part ways. While Foucault clearly advocates liberal values, Lyotard just as clearly bids them adieu. Like political-ethical values and systems generally, autonomy, freedom, rights, and democracy exert hegemonic effects. A fighter against hegemony, consequently, cannot endorse them. Indeed, Lyotard is unwilling to advocate any specific political-ethical values. He embraces the Idea of Justice as diversity because it articulates the sublime feeling "we" experience in witnessing the dissolution of metanarratives. And it is in the name of diversity that he opposes hegemony and therewith liberalism along with all other more specific systems of values. Of course, it remains an open question, unaddressed by Lyotard, whether democracy is the political system, and freedom and autonomy the values, most compatible with diversity.[18] Lyotard himself argues that deliberative politics admits the heterogeneity of language games (*TD*, 210, 217, 253). Further, since he conceives the political good to be the least hegemony, he could favor democracy on the grounds that it is the political system that best realizes this state of affairs. This is not, however, the place to pursue these questions further.[19] Too many issues announce themselves, for example, does Lyotard's call for diversity allow for community, and, if so, what sort of community? Does Lyotard's call for diversity entail the separation and segregation of groups?[20] Doesn't Lyotard's analysis of the inherent instability of pluralistic deliberative politics problematize the viability of a democracy which valorizes diversity (see *NOL*)? It is not at all clear that Lyotard can endorse democracy as we know it. Similarly, although democracy seems to be the system most capable of upholding the other liberal values Foucault endorses, he nowhere avers, so we must beware attributing to him, an allegiance to this system of government.

Forsaking the conception of political-ethical theory promulgated in modernity is a third dimension of philosophical postmodernity rigorously defined. Most, though not all, modern philosophers supposed that theory could and should not only specify the nature of social reality and discern political and ethical concepts and ideas, but also justify and defend these values; prescribe to people generally what they should be and do; and outline utopias, systems, and general strategies for action. These philosophers adopted this position, moreover, because, when the ontological and teleological bases for values were left behind in the transition to philosophical modernity, it became incumbent upon reason and theory to fill the resulting lacuna.[21] In abandoning the need for secure mooring and therewith theory's function in providing this, Lyotard and Foucault exemplify a postmodern approach to political-ethical matters.

Concluding Remarks

Having adopted a generally laudatory voice in this chapter, I want to conclude by offering several general and straightforward criticisms of Foucault's or Lyotard's ideas on politics and political theory. It is hard to quarrel with their general idea of struggles against local forms of oppression. Nor do I personally have any difficulty with their refusal to articulate or defend criteria that identify which local struggles should be fostered. I do think, however, that Foucault's specific conception of these struggles is more sensible than Lyotard's. For instance, Lyotard's notion that wrongs are signaled by feelings is both too broad and too narrow. It is too broad because people have and share feelings for many reasons, including spite, envy, and ignorance, and at least some feelings presumably also have physiological causes. So feelings, including those we have difficulty expressing, do not always signal hegemony and oppression. His notion is too narrow, on the other hand, because wrongs emanating from hegemony and oppression are not always signaled by feelings, for example, when the people suffering them are unaware of the hegemony and oppression at work. By contrast, Foucault's depiction of the tangible ways in which power relations contribute to the formation, subjugation, and domination of individuals offers a solid framework for possible intervention. In addition, his appeal to "commonly valued freedom-autonomy" is more congruent with my own feelings than is Lyotard's plea for diversity.

Moreover, although Foucault and Lyotard deny that there is a criterion for distinguishing between permissible and impermissible forms of power or hegemony, I am sure that Foucault would have agreed that not all forms of power are unacceptable. Lyotard's espousal of diversity, however, means that all forms of "oppression" and "hegemony" are ruled out of court: a wrong occurs whenever a conflict is resolved by rules inadmissible to one of the parties. Surely this blanket condemnation runs afoul of our experience and knowledge of areas and moments of life where "wronging" someone can be either for his or her own good, for example, children, or for our good, for example, fascists. Set against experience, justice as diversity seems fantastic.

Lyotard's analysis of local oppression is more doctrinaire and hence less realistic and practically fruitful than Foucault's. At the same time, Foucault's incessant focus on local politics can numb one's appreciation of the crucial roles that governments and economic systems play in individual lives and systems of power. Foucault does not deny these roles. But, unlike Lyotard's analysis of the political realm, which secures a place for systemic oppression, Foucault's drive to promote local politics obfuscates the complementariness of local activity with resistance to governmental and economic (as well as religious, ethnic, and racial) oppression. Foucault is mistaken to favor local struggles at the expense of resistance to the state or economic systems. Maybe all modern economies and states exploit the disciplinary- and bio-power mechanisms he describes, but surely Walzer is correct that they do not do so in the same ways.[22] Overthrowing an economy or government might not only be good for its own sake, but also lead to changes in at least some of these power relations.

This is an obvious point, one it is hard to imagine Foucault having denied. Perhaps, therefore, we should read his disinterest in general struggle differently. Perhaps Foucault believed that the entrenchment of the global capitalist system is so advanced that it has become hopeless to struggle against it. If so, then local struggle is the only sensible form of economic counteractivity. I do not know if Foucault believed this (but see *RA*, 230). Even if he did, however, parallel claims cannot be made about the political realm. Here, so long as the nation-state remains a central player on the world scene, local struggle cannot be the sole focus of political activity.

Finally, I also believe, contra both Foucault and Lyotard, that theories of government and economics have an important role to play in the opposition to governmental and economic oppression. I agree with them

that it is not the business of theory to justify or even defend basic political-ethical values. But this struggle is informed by, and its success partly
tied to, its ability to offer alternative visions of the organization of government and the economy. It is the function of theory to provide these
visions. It is probably true that theoretical activity of this sort in the political though not the economic realm has been moribund since the middle
of the previous century (in comparison to the previous two hundred
years). And Foucault and Lyotard, like so many others in recent decades,
call attention to dangers attending the implementation of large-scale
visions. But there is need today for both the development and aggressive
promotion of such visions, however unlikely their chances for success.[23]

Notes

1. See, for instance, Eugene Lunn, *Marxism and Modernism* (Berkeley:
University of California Press, 1983).
2. My use of this Heideggarian term parallels that made of it by Richard
Bernstein in "An Allegory of Modernity/Postmodernity: Habermas and Derrida,"
in his *The New Constellation: The Ethical-Political Horizons of Modern-
ity/Postmodernity* (Cambridge: MIT Press, 1992).
3. References in this chapter to works by Foucault are as follows:

CT	"The Concern for Truth," in *Michel Foucault: Politics, Philosophy, Culture*, ed. Lawrence D. Kritzman (New York: Routledge, 1988), 255–67.
CTIH	"Critical Theory/Intellectual History," in *Michel Foucault: Politics, Philosophy, Culture*, 17–46.
HS1	*The History of Sexuality, Vol. 1: An Introduction*, trans. Robert Hurley (New York: Vintage, 1980).
HS2	*The History of Sexuality, Vol. 2: The Use of Pleasure*, trans. Robert Hurley (New York: Vintage, 1986).
IP	"Intellectuals and Power," in *Language, Counter-Memory, Practice*, ed. Donald F. Bouchard (Ithaca, N.Y.: Cornell University Press, 1977), 205–17.
NGH	"Nietzsche, Genealogy, History," in *The Foucault Reader*, ed. Paul Rabinow (New York: Pantheon, 1984), 76–100.
OGE	"On the Genealogy of Ethics," in *Michel Foucault: Beyond Structural-ism and Hermeneutics*, 2d ed., ed. Hubert L. Dreyfus and Paul Rabinow, (Chicago: University of Chicago Press, 1983), 229–52.
PaS	"Power and Sex," in *Michel Foucault: Politics, Philosophy, Culture*, 110–24.
PC	"Practicing Criticism," in *Michel Foucault: Politics, Philosophy, Culture*, 152–6.
PPP	"Polemics, Politics, and Problemizations," in *The Foucault Reader*, 381–90.

PS	"Power and Strategies," in *Power/Knowledge*, ed. Colin Gordon (New York: Pantheon, 1980), 134–45.
RA	"Revolutionary Action: Until Now," in *Language, Counter-Memory, Practice*, 218–33.
SP	"The Subject and Power," in *Michel Foucault: Beyond Structuralism and Hermeneutics*, 208–26.
TP	"Truth and Power," in *Power/Knowledge*, 109–33.
2L	"Two Lectures," in *Power/Knowledge*, 78–108.
WiE	"What is Enlightenment?" in *The Foucault Reader*, 32–50.

References to works of Lyotard are as follows:

DGR	"La Deflexion des grand recits: Entretien avec Jean-François Lyotard," Etienne Tassin (interviewer) *Intervention* no. 7 (November–December 1983, January 1984).
JG	*Just Gaming*, with Jean-Loup Thebaud, trans. Wlad Godzich (Minneapolis: University of Minnesota Press, 1985).
LL	"Levinas' Logic," in *The Lyotard Reader*, ed. Andrew Benjamin (Oxford, England: Blackwell, 1989), 275–313.
LP	"Lessons in Paganism," in *The Lyotard Reader*, 122–54.
NOL	"Notes on Legitimation," trans. Cecile Lindsay *Oxford University Review* 9, nos. 1–2 (1987): 106–18.
PMC	*The Postmodern Condition*, trans. Geoff Bennington and Brian Massumi (Minneapolis: University of Minnesota Press, 1984).
RPS	"Rules and Paradoxes and Svelte Appendix," trans. Brian Massumi, *Culture Critique* 5 (1986), 209–19.
SH	"The Sign of History," in *The Lyotard Reader*, 393–411.
TA	"Theory as Art," in *Image and Code*, ed. Wendy Steiner (Ann Arbor: University of Michigan Press, 1981), 71–77.
TD	*The Differend*, trans. Georges Van Den Abbeele (Minneapolis: University of Minnesota Press, 1988).
UHCD	"Universal History and Cultural Differences," in *The Lyotard Reader*, 314–23.

4. David Carroll's claim that Lyotard abandons Wittgenstein's notion of language games overlooks the fact that, in *The Differend*, this notion is reproduced in the twin notions of a regime and of a genre, which diversify it while retaining the full range of pragmatic valencies Lyotard discusses in earlier works. See "Rephrasing the Political with Kant and Lyotard: From Aesthetic to Political Judgments," *Diacritics* 14, no. 3 (Fall 1984): 74–88, esp. 77. See also David Ingram, "Legitimacy and the Postmodern Condition: The Political Thought of Jean-François Lyotard," *Praxis International* 7, nos. 3–4 (Winter 1987–88); 286–305; esp. 294.

5. The complications attending Lyotard's notion of a phrase (a meaningful "articulation . . . of separate [discrete] elements" [*RPS*, 212]) cannot be discussed

here. Suffice it to say that denotative phrases whose addressor (and maybe also addressee) poles are empty are occurrent states of affairs. The question of what phrase links onto such a phrase is the question of what state of affairs succeeds a previous one. I will speak of "states of affairs or phrases" succeeding one another to indicate that Lyotard is concerned with linkages onto both states of affairs and statements.

6. When power is conceptualized as the structuring of others' possibilities of actions, the freedom to choose among possibilities, to act otherwise, confronts every relation of power. Hence, the possibility of resistance is inherent in every instance of power. See SP, 219–25.

7. Lyotard does not clearly differentiate between articulating wrongs and eliminating them. Perhaps he believes that a wrong cannot be articulated unless the social world has been altered in a manner that also permits its elimination. His lack of clarity here opens him to objections of the sort leveled by Seyla Benhabib (with a different point in mind), that his politics naively ignores the structural sources of inequality, influence, and resource. See "Epistemologies of Postmodernism: A Rejoinder to Jean-François Lyotard," New German Critique 33 (Fall 1984): 124. On the other hand, his analyses in various works of, among other things, capitalism and economics clearly demonstrate that Nancy Fraser and Linda Nicholson err in claiming that he rejects both the "project of social theory" and large-scale, nonimmanent critique. Whether he grants legitimacy to theoretical accounts of "macrostructures" is a more complicated issue, tied to the nature of macrostructures. See "Social Criticism without Philosophy," in Universal Abandon? The Politics of Postmodernism, ed. Andrew Ross (Minneapolis: University of Minnesota Press, 1988), 83–104, esp. 85–91.

8. Thomas Flynn, "Foucault and the Politics of Postmodernity," Nous 23 (1989): 197. Flynn's characterization of Foucault as a parrhesiast in the tradition of the cynics throws interesting light on Foucault's postmodern sensibilities.

9. Foucault calls freedom "liberation" and autonomy "liberty" in "The Ethic of Care for the Self as a Practice of Freedom," in The Final Foucault, ed. James Bernauer and David Rasmussen (Cambridge: MIT Press, 1988), 1–20.

10. For Foucault, therefore, autonomy is not something "which all human beings have within them and which society can release by ceasing to repress them" (Richard Rorty, Contingency, Irony, and Solidarity [Cambridge: Cambridge University Press, 1989], 65). This is an older, more metaphysical conception of autonomy rejected by Foucault. Foucault in fact agrees with Rorty that autonomy is an achievement attained through self-creation, a self-creation that requires the acquisition of capacities and is limited in scope.

11. Flynn, "Foucault and the Politics of Postmodernity," 196, note 8.

12. Nancy Fraser, "Foucault's Body Language: A Posthumanist Political Rhetoric?" in her Unruly Practices (Minneapolis: University of Minnesota Press, 1989), 56.

13. Lyotard alludes here to the feeling of enthusiasm had by observers of the French Revolution, which Kant interprets as evidence for progress in human history on the grounds that having this feeling requires advancement in "the culture of skill and will." (See "An Old Question Raised Again: Is the Human Race

Constantly Progressing?" [Part II of *The Conflict of Faculties*], in Immanuel Kant, *On History*, ed. Lewis Beck White [Indianapolis, Ind.: Bobbs-Merrill, 1963], 137–54.) One can criticize Lyotard for basing the content of justice on a feeling which some indeterminate group of observers experience. He might reply that the judgment, that diversity is the content of justice, is of the same sort as ethical judgments generally, hence can be based only on feeling. It is unclear to me, however, why it is of the same type.

14. I note in passing another way to attempt justifying the label "postmodern" for Foucault's and Lyotard's preferred politics. Both thinkers believe that local struggles are especially pertinent in the contemporary age. If this is true, for instance, in the largely democratically stabilized nations of the modern West, and if, moreover, the current age, and not just its culture, can justifiably be analyzed as postmodern, then there is a sense in which local struggle is the postmodern political activity *par excellence*.

15. For concise statements of most of these points, see "What Is Practice? The Conditions of Social Reason" and "Hermeneutics as Theoretical and Practical Task," in Hans-Georg Gadamer, *Reason in the Age of Science*, trans. Frederick G. Lawrence (Cambridge: MIT Press, 1981), 69–87, 113–38.

16. A similar approach to defining postmodernity is found, for example, in Chantal Mouffe, "Radical Democracy: Modern or Postmodern?" in *Universal Abandon?: The Politics of Postmodernism*, 31–45, note 7; and in Gianni Vattimo, Introduction, *The End of Modernity*, trans. Jon R. Snyder (Baltimore: Johns Hopkins University Press, 1988).

17. See Hans Blumenberg, *The Legitimacy of the Modern Age*, trans. Robert M. Wallace (Cambridge: MIT Press, 1983).

18. This is, for example, Mouffe's position in "Radical Democracy: Modern or Postmodern?" note 16. See also Fred Dallmayr, "Modernity under Crossfire," chapter 2 of this volume.

19. Ernest Yanarella discusses the political problem of community and unity in diversity in his contribution to this volume.

20. Unless mutual indifference and lack of interaction are forms of community, David Carroll attributes too much to Lyotard's views in suggesting that the prime political problem in Lyotard's eyes is "how to link . . . heterogeneity . . . to a notion of 'sociability' or community that is open but not simply pluralistic, how to develop a narratological-political strategy that neither suppresses this heterogeneity in the name of a historico-political ideal nor makes it an end in itself at the expense of the social community" ("Narrative, Heterogeneity, and the Question of the Political: Bakhtin and Lyotard," in *The Aims of Representation: Subject/Text/History*, ed. Murray Krieger [New York: Columbia University Press, 1987], 80). The complexity in understanding Lyotard's position here is nicely captured by David Ingram when, after first suggesting that the experience of heterogeneity signifies for Lyotard a "community of discourse in which integrity, harmony, and justice . . . ideally prevail," he almost immediately thereafter notes that for Lyotard "the ideal of a just society resides as much in the form of a negative disassociation of reified appearances as in the positive projection of community"; see "Legitimacy and the Postmodern Condition," 299–300, note 3.

21. This sort of analysis is exemplified in Alasdair MacIntyre, *After Virtue* (Notre Dame, Ind.: University of Notre Dame Press, 1981).

22. Michael Walzer, "The Politics of Michel Foucault," in *Foucault: A Critical Reader*, ed. David Couzens Hoy (New York: Blackwell, 1986), 66.

23. I would like to thank Les Thiele for comments on an earlier version of this essay.

4

Whither Hegemony?: Between Gramsci and Derrida

ERNEST J. YANARELLA

Reflecting on the cultural and political conditions of the early twentieth century in his squalid prison cell in Turi, Italy, Antonio Gramsci penned a sentence on the nature of organic crisis that would express for many later in this century the mood and experience of a period suspended between imminent change and continuing blockage. "The crisis," he wrote, "consists precisely in the fact that the old is dying and the new cannot be born; in this interregnum a great variety of morbid symptoms appear[s]."[1] Within scholarship and other forms of cultural production today, the complex and multitiered debates over modernity and modernism launched by postmodern writers in diverse fields and across national boundaries have provoked a host of questions, not only about the legitimacy of the modern age and the viability of the Enlightenment project of modernity, but also about the character and virtues of postmodernism, poststructuralism, and one of its variants, deconstructionism.

As N. Katherine Hayles has aptly observed in her splendid study of disorderly order in chaos theory and in postmodern philosophy and literature, the privileging of disorder over order (or better, the reciprocal intertwining of disorder within order) in the current cultural conjuncture has not been univocal. Rather, "disciplinary traditions [have played] crucial roles in determining how isomorphic ideas are valued and interpreted."[2] Thus, she notes, "where scientists see chaos as the source of order, poststructuralists appropriate it to subvert order."[3] Likewise, the reception of varieties of postmodern thought has been subject to disciplinary idiosyncracies. In some disciplines, schools of postmodern thought have come to exert such a hegemonic force on writing that, while scholars in fields like literary criticism, comparative literature, and architecture may write outside of the new mainstream, "the prevailing practices of the discourse community tend so strongly in contrary directions that anyone who attempts them feels an invisible pressure pushing against each paragraph, each sentence, each word."[4]

Happily, this condition does not define the intellectual force field of contemporary political theory. Yet, precisely because the relationship between postmodernism and politics has become a highly contested topic, especially with respect to Jacques Derrida's deconstructionist philosophy, the interrogation of postmodern currents and their import for the study of politics has become a more prominent task for political theorists like William Connolly, Fred Dallmayr, and a growing number of others in the field.[5]

This chapter seeks to participate in the critical appropriation of postmodern themes into contemporary political theory by investigating the relevance of Derridian deconstruction for political theory and practice. It will do so by exploring as its main thrust the concept of hegemony as it has been thematized in three recent works: William Corlett's *Community without Unity: The Politics of Derridian Extravagance*, Carl Boggs's *Social Movements and Political Power: Emerging Forms of Radicalism in the West*, and Ernesto Laclau and Chantal Mouffe's *Hegemony & Socialist Strategy: Towards a Radical Democratic Politics*.[6] My choice of these works was heavily influenced in part by the important insights each brings to the problematic of hegemony and in part by their varying sensitivity to the need within political theory and social practice to break with philosophical limitations and cultural compulsions of the crisis of modernity. *En passant*, this chapter will try to offer a provisional answer to whether deconstruction is one of those "morbid symptoms" of the crisis of legitimacy of late capitalism or an indispensable means for overcoming its deeper roots in Western thought and metaphysics.

Communitarian Reassurance in the Solvent of Derridian Extravagance: The Deconstructionist Political Theory of William Corlett

The relationship between deconstruction and politics is, and remains, the subject of lively and continuing controversy among both enthusiasts and critics of Derrida's work.[7] Derrida himself has bemoaned the fact that "available codes for taking a political stance are not at all adequate to the radicality of deconstruction." Still, he has in recent years taken political positions on a variety of topics—including women's liberation, neocolonialism, and apartheid—that would seem to point to the clear political relevance of deconstruction.[8] Moreover, he has promised, but not delivered, an encounter of deconstruction with "the text of Marxism" that would help illuminate where the "responsible anarchism" he has ambiguously embraced stands vis-à-vis that tradition.[9] The allusiveness (elusiveness?) and abstract nature of Derrida's writings to date on political theory and deconstruction suggest that the verdict is still out in regard to this issue. In any case, given Derrida's profession that his own work itself invites deconstruction, the answer will surely overflow the boundaries of the corpus of Derrida's deconstructive efforts. So, for the moment, the equivocal subtitle of a recent essay by Fraser on the work of some of his French students—"Politicizing Deconstruction or Deconstructing the Political?"[10]—would appear to be apt.

In this respect, a more intellectually challenging, provocative, and compelling work of political theory addressing this issue than William Corlett's *Community without Unity* would be hard to find. In the clearing he carves out on the pages of this work, Corlett admirably succeeds in filling his pages with analysis showing dialectical fealty to Derridian extravagance through a subtle interweaving of rational argumentation and the "barely natural drowsiness of reason," reason and its monstrosity, and provisional order and primordial chaos. The goal of his book is to subject the liberalism-communitarian debate to a deconstruction that opens up a space in the margins of this political discourse to the alternative of community without unity—or, as he calls it in various places, "mutual service and defense," "mutual service without domination," and more poetically, "joy before life" (pp. 12, 19, 208, respectively).

In the process of demonstrating the relevance and merits of Derrida's work to deconstructing the political, he draws out many salient threads within his writings for politicizing deconstruction in the sense of formulating a deconstructive political theory of community. As we shall see, in order for deconstruction to do its work, Corlett must drawn upon Foucault's writings on power—a treatment which opens up the main text of this chapter, the concept of hegemony.

Without trying to wrench his discussion of deconstruction out of the context of its use, I would like to highlight a number of his comments and observations about the relationship between deconstruction and political theory that nicely set up his sure and subtle exercise in applied deconstruction. Corlett's critique of the liberalism-communitarian con-

troversy is founded on his criticism of the way political theory as an
order-giving discourse tends to lapse into a form of reassurance about the
cosmos, the world, politics, community, time, and the subject. For him,
much political theorizing is prone to frame assumptions and categories
into theoretical and conceptual procrustean beds that push the unavoid-
able messiness of the natural world and social existence out to the margins of political analysis where they can be safely neutralized and effectively put out of play. Chaos, accident, chance, flux, irrationality—in general, the monstrosity immanent in reason and order—are effectively tamed by
generating binary oppositions (self/other, nature/culture, speech/writing,
man/woman, etc.) that typically privilege one pole over the other. Political
theorists, then, tend to place these bipolarities within continua or spectrums
apparently to resolve the dilemmas that bipolar thinking spawns.[11]

When liberals and communitarians, for example, debate the issues of
individualism and community or freedom and equality, their mutual
proneness to set up polar dualisms and to situate each polar concept on a
continuum merely hangs theorizing on the horns of self-imposed conceptual dilemmas or paradoxes. For, not only are debates about how much
individualism is possible within community or vice versa impossible to
resolve within the framework thus established, but the very order-giving
character of the framework itself leaves out the "excess" that Derridian
extravagance seeks to highlight through deconstruction. Though Corlett
ultimately reveals a family kinship with communitarians, he clearly
believes that the communitarian critique of liberalism has fallen into the
various philosophical and theoretical traps of reassurance that make this
body of thought ripe for deconstruction. Following the various renditions
of the communitarian critique offered by Sandel, Taylor, Walzer, and
others, he argues that liberal theorists, like Rosenblum, Benn, and Novak
(he calls them "rights-based theorists of communitarian individualism"),
build their political codifications upon an atomistic prejudice—the
assumption of an unencumbered, fully developed presocial self—founding an "instrumental community" he terms "remunity" (a portmanteau
word for remunerative community). But, he argues, this atomistic prejudice cannot withstand the communitarian assault on this ideological cari-
cature, an assault that demonstrates the situated, embedded nature of
the self and the inescapability of roots and traditions, and therefore the
inevitably socially and communally based character of subjectivity.

While acknowledging the superior strength of these and other communitarian arguments, Corlett wishes to take leave of the framing of the
liberalism–communitarian/remunity–communion debate in order to overcome the limitations posed by each stance and, in some cases, mutually
shared. "Both sides are deaf to the remainder," he argues, "the excess

territory not covered by their defenses of the individual and collective aspects of life." Thus, he continues, they "cannot sense the cost of keeping it out" (p. 33). Rejecting the bipolar thinking that conceptualizes the self as standing at some fulcrum point on a teeter-totter, balancing between the pole of individualism and the pole of communion, Corlett deconstructs this image by appropriating key insights from Foucault and Derrida.

For Foucault, ignoring the remainder eliminated by the individualism-collectivism continuum amounts to the suppression of the dark underside of the cozy and reassuring presuppositions of intersubjectivity or the situated self that governs communitarian theorizing. Exploring the subject in the double sense of identity and discipline, the Foucauldian project points to the multiple ways in which human beings are subjugated by "forces that dominate life in ways that hitherto have gone undetected because [political theorists in the production process of writing and theorizing] uncritically clean the factory of the page, eliminating all pieces that do not fit reasonable arguments" (p. 36). What Foucault and political theorists like William Connolly ask us do to is to "consider the scrap material and junk that piles up around the production of a piece of writing" (p. 37). Recognizing the subject as a double entendre, Foucault develops in his second lecture on power and elsewhere a postmodern theory of hegemony that supplements and displaces the arguments of remunity and communion theorists. As Corlett points out, while these two schools address the first two questions of power opened up by Foucault (domination and exploitation), only Foucault confronts the third question, the issue of subjugation, conceptualized in terms of the many disciplined ways in which "the state's domination is transmitted across time by the very subject it obliges" (p. 39).

Beginning with the "double bind" of modern power structures, that is, with the simultaneous totalizing and individualizing pressures unleashed by these far-reaching political constellations, Foucault adopts the strategy of traversing the "low road of everyday struggle, where he locates the play of domination" (p. 42). According to Corlett, this postmodern articulation of power takes discussion of subjectivity out of the dualistic framework that ensnares liberal and communitarian theorists alike (the subject as autonomous self vs. the subject as embedded self) and poses the situation of the double-edged subject as a hegemonic problem. As subjects and subjected, we embody a double bind flowing from the totalizing and individualizing pressures of modern power structures. Perceiving the bipolar structure created by the opposition of remunity and communion as a power play and refusing to choose between atomistic prejudice and situated subjectivity, Foucault portrays the double-bound subject as "forceably cut off from those aims and attachments s/he discovers everyday while acting as a vehicle of this subtle power" (p. 45).

What makes this postmodern theory of hegemony qua subjugation non- or even anti-Marxist are Foucault's interpretation of the character of the hegemon, the absence of a center for fixing the origins of domination, and the strategy for resistance. In Foucault's postmodern theory of subjugation, the hegemon is not some totalizing structure or process, but rather the "regime du savoir," that is, a regime, a technique, a structure of power (p. 45). Moreover, its hegemony is achieved in a very distinctive manner, through multiple, overlapping microstructures and micropractices that do not add up to any central totalizing process. Finally, since the power of modern structures inheres in a certain kind of knowledge, a counterhegemonic strategy appropriate to subverting its power and influence lies in the practice of genealogical resistance, a strategy that Foucault has championed in his works on the prison, the clinic, the knowledge industry, and sexuality.[12]

Corlett believes that communitarianism would benefit from Derrida no less than from Foucault. As a species of radical political theory, communitarian political theory, Corlett claims, "cannot seem to find its way out of thinking up politics that are either too good to be true or too true to be good" (p. 201). To overcome this disability, it needs to approach politics and political life by using abandon, "in the sense of losing control, giving in to the accidental, chaotic aspect of any structure" (p. 3), and by exploring in extravagant ways the "excess" that is systematically left out of thinking that divides the world in two and establishes hierarchies of dominance and subordination between the two poles. Derrida's deconstructive enterprise involves, then, *refusing to choose* between the two poles and *renouncing* their hierarchical positioning. It most emphatically does not mean, for Corlett, either engaging in destructive dismantlement (as he claims Connolly believes) or choosing the subordinate pole, thus installing a new hierarchy (as Theodore Roszak and Fritjof Capra urge).[13] Understood rightly, deconstruction means giving into the play of these theoretically constructed dualisms and significations without trying to reach closure or final resolution.

The infinite play of significations, for Derrida, flows from the radicalization of linguist de Saussure's insight that all signs are composed of signifiers (concepts) and signifieds (referents) and gain meaning only in relation to their difference from other signs. Because the meaning of any sign is continually deferred to other signs, to something absent, every sign carries with it a "trace" and must be "supplemented" by what is not present. Moreover, because presence is always deferred, there can be no "transcendental signified" which would otherwise establish an origin or foundation from which all other signs could be related. For political theory, this perpetual interplay of presence and nonpresence, of meaning and nonmeaning, means that "flux is in this sense the death of reason and also its most profound resource," and that "we are forced to confess that one makes sense only by provisionally postponing flux" (p. 160). Since this play of primordial flux is "always already" at hand in the margins, so to speak, the pure and fully present meaning of (say) identity or the self, human nature, time, community, politics—in short, Western metaphysics' "essence" or "the thing itself"—is "a sign, a trace, a difference" (p. 162).

Derrida, therefore, does not simply reverse the Platonic two-world schema of world of Pure Forms and world of Appearance. He intertwines form and appearance in an unending chain of significations, thus breaking down and dissolving the boundary separating them and refusing to install a new hierarchy. One implication for hegemony, then, is that any constituted totality, any totalizing form, involves an excess that is always already there and thus establishes its limit and makes it ripe for deconstruction. For Corlett, the reciprocal implication of order and chaos makes the notion of hegemonic dominance in political life indefensible. "It may become necessary," he says, "to use the words legitimacy, sovereignty, or powers-that-be in a minimalist sense that allows one to admit that political forms are vulnerable and not merely reversible" (p. 90).

Corlett's primary concern, though, is to deconstruct the remunity /communion binary opposition and to politicize the excess that Derrida would maintain in silence. Going beyond Derrida while remaining faithful to him, Corlett interprets this deconstructive move as "a will to confess that individual and collective lives as we know them are in principle incomplete; that these lives require a supplement; and that, if such considerations were not themselves always already postponed, such a supplement would completely undermine all that they stand for" (p. 162). Such a confession and its supplement, for him, lead to a third rendering of community: "community without unity." This alternative, for Corlett, does not stand alone, but instead mobilizes the space between the two poles of remunity and communion. Accepting the "full implication in the infinite difference of fellow beings" (p. 22) and refusing to embrace reassuring assumptions about community and politics that "are too good to be true," Corlett envisages a political space of community where mutual service without domination finds expression in the extravagance of gift giving. Such free gifts within the real community of flesh-and-blood human beings exists "without the unity of sharing anything in common" (p. 203) and erupts accidently and often surprisingly in the margins of institutional politics and business-as-usual where "the opposition between the caring 'in crowd' and the people in need 'out there'" (p. 208) is neutralized. In so doing, this cultivation of one's gifts in all directions, this madness of abandoning oneself in the practice of everyday life, manifests an "excentric subjectivity" that momentarily puts the forces of subjugation out of play and taps the primordial wellspring leading to a "joy before life" (p. 208).

In somewhat less poetic terms, Corlett identifies William Connolly's recent emendation of social democracy[14] in the direction of radical liberalism as closely approximating the requirements of community without unity (p. 216). He also suggests its close ties with communitarianism— but only as an extravagance to its reassurances. In the end, he acknowledges, "accidental community without unity is not designed to replace the other, more reassuring, usages of communion and remunity." It is intended, rather, "to thwart their claim to govern political theory" (p. 213).

As a work that disrupts, disturbs, and unsettles venerated ideas and hardening philosophical and ideological positions in contemporary political theory, Corlett's book surely stands out for its healthy iconoclasm. In terms of my opening question, it would seem to be a work that makes the double gesture toward deconstructing the political and politicizing deconstruction in ways that contribute to both enterprises. Although my criticisms of his study are concerned largely with matters of omission, I would like to begin with one glaring shortcoming that, for me, amounts to an error of commission.

In thematizing the concept of hegemony, Corlett, like Derrida, seems to defer engaging in a direct encounter with Marxism, and specifically, with the Gramscian rendering of ideological hegemony. In critically appropriating Foucault's postmodern analysis of subjugation and the "double bind" of modern power structures, Corlett veers toward a modernist, Weberian analysis of power and an individualist strategy of resistance. By identifying received theorizations of hegemony (including, I assume, Gramsci's) with the myth of total domination, Corlett gives the false impression that Gramsci's theory subscribes to this non-Marxist rendering, and he thus has an all-too-easy time dismissing as essentially politically vacuous a concept that in recent years has generated a rich corpus of theory. At one point, for instance, he even makes the perfunctory criticism that "the principle of hegemony is a continual source of political conversations which do not seem to lead anywhere" (p. 70). Whatever limitations the Gramscian notion of hegemony may have (and these will be explored later), it certainly rests upon a subtle understanding of power that incorporates the elements of coercion and consent, force and legitimacy, and that overflows more facile characterizations, inside and outside Marxian orthodoxy, of hegemony as total domination that Corlett, by implication, imputes to it. Likewise, Gramsci's conception of the historical *bloc*, as we shall see, is an effort to gesture toward the possibilities of a counterhegemony without unity which, due to certain residues of Marxist essentialism in his thought, he was unable to completely overcome. Might it not be the case that remnants of liberal individualism informing Corlett's radical liberal/responsible anarchist stance still color his treatment of hegemony and his embrace of the Foucauldian interpretation?

A second line of criticism opens up questions and issues that were not, but might have been, developed in the text. For example, it is surprising that, for a work primarily focused on the politics of community in contemporary political theory, *Community without Unity* fails to develop in any systematic way the Derridian critique of phonocentrism in Western political thought. In defending writing against its subordination by speech, Derrida himself has taken on one of the Western political tradition's most ardent supporters of community: Jean-Jacques Rousseau.[15] While granting the persuasiveness of Derrida's lively critique of Rousseau's phonocentric position, it is not altogether clear that deeper and more complex issues in the identification of politics with speech and of community with face-to-face encounters are not being begged in the defense of "arche-writing" or writing in general. For those of us who were introduced to political philosophy through Hannah Arendt's *The Human Condition*,[16] the association of politics and community with speech and the space of appearance will not be given up lightly and without major contestation. The point is that the communitarian school carries on this Arendtian stance; and, to my mind, the absence of any treatment of the import of this major deconstructive move against the primacy of speech in politics for the politics of community presents a real lacuna in his analysis.

So too is the neglect of the theoretical writings of Niccolo Machiavelli—especially, his discussion of the role of Fortune in political affairs in his political theory of princely power. Who within the Western political tradition has offered a better thematization of the place of flux, chance, and accident in politics than Machiavelli? Certainly, the sexist overtones of his characterization of Fortune as a woman are obvious (see, for example, Pitkin[17]) and ready grist for the deconstructive mill. Yet, both Gramsci and Merleau-Ponty have approved the political realism of Machiavelli's musings on politics and flux, Orr has recently explored the time motif in Machiavelli, and Pocock has located the bases of civic humanism in Machivelli's political thought in ways that might meet with a favorable deconstructive reading.[18] If flux, according to Corlett, may be seen as the "death of reason and its most profound resource," surely Machiavelli was the first Western political theorist to recognize in the madness, the monstrosity, of Fortune at once the mortal enemy of political action and its most valuable potential ally.

Finally, for all of the emphasis on difference and its valorization by Corlett, it is suggestive, and indeed significant in light of the importance placed on marginal comments in deconstructive readings of texts, that he incidentally, almost casually, refers in his conclusion to human embodiment as the "literal common ground beneath all possible theorists of community" (p. 213). This theme of embodied subjectivity, for the initiate to deconstruction, points to the possible limits of that enterprise or to its need to foster a more direct engagement with the critical phenomenology of Merleau-Ponty, Paci, O'Neill, and Reid.[19] For it remains to be seen how deconstruction's interpretation of the body as text could plumb with comparable depth and subtlety the insights of these critical phenomenologists for the implications of embodiment for intersubjectivity, community, and politics.

Ideological Hegemony in Modernist Guise: The Post-Marxist Approach of Carl Boggs

Carl Boggs is a close and sympathetic student of Antonio Gramsci. In his recent book, *Social Movements and Political Power*, he offers a revised and updated formulation of hegemony that is not informed in any direct and studied way by the spirit and insights of deconstructionism specifically nor by those of postmodernism generally.[20] Instead, his is a revision and reconceptualization from within the tradition of Western Marxism that draws upon the observations of a situated theorist reflecting upon the divergent and contradictory forces shaping the contours of the political world of late modernity. In this sense, then, it is a distinctly post-*Marxist* approach to hegemony.

Oriented by a "Gramscian preoccupation with elaborating the conceptual basis of a new radicalism," Boggs aims to grapple with an emergent post-Marxist paradigm whose development remains "partial, limited, and fragmentary," whose theoretical basis is still "weak," and whose strategic articulation is, at best, "embryonic," at worst, "futile" (p. xi). Though he sees the eruption of radical-democratic insurgencies throughout the world in the last quarter of this century as a promising political development worth nurturing in theory and practice, Boggs makes the central argument that while such forms of insurgency cannot take concrete political form and substance "without the leverage made possible by control over state institutions (however remolded)," to date the "very process of winning and administering power imposes its own dilemmas and constraints" (p. xi). Thus, for him, the dominant motif of his work is captured in the apparent contradiction "between the rhythm and energy of the new movements and the political efforts to give them strategic efficacy" (p. xiii). So, he claims, emerging forms of radicalism in the West seem to oscillate between an increasingly antiquated paradigm of oppositional politics and a new one that has yet to fully crystallize and gain hegemony on the left.

Among the book's chief virtues is its dual critique of Marxism and liberalism. In Boggs's view, both are situated as ideological responses emerging from within the outmoded framework of capitalist development and its internal changes. He quickly disposes of twentieth-century liberalism, as he reviews its internal mutations in symbiosis with an ascendent and virtually unopposed corporate capitalist system leading to its final transformation into a "ritualized belief system barely masking a highly centralized and expansionist corporate system" (p. 6).[21] What makes his analysis post-Marxist is his embracement of the internal critique by Western Marxists in the twentieth century and his openness to the dramatic changes and novel forces erupting in this contemporary world that have put in radical doubt the credibility of certain Marxist assumptions, concepts, theories, and methods—including its scientism and objectivism, its reductionist theory of class domination, and its authoritarian/elitist temptations in the realm of organization and governance.

Drawing on the work of an impressive number of critical social theorists and political activists, he finds the outlines of a post-Marxist theory containing "a philosophy of praxis that is no longer wedded to the canons of scientific materialism or to the primacy of objective historical forces; a social theory that confronts the reality of multiple and overlapping forms of domination . . . without reducing that reality to one of its aspects; and a democratic political theory compatible with the idea of a nonbureaucratic, self-managed society" (pp. 16–17). At the same time, he is critical—indeed, in some places, sharply and insistently so—of the prevailing limitations and inadequacies of post-Marxist praxis as it informs the three "strategic options" or forms of radicalism (Eurosocialism, the new populism, and the Green alternative) emerging in symbiosis with the phenomenon of new social movements comprising the new terrain of radical politics. Along the way, he flatly rejects the varying Eurocommunist responses to the emergence of new social movements in the West— including that of sabotage in France, symbolic appropriation in Spain, and instrumental cooptation in Italy.

To each of the incipient forms of political radicalism, he brings to bear sophisticated political sensibilities and unwavering democratic commitments while evaluating their successes and failures. Informed by a keen awareness of the historical limitations of earlier strategies of radical political change, he sets in relief the high hopes and modest achievements to date of Eurosocialism and the new populism.

Whereas democratic socialism has remained on the periphery of American politics, Boggs's analysis shows how it found lively and plural form in the upsurge and political successes of Socialist parties in France, Spain, Greece, and Italy in the eighties. Eschewing the authoritarian temptations of European Communist parties, these Socialist parties succeeded in combining a nondoctrinaire socialist vision with a commitment to democratizing structural reforms in a way that gained strong popular support and linked up with the issues and demands of the new social movements. Despite the optimism and high expectations that were mobilized in the wake of their electoral victories at the beginning of that decade, however, by the mid-eighties Eurosocialists in power took a distinct turn toward political moderation and ideological retrenchment.

Boggs locates the reasons for the failure of Eurosocialism to live up to its promise mainly in the dilemmas of structural reform. Originally intended to reconquer and restructure state institutions along democratic and socialist lines, the structural reform measures of the various Eurosocialist parties were, in his view, increasingly compromised by economic, state administrative, and foreign policy "realities." Existing within a global political economy dominated by capitalism and experiencing serious economic doldrums, most of these parties adopted a "development first/socialism next" approach that propelled them toward institutionalizing an economic program characterized by technological restructuring, economic austerity, and neo-Keynesian economic practices. Politically, the priority given to state economic development during a global economic crisis meant that the political goals of democratic participation, decentralization, and *autogestion* took a back seat to administrative policies centered on the elite technocratic stratum intended more to streamline the accumulation process than to democratize the state apparatus itself. The result was mass demobilization and the decline of social movements, and with these consequences the loss of the democratic dynamic operating at the base. From these experiences Boggs concludes that, while the parliamentary road may have permitted these Euro-socialist parties to conquer governmental power, Eurosocialism is best characterized as a consolidation, rather than a supersession, of bourgeois hegemony, since it necessarily reinforces bourgeois hegemonic practices due to the fact that electoralism or parliamentarianism "rules out extraparliamentary activity" (p. 126).

Reviewing the eruption of progressive neopopulism in America in the seventies and eighties, Boggs presents a generally gloomy assessment of its political prospects as a counterhegemonic program. Identifying the substance of its strategy of democratic reform in its anticorporate stance, its attack on the state as the primary sphere of conflict and change, and its appeal to economic democracy, he points out how various neopopulist formations—including Tom Hayden's Campaign for Economic Democracy and the Santa Monica populist insurgency—adopted a series of tactics and strategies designed to mobilize citizens inside and outside the electoral arena behind concrete, "nonideological" issues affecting their everyday lives in their neighborhood, community, or region. Though impressed with the mass energy and enthusiasm generated at the grass roots and the episodic successes on individual issues by these various expressions of neopopulism, Boggs points to the greater limitations of this strategy of democratic reform and the Bernsteinian cast of its strategy—characterized by its stress on political evolutionism, electoral participation, and internal restructuring of the bourgeois state. While his judgment of the social democratic thrust of the new American populism is softened by his recognition of its key differences with traditional social democracy (see p. 137), his overall evaluation of its long-term potential is no less harsh than his assessment of Eurosocialism.

By restricting activity to the political-institutional sphere and by adopting an instrumental relation to political formations and mass constituencies, diverse neopopulist organizations routinely channeled political action into institutionally oriented politics and unduly narrowed the scope of conflict. Moreover, according to Boggs, neopopulism suffers from two other shortcomings. First, he argues, its organizational structure increasingly succumbs to Michels's iron law of oligarchy, as the internal organization of populist groups is transformed along the lines of the mass-based permanent organization model.[22] That is, local democratic structures become increasingly remote from populist representatives in power, grass-roots accountabilty disappears, and single-issue politics and a highly constrained political agenda come to inform elite strategies (p. 157). And, second, the popular revolt strategy implied in the "people vs. the state" and the "people vs. the corporations" slogans of the new populism leads to a disabling accommodation or deference to tradition, a distancing of or an alienation from the true harbingers of a new culture and a new politics on the margins of American society, and a "failure to spell out the political forms and the class content of cultural transformation" (p. 160). In so doing, the new populism actually works "against elements of a cultural and political radicalism that [would] enter into a broadening of the public sphere" (p. 163). In sum, by focusing almost exclusively on electoral politics, the new populism, for Boggs, fails to develop a genuine counterhegemonic politics and thus also fails to transform power relations shaping the institutional-political structure.

Without abandoning critique for mere celebration, Boggs finds in the rise of the West German Greens a novel and innovative political formation that reflects the true promise of post-Marxist currents. In his opinion, by forging and sustaining organic ties with popular struggles at the grass roots, the Greens have found organizational and political ways of establishing a more dialectical relationship between party and movement, national and regional spheres of activity, electoral politics and grass-roots mobilization. Unique among the inchoate strategic options explored, the Green alternative has found in the mechanism of the "antiparty party" a means for straddling the fence, for doing politics at the margins, between state and civil society, and for tying parliamentary politics to movement politics. This distinctive approach of the Greens is significant, because for Boggs the persisting flaw in so many new social movements has been "a seemingly inherent flight from politics," often taking the expression of "a simple assertion of civil society over the state, movements over party, the 'social' over the 'political'" (p. 13).

While recognizing the pluralism and continuing internal debate between the "fundis" and "realos" within the Greens, Boggs stresses the common ground informing the Green platform, political strategy, and vision of a new politics. Yet, simultaneously, he points to the key elements constituting what he calls "the Green predicament"—including the problem of formulating a sound and convincing transitional, trans-NATO defense policy (now made easier in the light of recent European developments); the tensions of the Red-Green coalition; and the difficulty of forging a meaningful Green-labor coalition. Curiously, Boggs highlights three other problems emanating from powerful ideological themes of Green philosophy: the danger of fetishizing democracy; the persistence of spiritualism and its "pathologies" evidenced among antimodern elements (especially the Rudi Bahro faction) within the Green movement; and the potentially disabling commitment of the Greens to Gandhian nonviolence. As we will see, not only are these concerns ex-plained in part by the continuing impact of the legacy of Marxism on Boggs's post-Marxist inclinations; they are also grounded in a largely unexplicated "anti-antimodern" commitment to a distinctly radical form of modernism and to certain covert Enlightenment assumptions.

In the end, Boggs's prescriptions drawn from the experience of success and failure of these strategic alternatives generated in late twentieth-century Western politics suggest that "these new phenomena amount to an emergent social bloc that would revitalize civil society" (p. 222). On the other hand, he acknowledges, they "possess no necessary or intrinsic ideological content, radical or otherwise," and their historical meaning and political import "will continue to depend upon . . . their relationship to one or another political formation shaped by particular visions and strategies" (p. 223). Critical to their ability to fulfill their radical potential will be "developing a unified theoretical and strategic perspective" by instituting a "dynamic process through which a merger of new movements and class forces might occur" (p. 231). The goal of this process would be to discover "new ways of understanding the formulation of collective interests in the struggle to transform the workplace, community, and state" (p. 237).

In addition, Boggs calls for a rejection of the "ideal of an unmediated civil society" standing outside of and against the "politico-institutional realm" and its replacement by a "dialectical interweaving of state and civil society" that grants the central role of the state "in the playing out of social conflict—and the corresponding importance of political strategy in the process" (p. 237). At the same time, he believes, new forms of local democratic authority in factories, neighborhoods, and other organizations must develop to permit the reconstitution of the national state on decentralized foundations of self-management. To bring about these developments, he believes, a genuinely counterhegemonic strategy will be needed to foster new values and symbolic attachments from within the new movements to replace, rather than adapt to, national and cultural traditions presently informing popular beliefs and opinions. In sum, the agenda of the new social movements requires the articulation of a radical-democratic theory of the state, a nonstatist strategy, and a counterhegemonic politics.

While Boggs's contributions to the updating and reconceptualizing of hegemony as a political concept and of counterhegemony as a political strategy bear the imprint of the Marxian heritage, his struggle to slough off antiquated philosophical assumptions and orthodox beliefs and prejudices in the light of changed social conditions and new historical developments is readily apparent. What is more doubtful is his success in extirpating some of these presuppositions and biases at deeper, more latent levels of his analysis. A deconstruction of Boggs's often penetrating study of the post-Marxist possibilities of these incipient forms of radicalism reveals a certain slippage in his analysis from time to time to more reassuring concepts and the dualisms of Marxist orthodoxy and an appearance of residues and remnants of modernist prejudices and Enlightenment errors that postmodernists from Derrida to Lyotard (as well as some of the Frankfurt school theorists and some phenomenologists and hermeneutic philosophers) have striven to illuminate and unseat.

Throughout his critical analysis Boggs continues to revert to outmoded Marxist language and Marxian totalizing gestures. For example, early in his study he refers to a "certain universal logic of capitalist development" (p. xiv) and then later he attempts to suggest the basis of a logic of social transformation in new social movements by appealing to Lucien Goldmann's notion of "potential consciousness" (p. 56)—a move that Laclau and Mouffe, operating from a genuine post-Marxist position, roundly criticize. In addition, here and there, Boggs sprinkles his critical reinterpretation of hegemony with references to "collective interests" (p. 237), "collective consciousness" (p. 243), and "subjective factors" (p. 249)—all part of the dualistic framework in which orthodox Marxism has been mired. Likewise, his critique of Jacobin-style revolution (pp. 7, 74–75) may be sincere and an outgrowth of his democratic commitments, yet he continues to appeal to revolution as total transformation and chastises the Greens at one point for lack of global economic or ecological models.

Second, in spite of his critique of the Enlightenment heritage in Marxism (p. 75), Boggs's thought still seems influenced by Enlightenment values and modernist illusions at deeper levels. The subterranean hegemony of the Enlightenment is evidenced, for instance, in his negative evaluations of the place of the antimodern in new social movements. Jacques Derrida once defined deconstruction succinctly as "an openness to the other"; and he and other postmoderns have underlined the need to rehabilitate those domains exiled by the Enlightenment conception of reason.[23] As a post-Enlightenment/postmodern gesture, might we not openly consider the antimodern religious-spiritual other as a marginalized other? If so, Boggs's persistent antimodern baiting (see pp. 14, 164–165, 211, 212) would strike one as distinctly modernist in its antireligious prejudice, as well as overly tendentious in identifying the elements that might constitute a left hegemonic bloc.[24]

To my mind, Ernst Bloch's view of premodern and antimodern elements as remnants of old being and noncontemporaraneous contradictions offers a far more subtle and radical interpretation of their political potential.[25] Regarding farmers, small business, and religious folk as continuing repositories of older ideas of land, community, work, and home subverted by the advance of industrializing forces and secularizing trends, Bloch pressed Marxists to shoulder the radical task of active inheritance as a form of hegemonic rearticulation of the cultural surplus of these ideas. That is, he urged Marxists to "pay the debts of the past in order to receive the present" by articulating the futurity contained in every value and ideal expressed by existing remnants of older economic being and political consciousness—a futurity that could only be truly realized in a socialist society.[26] In this respect, whatever one's evaluation of Boggs's critique of the new populists, his anti-antimodernism and urban modernist biases (reminiscent of Marshall Berman's[27]) clearly cloud his treatment of the last indigenous movement against the crystallization of the corporate state in *fin-de-siècle* America, prompting him to issue a fleeting and rather facile criticism of the populist Farmers Alliance (p. 166).

In a similar vein, a third criticism of Boggs's reformulation of hegemony and his struggle to articulate a post-Marxist theory of counterhegemonic politics relates to his critique of tradition. Part of his assault on the dead weight of tradition is evidently mistargeted, since the object of his political scorn is really traditionalism, not tradition *per se* (pp. 164, 246).[28] But Boggs's theoretical problem with tradition goes deeper than a mere misidentification of tradition with traditionalism. David Kolb has recently taken Habermas to task for utilizing an unduly restrictive understanding of tradition to defend his evolutionary theory of modernity and the Enlightenment project of modernity generally.[29] Kolb, like Bloch before him, has emphasized the symbolic "spaciousness" or multivocity of traditions and their capacity to carry internal standards of evaluation that do not require critique to reside outside and above cultural heritages. By embracing a modernist interpretation of tradition, Boggs puts himself in a peculiar dilemma: if one of the requisites of a "viable counterhegemonic politics" is the "success of activists in making concrete—making alive —issues that can attract the vast majority of people to the ideal of a democratic, egalitarian, nonviolent world" (p. 249), it would appear that that road can be found only by way of the avenue of spacious indigenous traditions, not via a detour around them. This is precisely what Boyte's neopopulist strategy is attempting to do.

Fourth, these modernist biases and blind spots also undercut the sophistication of his strategy of counterhegemony. For one thing, they lead him to oscillate between the pre-Gramscian, proto-Leninist language of counterhegemony qua alliance (pp. 56–57) and a modernist view of hegemony qua integrated culture based on collective interests and values (p. 162). Lacking an appreciation for deconstruction's sensitivity and insights into the trap in which the collective/individual bipolarity situates him, Boggs tacitly embraces, as I will discuss in the next section, aspects of his mentor Gramsci's own latent essentialism. For another thing, Boggs's modernism vitiates his understanding of how hegemonic processes actually operate. In his penetrating essay on ways of thinking about "the popular" and popular culture in socialist theory, Tony Bennett stresses that "such processes neither erase the cultures of subordinate groups, nor do they rob 'the people' of their 'true culture': what they do do is shuffle those cultures on to an ideological and cultural terrain in which they can be disconnected from whatever radical impulse

which may (but need not) have fuelled them and be connected to more
conservative or, often, downright reactionary cultural and ideological tendencies."[30] It is precisely the ambivalent, open-ended, multivocal character of tradition as its operates in forms of hegemonic articulation that
Boggs seems to miss.

These and other shortcomings, finally, exact their toll on Boggs's critique of the Green alternative. Most tellingly, his offhanded side comment criticizing the potentially destabilizing impact of direct democracy,
spiritualism, and a commitment to nonviolence, points to a latent mobilization of shopworn assumptions and beliefs within the Marxist heritage
and to a modernist skepticism that fundamentally undercuts his democratic commitments. Ultimately, Boggs fails to clarify the outlines of a
Green counterhegemonic strategy transcending the *realo/fundi* split within the movement by leaving suspended the questions: Can it be overcome? Should it be overcome? Might its irresolution or lateral entwine-
ment not be more in keeping with a deconstructionist double gesture to
hegemony and antihegemony, to the political center and to the margins,
the twilight world between Gramsci and Derrida?

Hegemonic Articulation and
Democratic Equivalence Beyond
the Positivity of the Social:
The Deconstructive/Marxist Logic
of Hegemony in Laclau and Mouffe

Working in the margins of political discourse between Corlett's non-
Marxist, postmodern interpretation of hegemony and Boggs's post-
Marxist rendition of hegemony and counterhegemony, Ernesto Laclau
and Chantal Mouffe set themselves the ambitious task of recasting the
Gramscian problematic of ideological hegemony in their book, *Hegemony
& Socialist Strategy*, by drawing upon the implications of the postmodern
critique of Enlightenment foundationalism and Western dualistic
thought *without* abandoning the political project of modernity informing
Enlightenment thinking and its intellectual heirs, including Marxism. In
relentlessly pursuing the deconstructive logic of Derridian extravagance
and by supplementing it with a post-Marxist reading of structuralist logic
of Althusserian overdetermination, they dispose of the essentialist foundations of nineteenth-century Marxism, leaving only its animating goals
of human emancipation, social egalitarianism, and democracy. Along the
way, they renounce any Jacobin-style model of revolution as the basis for
social change, the ontologically central and epistemologically privileged

status of a "universal class," and a unitary and homogeneous collective will underpinning and solidifying some new hegemonic "historic bloc" that will organize social and political relations in the future.

Although Laclau and Mouffe regard Gramsci's writings as a "watershed" in Marxian theorizations on ideological or cultural hegemony, their genealogy of the concept begins with the context of its emergence in the *fin-de-siècle* crisis of Marxism experienced by second-generation orthodox and revisionist Marxists who had to come to grips with "a new awareness of the opacity of the social, of the complexities and resistances of an increasingly organized capitalism, and the fragmentation of the different positions of social agents which, according to the classical paradigm, should have been united" (p. 18). Thus, the concept of hegemony is first introduced into Marxian discourse, as Fred Dallmayr has put it, as a "stop-gap measure or as mere supplement designed to patch up evolutionary anomalies."[31] Their discussion shows how revisionist and orthodox Marxists alike contributed to the unfolding of the hegemony concept in a number of interesting and sometimes surprising ways that prepared the theoretical and conceptual ground for Gramsci's reformulation. They give credit to Rosa Luxemburg for recognizing that the multiplication of social antagonisms and forms of struggles generated by tendencies toward fragmentation within a new phase of capitalism overflows the boundaries of the working class and shatters the capacity for simple class representation and control of these many points of social conflict. This lack of any necessary overlap between political subjectivity and class positions, this "overflowing of the signifier by the signified" (p. 11), lead Luxemburg to posit the unity of the working class as a symbolic unity through the theory of spontaneism, a theory that Laclau and Mouffe find illogical in terms of Luxemburg's reassuring classicist conclusion.

This experience of the proliferation of social cleavages and the indeterminancy of the articulations between different struggles and points of antagonism prompts the orthodox Marxist school represented by Kautsky, Plekhanov, and the Austro-Marxists to open up orthodox discourse to a dualism between a realm of necessity, where objective laws operate, and a realm of contingency, where the autonomy of political will and initiative takes place, and to find a new role for theory as guarantor that the tendencies described above "will eventually coincide with the social articulations proposed by the Marxist paradigm" by way of changes in the economic base (p. 19). The second response—especially, the revisionism of Bernstein—makes the bold theoretical move of breaking with the rigid base/superstructure dichotomy and theorizes the autonomy of the political from the base—a move that proved decisive to the opening up of the social topography for the assertion of hegemony as a form of political action. In Bernsteinian revisionism, this bold theoretical stroke is vitiated, according to the authors, by two mistaken assumptions: the *transcendental* premise of the autonomy of the ethical subject as the basis of the party's role as the source of symbolic unification of diverse social struggles; and the *evolutionary* assumption of the forward and ascendent nature of socialist struggle such that every concrete political gain or victory is deemed *per force* progressive and nonreversible. With these assumptions, evolutionary socialism ironically closes off the political space it initially opened up and therefore shuts the door to a theory of hegemonic articulation, since its liberal assumption of linear progress and irreversibility removes the task of consolidating unstable and indeterminate social forces as a political problem.

For Laclau and Mouffe, the crystallization of the concept of ideological hegemony in Gramsci's work awaited the synthesis of the concept of the *bloc* originating in the revolutionary syndicalism of Sorel and the idea of "hegemony" deriving from the voluntarist Marxism of Leninism. With his conception of moral qualities as the binding cement of an ascending society and his view of Marxism as an ideology as well as a science, Sorel came to see the unification of society as a consequence of the capacity and will of various groups to impose their conceptions of social structure and economic organization upon other groups and society at large. For Sorel, the growing decomposition of the sharpness of class divisions and the dispersion of social struggles and multiple antagonism necessitate the generation of forms of reaggregation that he calls blocs, defined in terms of "expressive supports" that "operate as elements aggregating and condensing the historical forces" presently scattered through the social *melange* (p. 38).

Although Leninist discourse virtually begins with the centrality of hegemony, it ultimately reduces class relations to a supplement to class relations. Still, for Lenin, hegemony is conceived in terms of political leadership within a class alliance. And the political nature of the hegemonic link, though seen as external to the class identity of the social agents, is fundamental and controlling, since "the terrain on which the link establishes itself is different from that on which the social agents are constituted" (p. 55). Though potentially more democratic than other conceptions of politics found in orthodoxy or revisionism, Lenin's view of hegemony succumbs to authoritarian tendencies due in part to the vanguardist role imputed to the proletariat (or, better, its leaders) in the class alliance, and to the unchanged identities of the various elements represented in the alliance based upon ultimately incompatible "interests."

In the hands of Antonio Gramsci, according to Laclau and Mouffe, these ingredients of an inchoate strategy of hegemony take on a new level of theoretical sophistication and practical significance. Superseding the essentialist compulsions of rigid class identities while facing up to sociohistorical anomalies that triggered the turn-of-the-century crisis of Marxism, Gramsci's theoretical innovations did much to deepen the democratic core of hegemony. His key move in refurbishing the problematic of hegemony was to shift the terrain of political recomposition and hegemony from "the political" to what he called "the intellectual-moral plane." In relocating hegemony beyond the Leninist notion of class alliance, he removed the problem of achieving unity among diverse subordinate groups from the field of class structure, supplanting the principle of representation by the principle of articulation. Gramsci also transformed the Sorelian notion of bloc from its ultimate grounding in the myth of the general strike by conceptualizing "historical blocs" in terms of broader social groupings traversing a number of class sectors who were bound together by an ensemble of ideas, beliefs, and values constituting a higher synthesis or a "collective will." As an organic ensemble of beliefs and practices, ideology provided the means by which the new historical bloc could be cemented and its intellectual-moral leadership could be articulated in the field of political contestation and its hegemony exerted over the rest of society.

For Laclau and Mouffe, Gramsci's theorization of hegemony represented a clear advance over previous articulations. Its novelty and superiority, for them, rest on two innovations: (1) his emphasis on the materiality of ideology, where ideology is understood as "an organic and relational whole, embodied in institutions and apparatuses, which welds together a historical bloc around a number of articulatory principles" (p. 67); and (2) his rupture with the reductionist problematic of political subjectivity, where for Gramsci "political subjects are not . . . strictly speaking classes, but complex 'collective wills,'" and where the "collective will is a result of the politico-ideological articulation of dispersed and fragmented historical forces" (p. 67).

If the democratic practice of hegemony requires the decoupling of the democratic tasks from any necessary class belonging and the renunciation of stagism in any of its multiple forms, Laclau and Mouffe hold that Gramsci's thought represented a tremendous advance in the democratic project. Yet, they acknowledge, his problematization of hegemony retained a lingering remnant of Marxist essentialism: "[E]ven though the diverse social elements have a mere relational identity—achieved through articulatory practices—there must always be [for Gramsci] a *single* unifying principle in every hegemonic formation, and this can only be a fundamental class" (p. 69).

What would a post-Marxist formulation of hegemony as an articulatory practice, stripped of all essentialist residues from the Marxist tradition, look like? And how do postmodern insights and innovations contribute to the deconstruction and supersession of these and other residues deeply rooted in Western metaphysics?

In tracing out the ramifications of deconstruction and postmodern antifoundationalism in their effort to rework the Gramscian problematic, Laclau and Mouffe offer a conception of hegemony as a deconstructive logic and a form of articulation that strives to overcome the antinomies of Marxism (base/superstructure, ideas/matter, essence/appearance, etc.); affirm the unfixity of every social identity (including the multiformity and nonunitary character of the subject) and the incompletenss of every totality (including and especially society); and defend the primacy of politics over all versions of economism and sociologism. In the process, they introduce a set of categories developed from the cross-fertilization of Marxism and deconstruction that prepares the way for their engagement with the radical and deconstructive potential of the phenomenon of new social movements as an aspect of the unfolding "democratic revolution" in our times.

Laclau and Mouffe work to dissolve all those "necessary" structural connections and "essential" conceptual and metaphysical anchorages in order to allow the logic of hegemony to complete its deconstructive work on Marxism begun by Gramsci. Deconstructing Gramsci's essentialist belief that "the ultimate core of the hegemonic subject's identity is constituted at a point external to the space it articulates" (p. 85), the authors draw the postmodern inference of the radical unfixity and constant deferral of every social identity. With the decoupling of the democratic task and the class that was supposedly its necessary agent, every social identity becomes an unstable and incomplete identity articulated as a hegemonic relation. Thus, for example, rather than impute *either* a peripheral status to new social movements (feminist, ecological, peace, etc.) to some privileged class agency *or* proclaim their a priori progressive or hegemonic character, Laclau and Mouffe argue that their political meaning and import is radically dependent upon their hegemonic articulation with other struggles and demands (p. 87).

Nor do they believe that the logic of detotalization rightfully implies that existent and new points of antagonism and forms of social contestation—now called "subject positions"—should be seen as dissimilar and fully constituted elements that can be linked through hegemonic articulation without their identities—already unstable and unfixed—being modified in the process. Here, these two theorists radicalize Althusser's notion of overdetermination. Althusser has argued that everything existing in the social realm is shaped by a multitude of causes that cannot be reduced to explanation by a single causal agent. Rejecting Althusser's incompatible structuralist Marxist assertion that, despite overdetermination, the economy is determinant in the last instance, Laclau and Mouffe unfold the deconstructive effects of this position by arguing that the thesis of overdetermination implies, first, that the social constitutes itself as a symbolic order and, second, that the symbolically articulated and overdetermined character of these social identities, subject positions, and social relations are always already mutually implicated with, and subverted by, some, if not all, of the others.

This critical insight for radical democratic praxis may be illuminated by exploring another postmodern insight appropriated by Laclau and Mouffe for their larger political purposes: the multiformity and nonunitary character of the subject. As against the rationalist and liberal conceptions of the human being as a unitary subject, contemporary philosophical stances informed by postmodern thought have come to recognize the subject as a multifaceted, detotalized, and decentered agent constituted, as Chantal Mouffe puts it, "at the point of intersection of a multiplicity of subject-positions between which there exists no a priori or necessary relation and whose articulation is the result of hegemonic practices" (p. 35). The increasing differentiation of modern industrial societies and the attendant growing complexity of modern life, among other things, have prompted the incredible multiplication and dispersion of subject positions along with the other subject positions inherited from earlier periods that continue to influence and shape social life.

As opposed to the facile theorists of the "fully integrated" human personality or of structuralist stage theories of human development vesting a unity or centeredness to human subjects,[32] Laclau and Mouffe see the subject as "penetrated by the same ambiguous, incomplete and polysemical character which overdetermination assigns to every discursive identity" (p. 121). But, for them, the problem of the fragmentation of the unitary subject is at one and the same time a source of the experience of subjugation *à la* Foucauldian analysis and a precondition of the democratization of the contemporary social world. "Renunciation of the category of subject as a unitary, transparent and sutured entity," they argue, "opens the way to the recognition of the specificity of the antagonisms constituted on the basis of different subject positions, and, hence, the possibility of the deepening of a pluralist and democratic conception" (p. 166).

Before probing the implications of these notions for radical democratic politics, I will need to analyze the difficult, and sometimes dense, treatment by Laclau and Mouffe of the necessity of going beyond the positivity of the social and its import for the Marxist idea of totality. Adhering to the nonfoundationalist and nonessentialist mooring points of postmodern philosophy, Laclau and Mouffe undertake to deconstruct the category of society as totality in order to derive important political inferences for democratic practice. Denying sociology a privileged role as master social science, they argue that, if hegemony is a form of articulation and every social identity is unfixed and overdetermined, then they must repudiate the idea of society as a foundational totality of its partial or mediating processes. If the social has no essence, is constituted as a field or plenum of identities and differences, of presence and nonpresence, of order and disorder, and is therefore riddled by antagonisms that pose the limit of its positivity, it cannot achieve the status of full presence, and "the objectivity of its identities [including "society"] is permanently subverted" (p. 129). As a result, there can be no sutured space distinctive to society that would establish a fixed anchorage or foundation from which sociological analysis could derive general laws or objective strategems that relieve hegemonic practice of its need for political articulation.

Laclau and Mouffe, then, do not deny that "society" needs to be organized and given shape. What they argue is that this task must be assigned to politics as a kind of hegemonic articulation. The political problem, for them, is "the problem of the institution of the social, that is, of the definition and articulation of social relations in a field criss-crossed with antagonisms" (p. 153). Converging with Derrida's abandonment of the transcendental signified as a possible means of closing off discourse and establishing some ultimate meaning or foundation, Laclau and Mouffe turn to the idea of "nodal points" as partial fixations in the practice of hegemonic articulation. Since articulation "does not have a plane of constitution prior to, or outside, the dispersion of the articulated elements" (p. 109), nodal points are necessary to the practice of hegemony to selectively structure the social field precisely because the infinitude of the field of discursivity constantly overflows every discourse. Without them, the infinite play of significations and the excess of every sign that constantly defers its meaning might forever postpone hegemonic intervention, tempting theorists and other agents who practice deconstruction (as Corlett warns) into "becoming bogged down in the endless wordplay and punning—or substitution of signs—that their ways of reading and writing make possible."[33]

Having submitted the Gramscian problematic of hegemony to the full impact of deconstructive critique and reformulation, Laclau and Mouffe turn in their concluding chapter to unfolding the ramifications of hegemonic articulation as political practice for the project of radical and plural democracy. This project was opened up, in their view, by the democratic revolution triggered by the French Revolution that installed a new political imaginary of Western societies based upon the democratic principle of liberty and equality. With the simultaneous and ambiguous experiences of tendencies toward totalization and toward fragmentation that have attended the hegemonic formations within the Western world and extended their global reach, new subject positions have erupted, political spaces have proliferated, and the field of social conflict has expanded.

Among those new subject positions that have emerged and taken political form are the new social movements spanning the fields of feminist, ecological, peace, local community, and gay and lesbian concerns. With Claude Lefort, the authors argue that these new social movements must be seen against the background of the democratic revolution's inauguration of a new form of institution of the social: "the experience of a society which cannot be apprehended or controlled, in which the people will be proclaimed sovereign, but in which its identity will never be definitively given, but will remain latent" (p. 187). Yet, they caution, the new imaginary brought into being by the democratic revolution does not predetermine its specific ideological form or political direction. So, "we are faced here with a true polysemia" (p. 168), and the forms of articulation that these social movements may take are truly polymorphous since "every antagonism, left free to itself, is a floating signifier, a 'wild' antagonism which does not predetermine the form in which it can be articulated to other elements in a social formation" (p. 171). In this respect, these two theorists are particularly convincing in their analysis of the recent success of the New Right in disarticulating and rearticulating populism in a reactionary direction in the effort to mold a new historical bloc combining themes of an antiegalitarian social conservatism, the exaltation of the myth of the market, and the further depoliticization of key issues of social welfare and political economy (pp. 169–175).

In presenting a left alternative to this New Right hegemonic strategy, the authors introduce the concept of "democratic equivalence" as a crucial tool in the struggle to advance this new phase in the democratic revolution in a left-libertarian direction. In offering this concept, they raise the knotty theoretical question, "[I]s there not an incompatibility between the proliferation of political spaces proper to radical democracy and the construction of collective identities on the basis of the logic of equivalence?" (p. 181). For them, because antagonisms do not emerge merely in the dichotomized space constituting it but as well in the field of discursivity and plurality of the social that forever overflows it, the logic of equivalence always stands in tense relation to the logic of difference or autonomy. That is, through the process of hegemonic practice, aspects of plural and semiautonomous subject positions can be articulat-

ed so that their symbolization will be seen by the social agents as equivalent and mutually supportive. For example, the work of Carolyn Merchant has done much to promote democratic equivalence between the
discourse formations of the ecological and feminist movements by articulating the modern scientific roots of sexism, patriarchy, and the domination of nature through the historic Western identification of nature as
female and its transmutation by early modern scientists and philosophers
of science.[34]

The expansion of such webs of equivalence across diverse social
movements and other antagonisms holds the promise of strengthening
specific democratic struggles and potentially consolidating them into a
new historical bloc. But, the authors point out, the logic of autonomy
operating within these struggles to retain their differential specificity
militates against full integration or total fusion. For as opposed logics that
are at the same time mutually implicated in one another, the logic of
equivalence and the logic of autonomy "intervene to different degrees in
the constitution of every social identity" and "partially limit their mutual
effects" (p. 183).

Crucial to the generation of democratic equivalence, for the authors,
is construction of a new "common sense" which alters the identities of
the different subject positions so that the claims and demands of each are
articulated in an equivalent manner (p. 183). The modification of the
identities of the social groups engaging in equivalential articulations is
what distinguishes hegemonic practices from typical alliances conjoining
interests and what makes equivalence always hegemonic. So, to illustrate, the work of Environmentalists for Full Employment may be distinguished from the Clean Air Coalition by the struggle of the former to foster democratic equivalence while the latter has merely sought to rally different environmental interest groups around a shared villain (polluting
industries).

The precariousness of the relation between equivalence and autonomy means, for Laclau and Mouffe, that the project of radical and plural
democracy requires both the hegemonic articulation among new and old
antagonisms as an absolutely essential means of integrating potential
democratic struggles and deepening the new democratic revolution *and*
"the autonomization of the spheres of struggle and the multiplication of
political spaces" to further radical pluralism (p. 178). From this position,
they draw a number of important conclusions. First, they conclude that
this democratic project entails that socialism be only one nonprivileged
component within any incipient historical bloc and that this project pre-
cludes both the concentration of power and knowledge and the "war of
maneuver" implied by the Jacobin revolutionary model and its socialist

variants (p. 178). Further, in contrast to Boggs's view of liberalism as a politically empty facade for a technocorporate political economy, Laclau and Mouffe argue that the project of radical democracy must not "renounce liberal-democratic ideology, but on the contrary . . . deepen and expand it in the direction of radical and plural democracy" (p. 176). Acknowledging the spaciousness of the liberal tradition and certain "intimations" sedimented within it, they emphasize that, since the meaning of liberalism as a discourse is in no way univocal or definitively fixed, part of the democratic agenda is the articulation and redefinition of certain liberal categories. By implication rejecting Christopher Lasch's communitarian claim that "the vocabulary of rights [is] fundamentally incompatible with the vocabulary of virtue,"[35] the authors press for the disarticulation and rearticulation of individual rights as "democratic rights." As Mouffe explains in a later essay, what is required are new rights that "are the expression of differences whose importance is only now being asserted" by groups on the margins and "are no longer rights that can be universalized."[36]

Adhering both to the spirit of democratic revolution and to the sobering implications of the deconstruction of the Marxist tradition and the Gramscian problematic of hegemony, Laclau and Mouffe conclude with an affirmation of a form of politics fully compatible with an antiessentialist and postfoundationalist project of radical and plural democracy—one that "is founded not upon dogmatic postulation of any 'essence of the social,' but, on the contrary, on affirmation of the contingency and ambiguity of every 'essence,' and on the constitutive character of social division and antagonism"; one affirming "a 'ground' which lives only by negating its fundamental character"; one pursuing "an order which exists only as a partial limiting of disorder"; one articulating "a meaning which is constructed only as excess and paradox in the face of meaninglessness—in other words the field of the political as the space for a game which is never 'zero-sum,' because the rules and the players are never fully explicit." "This game," they say, "does at least have a name: hegemony" (p. 193).

With the publication of *Hegemony & Socialist Strategy*, the strategic concept of hegemony for a radical democratic politics has undoubtedly achieved a new level of theoretical articulation and political expression. In the light of perspectives opened upon the idea of ideological hegemony by earlier works examined and from the vantage point of the living present, latent modernist assumptions and Marxian residues continue to stand out against the background of this remarkable work of political theory. Like Boggs's work, the postmodern and post-Marxist approach of the analysis and argumentation is sometimes hobbled by reversions to antiquated terminology and unsurpassed dualisms rooted in Western metaphysics and the Marxist legacy. In discussing the nature of discursive structures, Laclau and Mouffe play off of the mental/material dichotomy so deeply ensconced in the classical Marxist paradigm (p. 108). Similarly, even as they proceed to demolish any foundationalist misapprehensions about the constitution of the social for an embracement of equivalence and autonomy as social logics intervening in the formation of every social identity, they revert to the essentialist language of collective identities elsewhere to introduce the aforementioned subtle articulation of the two logics (pp. 183 and 181, respectively). In addition, their treatment of positivity and negativity and accompanying use of presence and nonpresence, of meaning and nonmeaning, in places slips out of a Derridian formulation so well rendered by Corlett[37] into Sartrean antinomies of being and nothingness and of meaning and meaninglessness (e.g., pp. 126, 128, 193). So too does their analysis hang suspended on the dualities of freedom and necessity and of determinism and contingency, at times embracing a simple reversal of the bipolarities, which on other occasions, as Fred Dallmayr has noted, is overcome by a "complex and fascinating conceptualization of hegemony in terms of an intertwining and mutual subversion of necessity and contingency."[38]

The authors also share certain modernist, secular prejudices against antimodern, religious subject positions which, I would argue, blunt their strategy for promoting a new majoritarian/democratic historical bloc to advance the democratic and plural project. If, as they claim, radical democracy as a project "cannot consist of the affirmation, from positions of marginality, of a set of anti-system demands" (p. 189), then the unfixity of every social identity and the surplus of meaning in every discursive formation imply clearly that in the spaciousness and cultural surplus of the pastoral tradition of small farmers, for example, in traditional religions (even and especially Gramsci's *bête noire*, Catholicism!), and in the free-market world of small business people, must be found the cultural symbols and political resources of hegemonic articulation.[39] Precisely the avoidance of this task by the left ceded enormous ideological terrain to the New Right's hegemonic practices in the late seventies and early eighties.

Given Laclau and Mouffe's appreciation of the nonunitary nature of subjects and the often many subject-positions and community bases constituting the subject, it is surprising that they fail to follow the enormously complex ramifications of promoting democratic equivalence linking groups as diverse as working-class Catholics and middle-class Protestant professionals on admittedly delimited issues—say, the threat from a toxic waste dump to a local community—with articulatory consequences for their social identities and differences which may radiate outward and have long-term equivalential effects even on their proximate differences. Such a possibility is broached, but not developed, in Laclau and Mouffe's brief, but suggestive, discussion of "demonstration effects" (p. 181). At the very least, enlarging and expanding the strategic terrain of hegemonic articulation to other subordinate groups would do much to bring radical left politics, especially in the United States, out of its reassuring and comforting political enclaves and into the realm of excess where an extravagant politics might make the work of the left a more politically significant force than it is or has been for a long time.

Finally, the authors are mute on the topic of the relationship between the project of radical and plural democracy and the question of party organization—an issue animating Boggs's critique of the antipolitical character of the strategy and tactics of many of the new social movements. The need and importance of counterhegemonic institutions was a major facet of the Gramscian problematic of ideological hegemony and was drawn by Gramsci out of his experience and reflections on the worker's councils in Turin during the late 1910s. The Turin factory councils and their failure to achieve coordination nationally compelled Gramsci to rethink his views on party organization. As his prison notes reveal, he came to see the party organization as a "historical laboratory" capable of forging an organizational network nationwide that could facilitiate coordination and direction of the workers' movement as a whole so that small-scale victories once won could be consolidated at the national level and sedimented into institutional practices.[40] Boggs's discussion of the West German Green's antiparty party structure and its commitment to rooting party organization within hegemony of the movement as a whole points to a major area of neglect in Laclau and Mouffe's otherwise wide-ranging contribution to the realm of democratic political theory and practice. [41]

Conclusion

In critically reappropriating the concept of hegemony originally fashioned by Antonio Gramsci, Corlett, Boggs, and Laclau and Mouffe have impressed their own individual stamps and offered their unique contributions to the ongoing debate over the structure of power in late capitalist societies.

In the process of introducing students of political theory to Derrida's—and, to an extent, Foucault's—work in thought and practice, the deconstructive political theory of William Corlett has dissolved radical communitarian thought in the solvent of Derridian extravagance—and with insightful and sobering results. Not least of all, Corlett uses deconstructive tools to subvert the remunity/communion bipolarity and institutionalize a politicization of the excess that escapes major protagonists in the liberalism/radical communitarianism debate. Unfortunately, when he approaches the experience of domination and subjugation by way of Foucault's "low road of everyday struggle," Corlett reconstructs a postmodern modern theory of hegemony that, in my view, reverts to certain liberal individualist premises, fails to acknowledge how totalizing capitalist reifying processes truly are, and fails to confront the full challenge of Gramsci's reconstituted Marxist interpretation.

Carl Boggs's post-Marxist approach, while weighted too heavily by antiquated Marxist assumptions, reminds the situated political theorist of the ineluctability of politics in every theoretical praxis and counsels the agents of new social movements about the necessity of articulating a radical-democratic theory of the state, a nonstatist political strategy, and a genuinely counterhegemonic politics. Although his modernist and Enlightenment shortcomings sometimes undercut his often keen sense of the political, Boggs forces political thinkers and thinking political agents to confront Marx's insight in his "Theses of Feuerbach" about the "this-sideness" of all thought and strategizing.

But it is to Laclau and Mouffe that I have turned for a truly post-Marxist interpretation of hegemonic articulation that successfully entwines the deconstructive logic of Derridian extravagance with a poststructuralist reading of the Althusserian logic of overdetermination. The essentialist foundations of nineteenth-century Marxism and Enlightenment are radicalized and overcome by them while concomitantly the Gramscian problematic of ideological hegemony is conceptually recast and thereby stripped of modernist residues. Where Boggs's ambitions to rehabilitate the Gramscian problematic for radical-democratic politics were frustrated by his regression to Marxian reassurance, Laclau and Mouffe have largely succeeded in thematizing a hegemonic politics informed by the radical unfixity and constant deferral of every social identity and the excess of every symbolic articulation. While some may surely shrink from the world of politics implicit in their work and demand safe havens from the implications of this outlook for identity and political action, others will recognize this world as *their* world—the world within which the risks and hazards of political action must be chanced if its benefits and rewards are ever to be tasted.

The situating of hegemony in the twilight world between Gramsci and Derrida has reaped enormous benefits for rearticulating the Gramscian problematic in postmodern terms that have allowed the deconstructive impact of Derridian thought upon this Marxian category to be felt. It has also clarified the uncertain relationship between deconstruction and politics. If hegemony is best conceived as an articulatory practice and a deconstructive logic, deconstruction's relationship with politics is, in my opinion, best understood as an extravagant approach to the excess of every political intervention carrying limited political intentions and widespread philosophical implications. That is, deconstruction as a guard over the fallacies of the metaphysics of full presence and excess of every ontological dualism obviously has ethical intimations and suggestive political implications; but it is not itself an ethical system or a political philosophy.

To do its work, then, deconstruction must not congeal into a reified system. It does its work best with a sense of vigilance in symbiosis with other disciplines, fields of inquiry, and traditions of discourse—not least of all, political theory. To ask it to do more is to burden the deconstructive imagination with a metaphysical or onto-theological weight it could never bear without renouncing its radical philosophical intent and arresting its infinite play within an endlessly unfolding field of political and other significations.

Notes

1. Antonio Gramsci, *Selections from the Prison Notebooks*, ed. and trans. Quintin Hoare and Geoffrey Nowell Smith (New York: International Publishers, 1971), 276.

2. N. Katherine Hayles, *Chaos Bound: Orderly Disorder in Contemporary Literature and Science* (Ithaca, N.Y.: Cornell University Press, 1990), xiv.

3. Ibid., 176.

4. Ibid., 233.

5. See William Connolly, *Politics and Ambiguity* (Madison: University of Wisconsin Press, 1987); and *Political Theory and Modernity* (Oxford, England: Blackwell, 1988); and Fred Dallmayr, *Polis and Praxis* (Cambridge: MIT Press, 1984), *Twilight of Subjectivity: Contributions to a Post-Individualist Theory* (Amherst: The University of Massachusetts Press, 1981); *Polis and Praxis* (Cambridge: MIT Press, 1984); and *Margins of Political Discourse* (Albany, N.Y.: The State University of New York Press, 1989).

6. William Corlett, *Community without Unity: A Politics of Derridian Extravagance* (Durham, N.C.: Duke University Press, 1989); Carl Boggs, *Social Movements and Political Power: Emerging Forms of Radicalism in the West* (Philadelphia: Temple University Press, 1986); and Ernest Laclau and Chantal Mouffe, *Hegemony & Socialist Strategy: Towards a Radical Democratic Politics* (New York: Verso, 1985); references to the three works will be cited in text by page number only in the three sections devoted to their analysis.

7. Jacques Derrida, "The Politics of Friendship," *Journal of Philosophy*, 85 (November 1988): 632–44; Thomas McCarthy, "On the Margins of Politics,"

96 Postmodern Contentions

Journal of Politics, 85 (November 1985): 645–48; Jürgen Habermas, *The Philosophical Discourse of Modernity: Twelve Lectures*, trans. by Frederick G. Lawrence (Cambridge: MIT Press, 1990), esp. 161–210; Thomas McCarthy, "The Politics of the Ineffable: Derrida's Deconstructionism," *Philosophical Forum* 21 (Fall–Winter, 1989–90): 146–68; Richard Bernstein, "Serious Play: The Ethical-Political Horizon of Jacques Derrida," *Journal of Speculative Philosophy*, 1 (1987): 95–113; Michael Ryan, *Marxism and Deconstruction* (Baltimore: Johns Hopkins University Press, 1982); and Bernstein, "An Allegory of Modernity/Post-Modernity: The New Constellation," (Cambridge: MIT Press 1992): 199–229.

8. Derrida, "Deconstruction and the Other" (Interview with Richard Kearney), in *Dialogues with Contemporary Thinkers*, ed. Richard Kearney (Manchester, England: Manchester University Press, 1984), 119. His deconstructive comments on these issues have appeared in a number of writings, including "Choreographics," *Diacritics* 12 (Summer 1982): 66–67; "Racism's Last Word," trans. Peggy Kamuf, *Critical Inquiry* 12 (Autumn 1985): 290–99; "The Ends of Man," in *Margins of Philosophy*, trans. Alan Bass (Chicago: University of Chicago Press, 1982): 109–36; and "The Laws of Reflection: Nelson Mandela, in Admiration," in Jacques Derrida and Mustapha Tlili, eds., *For Nelson Mandela*, trans. Franklin Phillip *et al.* (New York: Henry Holt and Company, 1987): 13–42.

9. Derrida, "Positions: Interview with Jean-Louis Houbedine and Guy Scarpetta," in *Positions*, ed. Alan Bass (Chicago: University of Chicago Press, 1981): 37–96.

10. Nancy Fraser, "The French Derridians: Politicizing Deconstruction or Deconstructing the Political?" *New German Critique*, no. 33 (Fall 1984): 127–54.

11. For a convergent perspective on dualistic thinking in philosophy and political theory and the need for a postmodern turn, see Herbert G. Reid and Ernest J. Yanarella, "Toward a Post-Modern Theory of American Political Science and Culture: Perspectives from Critical Marxism and Phenomenology," *Cultural Hermeneutics* 2 (August 1974): 91–166.

12. Michel Foucault, *Discipline and Punish: The Birth of the Prison*, trans. A. M. Sheridan Smith (New York: Vintage Books, 1979); *The Order of Things: An Archeology of the Human Sciences* (New York: Vintage Books, 1973); *The History of Sexuality*, trans. Robert Hurley (New York: Pantheon, 1980).

13. Connolly, *The Terms of Political Discourse* (Princeton, N.J.: Princeton University Press, 1983), 243; Roszak, *The Making of a Counterculture* (Garden City, N.Y.: Anchor Books, 1969); and Fritjof Capra, *The Turning Point: Science, Society, and the Rising Culture* (New York: Bantam Books, 1982).

14. Connolly, *Political Theory and Modernity* (Oxford, England: Blackwell, 1988).

15. See Jacques Derrida, *Of Grammatology*, trans. Gayatri Chakravorty Spivak (Baltimore: Johns Hopkins University Press, 1976), esp. part 2.

16. Hannah Arendt, *The Human Condition* (Garden City, N.Y.: Doubleday Anchor Books, 1959), esp. ch. 2.

17. Hannah Fenichel Pitkin, *Fortune Is a Woman: Gender and Politics in the Thought of Niccolo Machiavelli* (Berkeley: University of California Press, 1984).

18. Gramsci, "The Modern Prince," *Selections from the Prison Notebooks*,

123–205; Maurice Merleau-Ponty, "A Note on Machiavelli," *Signs*, trans. Richard C. McCleary (Evanston, Ill.: Northwestern University Press, 1964), 211–23; J.G.A. Pocock, *The Machiavellian Moment: Florentine Political Thought and the Atlantic Republican Tradition* (Princeton, N.J.: Princeton University Press, 1975); and Robert Orr, "The Time Motif in Machiavelli," in *Machiavelli and the Nature of Political Thought*, ed. Martin Fleisher (New York: Atheneum, 1972), 185–208.

19. Merleau-Ponty, *Phenomenology of Perception*, trans. Colin Smith (New York: Humanities Press, 1962), and *The Visible and the Invisible*, ed. Claude Lefort and trans. Alphonso Lingis (Evanston, Ill.: Northwestern University Press, 1968); Enzo Paci, *The Function of the Sciences and the Meaning of Man*, trans. Paul Piccone and James E. Hansen (Evanston, Ill.: Northwestern University Press, 1972); John O'Neill, *Five Bodies: The Shape of Modern Society* (Ithaca, N.Y.: Cornell University Press, 1985); and Herbert G. Reid, "Critical Phenomenology and the Dialectical Foundations of Social Change," *Dialectical Anthropology* 2 (1977): 107–130.

20. Boggs has written extensively on the Gramscian problematic of hegemony: see *Gramsci's Marxism* (London: Pluto Press, 1976), and *The Two Revolutions: Gramsci and the Dilemmas of Western Marxism* (Boston: South End Press, 1984).

21. For a superb critique of the historical interweaving of American liberalism and the corporate state that clearly surpasses Boggs's perfunctory treatment, see Herbert G. Reid, "American Liberalism, Authority, and the Corporate State: A Critical Interpretation," *Annual Review of Political Science* 3 (1990): 134–59.

22. See Sheldon Wolin's critique of this model in the context of the peace movement in his essay, "Editorial," *democracy* 2 (July 1982): 2–4; and my criticism of the same model in the context of contemporary environmental groups, "Environmental vs. Ecological Perspectives on Acid Rain: The American Environmental Movement and the West German Green Party," in *The Acid Rain Debate: Scientific, Economic, and Political Dimensions*, ed. Ernest J. Yanarella and Randal H. Ihara (Boulder, Co.: Westview Press, 1985), 243–60, esp. 244–47.

23. Derrida, "Deconstruction and the Other," 124.

24. In this respect, the late Michael Harrington's secular Catholicism is more refreshing; see Harrington, *The Politics at God's Funeral: The Spiritual Crisis of Western Civilization* (New York: Henry Holt and Company, 1983).

25. Bloch, "Nonsynchronism and the Obligation to Its Dialectics," *New German Critique* 11 (Spring 1977): 22–38.

26. The quotation is from Dick Howard, "Marxism and Concrete Philosophy: Ernst Bloch," *The Marxian Legacy* (New York: Urizen Books, 1977), 78.

27. See Marshall Berman's celebratory paean to left urban modernism, *All That Is Solid Melts into Air: The Experience of Modernity* (New York: Simon and Schuster, 1982); and the devastating critique of the position that simultaneously respects the pre- and antimodern currents around the globe by Jackson Lears, "Ghetto of Illusion," *democracy* 3 (Winter 1983): 104–16.

28. For a critical appreciation of the differences between tradition and traditionalism, see Chantal Mouffe, "Radical Democracy: Modern or Postmodern?" in *Universal Abandon? The Politics of Postmodernism*, ed. Andrew Ross (Minneapolis: University of Minnesota Press, 1988), 38–41.

29. Kolb, *Postmodern Sophistications: Philosophy, Architecture, and Tradition*

98 *Postmodern Contentions*

(Chicago: The University of Chicago Press, 1990), 63–84, esp. 81–4.

30. Tony Bennett, "The Politics of the 'Popular' and Popular Culture," in *Popular Culture and Social Relations*, ed. Tony Bennett, Colin Menger, and Jane Woolscott (Philadelphia: Open University Press, 1986), 19.

31. Dallmayr, "Hegemony and Democracy: A Post-Hegelian Perspective," *Margins of Political Discourse*, 118.

32. For a critique of structural-developmental models from a critical phenomenological perspective, see Herbert G. Reid and Ernest J. Yanarella, "Critical Political Theory and Moral Development: On Kohlberg, Hampden-Turner, and Habermas," *Theory and Society* 4 (Winter 1977–8), 505–41.

33. Corlett, *Community without Unity*, 63.

34. Merchant, *The Death of Nature: Women, Ecology and the Scientific Revolution* (New York: Harper and Row, 1980).

35. Lasch, "The Communitarian Critique of Liberalism," in *Community in America: The Challenge of "Habits of the Heart,"* ed. Charles H. Reynolds and Ralph V. Norman (Berkeley: University of California Press, 1988), 173–84, quoted from 295 n.1.

36. Mouffe, "Radical Democracy: Modern or Postmodern?," 36. This reversal of the universality/particularity dualism is quickly reformulated in a postmodern way by Mouffe when she says that "universalism is not rejected but particularized" and goes on to state that "what is need is a new kind of articulation between universalism and the particular" (36).

37. Corlett, *Community without Unity*, 158–59, 146–49.

38. Dallmayr, "Hegemony and Democracy," 132.

39. See Gramsci's stinging criticism of Catholicism and the paradigm Catholic; *Selections from the Prison Notebooks*, 351–57. I have tried to rearticulate pastoralism as a political resource in "The Machine in the Garden Revisited: American Pastoralism and Contemporary Science Fiction," in *Political Mythology and Popular Fiction*, ed. Ernest J. Yanarella and Lee Sigelman (Westport, Conn.: Greenwood Press, 1988), 159–89, esp. 180–2.

40. Gramsci, *Selections from the Prison Notebooks*, 147–57, 210–18; and, more generally, Gwyn A. Williams's discussion, *Proletarian Order: Antonio Gramsci, Factory Councils and the Origins of Communism in Italy 1911–1921* (London: Pluto Press, 1975), esp. chs. 6 and 7.

41. In addition to his book, see Boggs's review essay, "The Green Alternative and the Struggle for a Post-Marxist Discourse," *Theory and Society*, 15 (1986): 869–99.

5

Postmodernism, Dialogue, and Democracy: Questions to Richard J. Bernstein

RICHARD J. BERNSTEIN
AND THE EDITORS

Eds. You have recently analyzed the *Stimmung* invoked by the terms "modernity/postmodernity" through a juxtaposition of Habermas and Derrida. Treating their work as elements of a "constellation" (in Adorno's sense), you propose to read them not as *either–or* but rather as *both–and*. Could you begin by summarizing this interpretation and the sense in which it provides an allegory for contemporary thought?

R.J.B. When I speak of the *Stimmung* invoked by the terms "modernity/postmodernity" I am deliberately employing Heidegger's suggestive expression. A *Stimmung*—a mood—is neither simply subjective nor objective. It is prereflective insofar as we have an inchoate sense of something that underlies and informs our conceptual distinctions. Nevertheless, a *Stimmung* exerts a powerful influence on the ways in which we think, act, and even feel. Anyone acquainted with recent debates can't help being struck by the instability of the signifiers "modernity" and "postmodernity." They are used in shifting, conflicting, and contradictory ways in different disciplines, and even within the "same" discipline. Many thinkers (e.g., Nietzsche, Heidegger, Foucault, Derrida) who are labeled "postmodern" by others rarely (if ever) use this expression or think of themselves as "postmodern." And yet there is a pervasive mood—shifting, amorphous, protean—a sense that something dramatic is happening that is changing the ways in which we think, act, and express ourselves. There are sharp disagreements about how to characterize this *Stimmung*. The reason why I speak of "modernity/postmodernity" is because—however one characterizes these two "moments"—they are, so I want to argue, inextricably interrelated and entwined with each other. In the essay to which you refer, "An Allegory of Modernity/Postmodernity,"[1] I attempt to characterize this *Stimmung* by probing the writings of Habermas and Derrida in order to highlight the ethical-political horizons of their thinking. Habermas is someone who is taken to exemplify and continue the Enlightenment legacy. He argues that modernity is an unfinished project. He emphasizes the themes of rationality and universality. He is concerned with the issue of the universal validity of norms that serve as the basis for critique. He argues that a major paradigm shift has taken place in the twentieth century—away from what he calls "the philosophy of consciousness" or "the philosophy of the subject" to a paradigm of communicative rationality and action. He is suspicious of the tendencies in "postmodern" thinkers who want to abandon the project of modernity and scorn Enlightenment ideals of justice and autonomy. He claims that when all forms of rationality and universality are damned then there is the danger that the critical impulse consumes itself. We are left with the *aporias* of "performative contradictions." And he thinks that this is the end result of those "postmodern" thinkers who attack the Enlightenment ideals that he defends.

Derrida is frequently read (mistakenly, I believe) as opposing everything that Habermas most strongly defends. He supposedly maintains that there is a deep rupture or break with this Enlightenment legacy and the project of modernity. It is only another variation of the flawed tradition of logocentrism which has characterized the "history of the West" and the metaphysics of presence. He thematizes *différance*, fragmentation, dispersal, and deconstruction.

For many who are drawn to one or the other of these thinkers, we seem to be confronted with a grand *Either–Or* where no reconciliation is imaginable or possible. Now I argue that this stark binary opposition is a gross oversimplification. Both of them are articulating something important and vital for understanding the "modern/postmodern" *Stimmung*. I propose a different reading of Habermas/Derrida where—to use the Hegelian expression—we highlight the "truth" in what they are saying and showing. Unlike Hegel, I do not think there is a grand synthesis or *Aufhebung* in which the tensions, differences, and oppositions between Habermas and Derrida can be finally reconciled. This is why I substitute

Adorno's metaphor of a constellation (which was also used by Franz Rosenzweig and Walter Benjamin) for Hegel's master metaphor of *Aufhebung*. A constellation is "a juxtaposed rather than integrated cluster of changing elements that resist reduction to a common denominator, essential core, or generative first principle." I also find Adorno's metaphor of a force field (*Kraftfeld*) illuminating for describing the *both–and* of Habermas/Derrida (and "modernity/postmodernity"). A *Kraftfeld* is "a relational interplay of attractions and aversions that constitute the dynamic transmutational structure of a complex phenomenon."

Habermas, I argue, is not a naive *Aufklärer*. He is profoundly aware of the ambiguities, conflicts, and treacheries of the Enlightenment legacy. He is not an uncritical champion of modernity. The Enlightenment legacy cannot be smoothed out into *either* a grand narrative of the progressive realization of freedom and justice *or* the cosmic might of ineluctable nihilistic self-destruction. With a stubborn persistence, he seeks to keep alive the memory/promise and hope of a world in which justice, freedom, and dialogical rationality are concretely embodied in our everyday social practices.

As I read Derrida he doesn't "oppose" or "reject" this memory/promise. Rather he is profoundly aware of the fissures and double binds of this project. Few contemporary thinkers have been as incisive and nuanced as Derrida in tracking the varieties of alterity and otherness, and *showing* how otherness ruptures, disrupts, and eludes our logocentric conceptual grids. One reason why I think that Derrida "speaks" to many of "us" and is so important for understanding the "modern/postmodern" *Stimmung* is because the question of otherness and difference (in all of its variations) has become a central issue for our time. The question that obsesses Derrida is; How can we be open to, and respond responsibly to the singularity and threat of otherness? This is primarily an ethical-political question for which there cannot be a final answer.

My reading of Habermas/Derrida is intended to be an allegory of the *Stimmung* of "modernity/postmodernity" in the sense that it is not exclusively about two "authors" or sets of texts, but about two intertwined moments of what I have called "the new constellation."

Eds. In fashioning this allegory, you combine selective elements of Habermas's and Derrida's thought so as to read each as the "other's other." This procedure implicitly enjoins the reader to choose which of these elements he or she affirms. Given the often sharp disagreements separating Habermas's and Derrida's positions, can one in fact treat them as a *both–and* without falsifying central elements of their thinking? What constitutes the particular standpoint from which you are able to combine them?

R.J.B. Before attempting to answer your question, let me first comment on your phrasing of the question. There is, of course, a generic sense in which any reading or interpretation is necessarily "selective." But I have tried to do justice to those "elements" of their thinking which *appear* to be most antithetical to each other. I do not want to downplay their differences but rather highlight them in order to discern the precise points where they "supplement" each other. I would resist the suggestion that "this procedure implicitly enjoins the reader to choose which of these elements he or she affirms"—as if one could arbitrarily pick and choose. This would miss the force of my insistence on a constellation of *both–and*. It would distort my intention to characterize the *Stimmung* of "modernity/postmodernity" as one where we must hold on to antithetical elements without succumbing to a false and facile reconciliation. I am fully aware that if we restrict ourselves to how Habermas and Derrida (and many of their followers) read each other we are confronted with something worse than "sharp disagreements." There is mutual distortion and at times almost total incomprehension of what the other is saying. But I do think we can move beyond this apparent standoff. I do not think that I have falsified "central elements of their thinking" but have attempted to bring forth their insights and blindnesses.

I come to what I take to be your basic question: "What constitutes the particular standpoint from which you are able to combine them?" I reject the very idea that there is or can be a neutral "standpoint" from which we can interpret, evaluate, and judge a thinker. We are always already participants in an ongoing critical encounter and dialogue. But I can try to answer your question in three ways. Like Gadamer (and Peirce) I believe that all critical understanding is informed by one's prejudgments and prejudices—which are themselves shaped by the traditions to which one belongs. Prejudgments are both enabling and at times blinding. We can only test and risk our prejudgments in the to-and-fro movement of hermeneutical understanding in our critical encounters with the other. What I attempt to do is to enter into dialogue with Habermas and Derrida—seeking to understand them in the strongest possible way in order to learn from them. My "standpoint" is not something which is fixed and given but rather *emerges* from this encounter. And it is, of course, open to criticism.

Alternatively, I can characterize my approach as an immanent critique—one in which I seek to enter their own projects and think through the consequences of what they are saying—and to do this in a way where one can discern the precise points of strength and weakness, the places where they "supplement" each other and require each other.

More informally, I can say that after years of close study of their texts

I came to the realization that each is telling us something important about our "modern/postmodern" predicament. Given their manifest sharp differences, the task became how "to do justice" to their apparent oppositions. This led to the idea that together they form a new constellation which enables us to understand the *Stimmung*, "modernity/postmodernity." Here too I would say that my "particular standpoint" is itself a *result* of these critical encounters. As a committed fallibilist I would insist that this standpoint is open to criticism by others.

Eds. Many writers argue that postmodernity is in some sense continuous with modernity. We were struck by the convergence between your juxtaposition and the idea, discussed in our introduction, that two streams of thought arising at the time of the French Revolution have to this day set broad parameters for continental philosophy. Can Habermas and Derrida be considered leading contemporary representatives of these still-opposed lines of thought? How does this bear on the alleged continuity of postmodernity with modernity?

R.J.B. I want to reiterate that the signifiers "modernity" and "postmodernity" are unstable and have been used in shifting and conflicting ways. They are "essentially contested" concepts. So we must be wary about slipping into a misleading essentialism where we explicitly (or implicitly) think we are talking about something definite and determinate. This bears on the question of "continuity" and "discontinuity." For whether we emphasize continuity or discontinuity will itself depend on what we take to be the primary characteristics of modernity and postmodernity. Continuity and discontinuity is always relative to how we describe or characterize the phenomenon that we are seeking to understand. Now much of the "rhetoric" of recent debates stresses the discontinuity, the rupture that supposedly has taken place. This is illustrated by the way in which Jean-François Lyotard opens his discussion in "The Postmodern Condition." Yet even Lyotard realizes that his dramatic contrast is an oversimplification. For he also tells us that the "postmodern" moment is "undoubtedly a part of the modern." "A work can become modern only if it is first postmodern."[2] From a very different perspective, Albrecht Wellmer argues that "modernity is for us an unsurpassable horizon in a cognitive, aesthetic and moral-political sense," yet he also declares that "postmodernism at its best might be seen as a self-critical—a skeptical, ironic, but nevertheless unrelenting—form of modernism."[3] I endorse what Derrida says when he claims:

> My own conviction is that we must maintain two contradictory affirmations at the same time. On the one hand we affirm the existence of rup-

tures in history, and on the other hand, we affirm that these ruptures produce gaps or faults (*failles*) in which the most hidden and forgotten archives can emerge and constantly recur and work through history. One must surmount the categorical oppositions of philosophic logic out of fidelity to these conflicting positions of historical discontinuity (rupture) and continuity (repetition) which are neither pure break with the past nor a pure unfolding or explication of it.[4]

This is what I have attempted to show when we seek to understand the new constellation of "modernity/postmodernity"; and this is the reason why I always juxtapose these terms together.

I do see some similarity with your analysis about the "two streams of thought" that have "set broad parameters for continental philosophy" (and perhaps even Anglo-American philosophy), but I have some serious reservations about your analysis. Even though I recognize that Mannheim uses the expression "conservative thought" in an idiosyncratic manner, I think it tends to obscure important oppositions and tensions. Let me bracket these reservations about Mannheim and focus on the binary oppositions that you specify. You write [in Chapter 1 of this volume]:

> Whereas rationalism stresses abstraction, generality, and universality, conservatism emphasizes concreteness, local particularity, and diversity. Whereas conservatism highlights holism as well as qualitative and/or "physiognomic" understanding, rationalism underscores atomism along with quantitative and/or "constructive" understanding. Moreover, while rationalism embodies a temporal understanding of history and seeks to grasp the actual via ahistorical norms, conservatism entertains a spatial understanding of history and seeks to understand norms via their embeddedness in actual history. Other oppositions characterizing conservatism versus rationalism include irrationality versus rationality of human reality, the historical embeddedness versus autonomy of reason, varying local versus universal truth, and becoming versus being.

You then add that "the affinities between postmodern and conservative thought should be evident even from this brief list." I have no doubt that the "rhetoric" of many "postmodern" discourses seems to fall on the side of what you and Mannheim call "conservative thought." But consider how misleading these stark oppositions are (aside from labeling them "conservative")—and how they fuel sterile debates. The "rationalism" you characterize above has nothing to do with the communicative rationality that Habermas articulates and defends. Indeed, he is a sharp critic of the type of rationalism you describe. It is closer to what he calls "instrumental" and "systems" rationality. Posing these stark contrasts makes it seem that postmodernism falls on the side of "irrationality" of human reality. And this is indeed a charge frequently made against so-called postmodern thinkers. But I don't see that Derrida, for example, defends "irrationality." On the contrary—as he himself tells us over and over again—he is engaged in *questioning* rationality, the principle of rationality and its ground. Questioning is not opposing or rejecting. And this questioning brings our hidden complexities of "rationality." Or consider the opposition of universality versus particularity.s Here too it initially seems that "postmodern" thinkers are drawn to particularity and seem to oppose all forms of universality. But is this true? I don't think so. Even Rorty and Lyotard who supposedly attack "universality" are proposing—in their utopian visions of society—a new type of universality where there is *universal* agonistic play without terror of incommensurable language games and vocabularies. Or again, I think it is misleading to associate rationalism with abstraction and "conservative thought" with concreteness. With all the talk of concreteness, specificity, and particularity, many "postmodern" discourses display an overgeneralized abstractness. If there is one clear moral to be drawn from "modern-postmodern" debates, it is that we should be wary of any and all stark binary oppositions. For when we think them through we see how they implicate and are entangled with each other. So I think it is more illuminating to ask precisely how each side (and there are more than two) conceives of rationality, universality, concreteness, particularity, temporality, spatiality, et cetera. Consequently, I would not consider Habermas and Derrida as "leading contemporary representative of these still opposed lines of thought" but rather as thinkers who cut across and undermine these oppositions.

Eds. Turning to politics, both Habermas and Derrida invoke democracy in their work. But whereas Habermas joins with Millian liberals in developing the notion of a public sphere centered on consensus, Derrida's "democracy to come" is aligned with those contemporary thinkers who, out of concern for preserving alterity and difference, promote a "federative" or "alliance"-based democracy. What do you see as the tasks for democratic theory in the contemporary modern/postmodern constellation? And what possible routes to the desirable form of democracy?

R.J.B. First, I think we must recognize that Derrida thus far has said very little about what he means by "democracy to come" while the meaning of democracy has always been a major thematic concern for Habermas. Nevertheless, in my essay "An Allegory of Modernity/ Postmodernity," as well as in my essay "Serious Play: The Ethical-Political Horizon of Derrida,"⁵ I have argued that from his earliest texts we can detect in Derrida a strong ethical-political concern that is relevant for understanding democracy. Derrida, unlike many of his followers, has always emphasized the political significance of deconstruction. Second, I think it can be misleading to say that "Habermas joins with Millian liberals in developing the notion of a public sphere centered on consensus." For this can distort the fact that Habermas's deepest intellectual roots are in the tradition of German philosophy: Kant, Fichte, Schelling, Hegel, Marx, and the Frankfurt critical theorists. He is a sympathetic critic of the liberal tradition. Sometimes I wish that Habermas had never employed the expression "consensus" because—especially in an Anglo-American context—it has so many misleading associations. What I see as most vital in Habermas's vision of democracy is not that we reach agreement or "consensus" but rather the willingness to develop public spheres in which we are committed to listen and argue with each other—where there is symmetry and reciprocalness, where we are aware of, and respect, genuine differences, where, as he says, the only force that is relevant is the force of the better argument. Of course, this is an ideal. He certainly realizes that empirically there are asymmetrical power relationships. Nevertheless, it is an ideal that can shape our political practices. And Habermas is also illuminating in showing and explaining how such communication is distorted in the contemporary world. He highlights what he calls the colonization of the life-world by systems rationality and relates this to developments in late capitalism.

Now although Derrida has not developed a well-articulated political theory, he is extremely incisive in exposing those tendencies in "the history of the West" which suppress and repress difference, alterity, and otherness. He exposes the hidden violence of marginalization and exclusion. This is why I think Derrida is so relevant for all those who have suffered from discrimination, oppression, and exclusion. The task for democratic theory today is to think through how to do justice to both universality and particularity, sameness and difference, to conceive and develop *practices* in which we recognize the interminableness of conflict and nevertheless can learn to respect the otherness of the other. I am not convinced that Habermas and Derrida have different conceptions of democracy. Rather, I see them as highlighting different aspects of a democratic polity. I wish I could say something illuminating about what "are possible routes to the desirable form of democracy," but I think we must honestly admit that this is one of the toughest and most complex practical questions that many of us are struggling with. The dramatic changes in the world situation in the past decade have placed on the agenda the meaning and practice of democracy. I also believe that there has been a "dialectic" in "modern/postmodern" debates where increasingly we are becoming aware of their ethical-political consequences and their relevance for rethinking what democracy means today. This is what I try to show in *The New Constellation*.

Eds. Many feminists fear that their political mission, arising out of unrealized Enlightenment ideals, is undercut by elements of postmodern thought. Other feminist political thinkers argue for abandoning Enlightenment ideals, which they see as inherently and unavoidably androcentric. Recognizing the plurality of feminisms, what do you see of the project of modernity in feminist politics today?

R.J.B. I would like to answer this question in two ways—from the perspective of what I am claiming about the "modern/postmodern" constellation, and from the perspective of what some feminists have argued. The apprehensions voiced on both "sides" make perfect sense to me. If one presses to an extreme those tendencies in "postmodern thought" which emphasize and indeed exaggerate particularity, difference, and alterity, then there is a real danger that we simply dissolve the very idea of feminism and a feminist perspective. We are left with an impotent nominalism that undercuts any collective political identity and action. On the other hand, no one can any longer ignore those tendencies in the Enlightenment legacy that have been entangled with patriarchy and the silencing of women. The task then—for an adequate feminism—is *neither* to throw out the baby with the bath, that is, not to completely condemn what is still viable in the Enlightenment ideals, the practical demand for justice, freedom, equality, and self-determination, *nor* to reify particularity, difference, and otherness. As I read feminist literature many feminists themselves are advocating such a *both–and*. They are showing us concretely what this means in the context of a feminist political struggle. Let me cite one example of what I mean. In a recent issue of *Praxis International*, there is a heated exchange among three feminists, Seyla Benhabib, Judith Butler, and Nancy Fraser, that is directly relevant to your question.[6] Seyla Benhabib, while not completely unsympathetic to "postmodern" feminism, nevertheless strongly opposes those tendencies in "postmodernism" which she claims are "not only incompatible with but would undermine the very possibility of feminism as the theoretical articulation of the emancipatory aspirations of women."[7] She is countered by a provocative and polemical critique by Judith Butler who strongly identifies herself with a feminist poststructuralist position. Commenting on their exchange, Nancy Fraser entitles her response

"False Antitheses." She notes that they seem to be "irreconcilably opposed" (just as others have argued that Habermas and Derrida are "irreconcilably opposed"). But then Fraser works through their oppositions and contends that "feminists do not have to choose between Critical Theory and poststructuralism; instead, we might reconstruct each approach so as to reconcile it with the other. Thus . . . I shall argue that the Benhabib–Butler exchange poses false antitheses and unnecessary polarizations."[8] I find myself in fundamental agreement with Fraser, and I think that the type of feminist perspective she has been developing is a viable project for a "modern/postmodern" feminist politics—one which is also compatible with my own reading of the "modern/postmodern" *Stimmung*.

Eds. A question about space. Foucault writes, "The great obsession of the nineteenth century was, as we know, history; with its themes of development and of suspension, of crisis and cycle, themes of the ever accumulating past. . . . The present epoch will perhaps be above all the epoch of space. We are in the epoch of simultaneity; we are in the epoch of juxtaposition, the epoch of the near and the far, of the side-by-side, of the dispersed" ["Of Other Spaces," *Diacritics* 16(1986): 22]. Jameson, meanwhile, avers that "a model of political culture appropriate to our own situation will necessarily have to raise spatial issues as its fundamental organizing concern" ["Postmodernism, or the Cultural Logic of Late Capitalism," *New Left Review* 146 (1984): 189]. Do you agree that spatial issues are especially pertinent in an account of the contemporary, and what relevance does this hold for your analysis of democracy?

R.J.B. At first glance, it might seem that I am in basic agreement with the "spirit" of these claims by Foucault and Jameson. I have entitled my recent book *The New Constellation* and acknowledge that "constellation" is primarily a spatial metaphor. I have even—echoing the passage from Foucault—characterized a constellation as "a *juxtaposed* rather than integrated cluster of changing elements." But I resist the claim that while the nineteenth century was the epoch of "history" the present epoch is above all the epoch of "space." It is important to note that when Foucault speaks of history here he is speaking of a very determinate concept of history "with its themes of development and of suspension, of crisis and cycle, themes of the ever accumulating past." Now Foucault is right insofar as he suggests that *this* conception of history has certainly been challenged—and some would say, exploded—in the twentieth century. But I don't see that this means (and I don't think Jameson would say) we today are any less concerned with history. Rather our understanding of history and its significance has been transformed. So too, for all its dramatic significance, I do not think it is correct to say the present epoch is "above all the epoch of space." For me, the primary question is how our understanding of space, time, and history, et cetera, have changed—and why?

Although there are multiple ways in which questions of space have been approached in our time, I would like to focus on two important conceptions of space which are relevant for the task of rethinking democracy: public space and ethical space. These concepts are explored in the work of Hannah Arendt and Charles Taylor.

"Public space" for Arendt is basic to an understanding of politics as a form of collective *action* (which she sharply distinguishes from work and labor). She argues that basic to the human condition is the plurality of human beings with their differing perspectives and opinions. The space she highlights is the "in-between" of this ineradicable plurality. It is in this public space of appearance where individuals act and speak together that freedom becomes a tangible reality. Action and speech take place *in-between* individuals. Speaking of the Greek polis, she tells us that "the polis, properly speaking, is not the city-state in its physical location; it is the organization of the people as it arises out of acting and speaking together, and its true space lies between people living together for this purpose no matter where they happen to be."[9] This public space both brings us together in a common world and separates us. "Action and speech create a space between participants which can find its proper location almost any time and anywhere."[10] Unlike those critics of Arendt who think she has a nostalgia for an idealized notion of the Green polis, I think her primary intent is very different. I read her as engaging in an act of retrieval and reclamation that is intended to serve as a critique of what has happened in the modern age. The danger she seeks to counter is one where our understanding of public space and political action are deformed. This is also her motivation in recovering "the lost treasure" of revolution where public space and freedom become tangible realities.[11] The reason why I think Arendt's analysis is so important and relevant for us (I have only given a brief sketch of what she means) is because we are threatened with what John Dewey called the "eclipse of the public." It is not surprising to me that many so-called postmodern thinkers are "rediscovering" Arendt and are drawn to her work. For her "thick description" of public space is a fertile source for thinking about democratic politics in which plurality, conflict, and difference are constitutive.

In Charles Taylor's *Sources of the Self* and in some of his other writings he thematizes the notion of "ethical space." He tells us that "a human being exists inescapably in a space of ethical questions; she or he cannot avoid assessing himself or herself in relation to some standard."[12] This is what he calls "strong evaluation" in which we necessarily make qualitative distinctions about what is good, bad, right, and wrong. Although Taylor claims that "human beings always have a sense of self which situates them in ethical space," he emphasizes that "the terms that define this space, and that situate us within it, vary in striking fashion."[13] Although he is critical of many "postmodern" thinkers, he nevertheless shares their critiques of the "modern" tendency to conceive of the human agent and subject as "monological" where the "subject is first of all an 'inner space,' a 'mind' to use the old terminology, or a mechanism capable of processing representations."[14] Although he sketches a history of changing ethical spaces and the growth of "radical reflexivity" he wants to highlight the emergence of the ethical space of the "dialogical self." And what is characteristic of this new ethical space is that an action is dialogical "when it is effected by an integrated, nonindividual agent." Much of our understanding of self, society, world, and language sets up "spaces of common action on a number of levels, intimate and public." "We define ourselves partly in terms of what we come to accept as our appropriate place with dialogical actions."[15]

There is a significant overlap between Arendt's analysis of public space and Taylor's analysis of dialogical ethical space (although there are also some striking differences). I have always thought that a primary motivation for many of the recent critiques of the monological tendencies of modern thought is not merely theoretical but practical. It is a justified reaction to what is an increasing tendency in contemporary life where we become isolated atomic monads—where we no longer practice or even understand what dialogical action even means. And I think both Arendt and Taylor in highlighting new ways of thinking about the space *in-between* human beings are helpful in countering the twin dangers of homogenization—or what Foucault calls "normalization"—and disintegration or complete fragmentation.

Eds. You once quoted Iris Murdoch's remark to the effect that it is revealing to ask what a thinker fears. What fears does your own work reflect?

R.J.B. Iris Murdoch remarked, "It is always a significant question to ask of any philosopher: what is he afraid of?" Now paradoxically, I don't know if I or any philosopher is in the best position to really answer the question "what is he afraid of?" Frequently it is others who are most perceptive in answering this question. Nevertheless, if pressed I would answer that my greatest fear is barbarism. And barbarism can come in many forms—some of the worst can be extremely sophisticated. You recall that Alasdair MacIntyre "concludes" *After Virtue* by warning us about the new barbarism which surrounds us today. To explain what I mean, let me cite a favorite passage of mine from John Courtney Murray. He writes:

> Barbarism . . . threatens when men cease to talk together according to reasonable laws. There are laws of argument, the observance of which is imperative if discourse is to be civilized. Argument ceases to be civil when it is dominated by passion and prejudice; when its vocabulary becomes solipsist, premised on the theory that my insight is mine alone and cannot be shared; when dialogue gives way to a series of monologues; when the parties to the conversation cease to listen to one another, or only hear what they want to hear, or see the other's argument only through the screen of their own categories . . . When things like this happen, men cannot be locked together in argument. Conversation becomes merely quarrelsome or querulous. Civility dies with the death of dialogue.[16]

Barbarism can manifest itself intellectually and theoretically as well as in deadly practical ways—and they are closely interrelated. I think that a primary reason why so many thinkers have been drawn to talking about incommensurability and relativism is because this reflects something fundamental about what is happening to our ethical-political practices. Too frequently we live as if we really are solipsists, prisoners within our own frameworks, vocabularies, language games, and paradigms. Our gestures toward communication degenerate to a "series of monologues" where we cease to listen to each other or hear only what we want to hear. This has been a tendency in recent philosophy and indeed in most of the cultural disciplines. We lack the willingness, imagination, and even the desire to listen to what the other is saying. And despite all the "postmodern" talk about the otherness of the other, I think that many of the so-called modern/postmodern debates exhibit this form of barbarism where we only see the other through the screen of our own entrenched categories. I do think that conflict is endemic in all human life. But the primary question is how we *respond* to these conflicts—how we learn to understand and live with our differences. And I am sympathetic with—and have sought to practice—a dialogical critical response which does not entail that we will agree with each other. For me this is not simply a theoretical issue but a practical one. For there is the ever-present danger of new forms of ethnic "tribalism" where, as we have witnessed recently in Yugoslavia, people begin killing each other. But we don't have to look abroad to witness this. We can see this manifested in the sexism, racism, and ethnic centrism which is manifested in our own society where we no longer even attempt to listen to each other and where we succumb to blinding prejudices. I see this type of fragmentation as posing one of the greatest threats to democracy. For democracy as an ethical-political ideal requires a commitment to serious engaged public debate that doesn't degenerate into devious manipulation or a series of monologues. For me the primary responsibility of an intellectual and a citizen is to oppose barbarism wherever it is encountered and whatever form it takes.

Notes

1. Richard J. Burnstein, "An Allegory of Modernity/Postmodernity: Habermas and Derrida," in *The New Constellation: The Ethical-Political Horizons of Modernity/Postmodernity* (Cambridge: M.I.T. Press, 1992).

2. Jean-François Lyotard, *The Postmodern Condition: A Report on Knowledge*, trans. Geoff Bennington and Brian Massumi (Minneapolis: University of Minnesota Press, 1984), 79.

3. Albrecht Wellmer, *The Persistence of Modernity* (Oxford, England: Polity Press, 1991), vii.

4. Jacques Derrida, "Dialogue with Jacques Derrida," in *Dialogue with Contemporary Continental Thinkers*, ed. Richard Kearney (Manchester, England: Manchester University Press, 1984), 133.

5. See Bernstein, *The New Constellation*.

6. See "An exchange on Feminism and Postmodernism," in *Praxis International* 11, no. 2 (July 1991): 137–194.

7. Ibid, 146.

8. Ibid, 166.

9. Hannah Arendt, *The Human Condition* (Chicago: University of Chicago Press, 1958), 198.

10. Ibid.

11. See Hannah Arendt, *On Revolution* (New York: Viking Press, 1965).

12. Charles Taylor, "The Dialogical Self," in *The Interpretive Turn*, ed. D. R. Hiley, J. F. Buhman, and R. M. Shusterman (Ithaca, N.Y.: Cornell University Press, 1991), 205.

13. Ibid, 306.

14. Ibid, 307.

15. Ibid, 311.

16. John Courtney Murray, S. J., *We Hold These Truths* (New York: Sheed and Ward, 1960), 14.

6

Postmodern Geographies and the Critique of Historicism

Edward W. Soja

A First Positioning

There are many modernities, many different processes of modernization, and many different modernisms; and the same can be said for their assertively *post*-prefixed expressions. Modernity and postmodernity are not singular and homogenous concepts to be categorized neatly by their opposing essences. Rather than being mutually exclusive, they are "in" one another in ways that make their intertwining as important as their differentiation. Every contemporary commentary on modernity and postmodernity must begin by recognizing this multiplicity of forms and meanings.

Accordingly, we must be open right from the start to the possibility of being both modern and postmodern at the same time, whether as individuals or as social groups. Indeed, it can be argued that every contemporary individual and social formation is simultaneously modern and postmodern, albeit with great variations in relative intensity and explicit proportion. Analyzing and interpreting these variations and combinations, the simultaneous and uneven development of modernity and postmodernity, is crucial to making practical and political sense of the contemporary world. Stated differently, modernity and postmodernity do not lend themselves very well to categorical polarization or simple binary opposition.[1]

Recognizing multiplicity and connectedness does not mean that we cannot generalize about modernity or postmodernity as separable concepts. Such generalization is most useful, however, not as an end in itself or as a means of exclusive categorical separation, but rather as a vantage point from which to gain perspective on the particularity and heterogeneity of their differentiated forms and meanings. Seen in this way, generalization assists in *contextualizing* modernity and postmodernity along three encompassing interpretive dimensions: the spatial, the temporal, and the social. More actively and expressively defined, these contextualizing dimensions describe the interconnected *spatiality*, *historicity*, and *sociality* of human life. All generalizations about human phenomena, from ontological statements on the conditions of being to theoretical arguments about the contingencies of the empirical world, revolve around these specifying and contextualizing fields of expression. Each provides a separate focus for generalization, but the fields also interact and combine with one another in a relational "trialectic," the best term I can find to denote their mutual determinations and oppositional unity.

I introduce this contextualizing trialectic of spatiality, historicity, and sociality for several reasons. First, it helps me to develop a useful working definition of *modernity-in-general*, an appropriately comprehensive conceptualization that can be used as a standard from which to assess the differentiation, specificity, and uneven development of modernities and postmodernities across time, space, and social practices. Modernity-in-general can be aptly described as a "culture of space and time," to recall Stephen Kern's felicitous phrase; or, in Marshall Berman's words, as a practical consciousness of the contemporary, an explicit awareness of the "perils and possibilities" inherent in being alive in a particular time, place, and social formation.[2] These evocative descriptions simultaneously generalize and particularize modernity within the framework of the trialectic.

This comprehensive definition of modernity also serves to outline the basis for the critical stance I will take in the remainder of this chapter, when I will argue that the particular forms of modernity and modernism that became dominant in the late nineteenth century, especially in the realms of critical theory and discourse, tended to privilege historicity and sociality at the expense of spatiality, thus distorting the interpretive trialectic and inhibiting the ability of modern movements to gain critical and potentially emancipatory insight from the "making of geographies" in the same way they more successfully did for the "making of history" and the intentional remaking of the social order.

I will also argue that the contemporary debates on postmodernity, postmodernization, and postmodernism have initiated the long-delayed reassertion of spatiality in critical thought and practice, thereby helping to rebalance the peculiar bias in critical thinking that has prevailed over the past century. Central to this reassertion of spatiality, as I see it, is the critique of a persistent ontological and theoretical historicism that has tended to subsume the spatial in its dominance over the critical discourse. My intention is not to replace historicism with an equally subsumptive spatialism, but to achieve a more appropriate trialectical balance in which neither spatiality, historicity, nor sociality is interpretively privileged a priori.[3]

The impatient reader will note that I have not yet provided either general or specific definitions of postmodernity in this "first positioning." To do so will require further elaboration regarding the development of modernity-in-general, for it is only by reference to this development that postmodernity can be defined and assessed.

The Succession of Modernities

The roots of modernity as a generalizable, periodizable, and spatializable form of collective consciousness are found in the European Enlightenment, although both roots and branches can be found in earlier times and in other places. Modernity-as-Enlightenment, as the first contextualization of modernity-in-general, revolved around the development of an explicit critical awareness of the then-contemporary world as a source of practical knowledge that could be accumulated and used to change the world, to make it "better," rather than simply to reinforce and faithfully maintain the status quo. Its driving questions were: What difference does today, what is going on right now, in this world and this period, introduce with respect to yesterday? How can we use our understanding of the contemporary to build a better future? In other words: What's new? . . . and what is to be done about it right now and here?[4] These remain the central questions defining all modernities and modernisms.[5]

The discourse on modernity has thus always been a critical, intentionally enlightening, and potentially emancipatory discourse. In its interpretive focus on the contemporary, its distinctive "presentism," if you will, this discourse is aimed at deriving practical knowledge from what it means to be alive in a particular place, time, and social nexus. In reaction both to classicism and theologism, the early Enlightenment turned to science and "modern" scientific understanding as the primary basis of praxis, the transformation of knowledge into presumably beneficial, progressive, social action. Ever since, the discourse on modernity has been traceable through what we still call the "philosophy of science" as well as through the more recent development of "critical theory."

Modernity-as-Enlightenment changed significantly, however, in the Age of Revolution, beginning most explosively with the first truly modern social revolutions, in the American colonies in 1776 and in France in 1789. More than ever before, the dynamics of modernity, modernization, and modernism became inextricably attached to capitalism and to its emergent political form, the capitalist nation-state. When Kant asked, *"Was ist Aufklärung?"* in 1784, he could answer with no mention of capitalism. After 1789, this became increasingly inconceivable, for the discourse on modernity-as-Enlightenment was significantly restructured into "another" general form and focus.[6]

This first comprehensive deconstruction and reconstitution of modernity, this profound *restructuring*, changed the critical discourse in nearly every field of knowledge and action. In particular, it redefined and refocused the politics and political philosophy of modernity and modernization. In 1848, both Marx and Comte would paper the revolutionary moment in Paris with their very different emancipatory "positivist" manifestoes, the former giving impetus to a revolutionary scientific socialism, the latter to a liberal social scientism, each in their own way a deconstructive and reconstitutive statement of the new (post?) modernism-as-Enlightenment. In the expansive Age of Capital that followed the revolutions of 1848–49, these two oppositional but nonetheless modernist movements would consolidate increasing power in their separate spheres and extend their influence—and their particular programs for what is to be done "just now"—around the globe in tune with the dynamics of capitalist urban and industrial development.

With the Paris Commune, the financial panics of the early 1870s, the rise of militant labor unionism and socialist political parties, the closing of the American frontier, the Long Depression in Europe, rapidly accelerated urbanization and industrialization, and many other disruptive events, the last three decades of the nineteenth century, the era of the *fin de siècle*, became another period of comprehensive restructuring and transformation, another transition to a new and different modernity. The more explicitly political discourses on modernity initiated by Marx and Comte continued to prevail but were significantly redirected, into an integrative (totalizing?) but now more Leninist Marxism and an instrumental and institutionalized social scientism that became increasingly disintegrated into specialized liberal disciplines, what the Marxists would call the "bourgeois" social sciences.

But I must cut short what deserves to be a much richer and more detailed discussion of the periodization and regionalization of modernity.[7] With egregious simplification, I will only note that a third restructuring and recomposition of modernity marked the second quarter of the twentieth century (the Great Depression, World War II, the rise of the Keynesian welfare state and Stalinist state socialism, the growth of Fordist mass production, consumerism, and suburbanization); and that the contemporary era, beginning as early as the mid-1960s, began yet another restructuring and recomposition, still in progress, still with its own distinctive perils and possibilities, and marked with the same complex mixture of continuity, change, and uneven development that characterized similar restructuring periods in the past.

For what I hope are now obvious reasons, one can describe the present period as the fourth restructuring in the sequence of contextualized modernities that began with the attachment of modernity-in-general (in the specific form of modernity-as-Enlightenment) to the dynamics of capitalist development and survival in the late eighteenth century. This attachment does not necessarily imply causal determination, one way or the other, nor should it suggest that the connections between capitalism and modernism are uniformly developed in all spheres of activity or that they are the same today as they were fifty years ago. The primary inference to be drawn, lest we forget, is that the complex and unevenly developed historical geographies of both capitalism and modernity continue to be conjoined in the present.

The Rush to the Post

Only at this point and with the preceding backdrop can we make appropriate sense of postmodernity, postmodernization, and postmodernism. As I already implied, the prefixing of *post* typically arises in conjunction with periods of restructuring and transition from one dominant form of modernity to another. Rather than signaling a complete break in the succession of modernities, it connotes a competitive shift in hegemony and direction. In terms reminiscent of Raymond Williams's neo-Gramscian treatment of hegemony,[8] each restructuring period can be characterized by at least three groups of modernist practices: a first group associated with the established but relatively declining dominant (unprefixed but usually described as "in crisis"); a second group developing rapidly along alternative paths to challenge the first group's dominance (prefixed with *post-* to mark its active opposition and potential supersession); and a third group, a mixed and markedly subordinated category of residuals (attached to other modernities of the past), ancients (antagonistic to modernity-in-general), and the excluded (completely outside the debate and discourse).

Today, to be Modern (capitalized here to distinguish the still-established hegemon) is thus to ascribe to one or another of the diverse modern movements that consolidated around the turn of the century and became increasingly hegemonic after the mid-twentieth-century restructuring. To be post-Modern is to ascribe to one or another of the diverse modern movements that have arisen in response to the particular conditions of the contemporary restructuring period. The two forms of practical consciousness coexist contentiously but are not mutually exclusive. To combine them together in practice, however, creates both constructive and destructive tensions that accumulate and push toward an explicit choice or identity. Individually and collectively, we may all combine aspects of the Modern and the post-Modern in our discourses and social practices, but we are being forced to make a discursive and practical choice by the increasing postmodernization of the contemporary world, the increasing success and rising power of those interest groups that have, contextually and strategically, chosen to pursue some variant of postmodernism, whether it be as a commodity-emblem, a strategy for progressive political practice, an aesthetic premise, or as a means to make war and win elections.

To be Modern versus post-Modern thus takes on new meaning as a contextual and strategic decision *internal* to the continuing discourse on modernity-in-general. It must be stressed, however, that this conjunctural choice does not hinge upon categorical assignments of responsibility for the continuation or destruction of the progressive Enlightenment project to one or the other camps, as so often occurs in the contemporary critical discourse, especially among those energetic categorizers who feel compelled to squeeze meaning into neat polar oppositions. Modernism and postmodernism as competitive social movements are much more complex and heterogeneous than established theories of them typically suggest. Each has the full capacity to engender the extremes of repressive-progressive political practice. Choosing between them is primarily a matter of practical efficacy, that is, how best to advance a particular project here and now, that same old question of "What is to be done?" that has always defined modernity-in-general. The critical division thus arises over whether the retention (with some reformative adaptation) and defense of the Modern or the adoption and strategic application of the post-Modern can best serve these specific projects.

A Little Bit of Baudrillard

Two interweaving time lines have been used to illustrate the succession of heterogeneous modernities that spring from the early European Enlightenment and conjoin with the dynamics of global capitalist development beginning in the late eighteenth century. To bring this sequence of modernities up to date and to help contextualize the particularity of the contemporary (What's now new?), I borrow from Jean Baudrillard his most significant discovery, what he has called the "precession of simulacra."[9] Baudrillard's insinuations about the changing relations between the signifying "real" and the representational "imaginary" supply another time line that can be used to help us make practical sense of the contemporary—which is, after all, the primary objective of any serious attempt to reassess the concepts of modernity and postmodernity.

Baudrillard defines four "successive phases of the image" which can be interpreted, for our purposes, as critical epistemes of modernity, modes of obtaining practical knowledge about the real lifeworld. The first critical episteme, often rooted in ancient Greek philosophy and generatively associated with the development of modernity-as-Enlightenment, is captured in the metaphor of the *mirror*. Making practical sense of the world in order to change it for the better comes from the ability to comprehend in rational thought the sensible "reflections" from that real empirical world, to sort out the accurate, good, useful information from the accompanying noise and distortion. This is essentially the epistemology of modern science and the scientific method, in their variously verificationist and falsificationist forms. It continues in force to this day in the human, biological, and physical sciences as the dominant epistemology, and is still recognizable, despite its detractors, as an important foundation for critical, emancipatory thought and practice.

An alternative critical episteme was developed most systematically in the nineteenth century, although again ancestral predecessors can be found. Its metaphorical embodiment is not the mirror but the *mask*, a belief that the "good" reflections potentially receivable from the world of the real are being blocked by a deceptive shroud of false or counterfeit appearances. Practical knowledge and understanding thus requires an unmasking, a demystification of surface appearances, a digging for insight beneath the empirical world of directly measurable reflections. The systematic exposition of this mode of critical discourse is closely related to the development of various forms of structuralism, from Marx, Freud, and de Saussure to more contemporary cultural criticism in art, literature, and aesthetics (where some might say an untheorized form of this discourse has always existed among creative artists of all kinds). This alternative episteme significantly shaped the discourse on modernity in the *fin de siècle* and has probably been the dominant counterepistemology for explicitly critical theory and practice throughout the twentieth century.

For Baudrillard, a third episteme emerges alongside the others in the late twentieth century, ushering in a new critical epistemology metaphorized around the *simulacrum* and indicative of a transition from the mere masking of appearances (dissimulation: feigning not to have what one really has) to the increasing "liquidation of all referentials," the substitution of signs or representations of the real for the real itself (simulation: feigning to have what one has not). The simulacrum, an exact copy of an original that has either been lost or did not exist in the first place, threatens to erase the very difference between the "true" and the "false," the "real" and the "imaginary," the "signifier" and the "signified." Around its increasing empowerment in the contemporary world (surely I need not footnote a list of demonstrative references) we have the reactive basis for much of what has been associated with the "postmodern condition" in critical discourse: the deconstruction of dominant epistemologies and the rise of more flexible, recombinant, and broadly poststructuralist critical theories; the resort to relativism, radical pluralism, eclecticism, and pastiche; the recognition of a pervasive hyperreality and the disappearance and dislocation of the subject and its referents; the crisis of representation and the radical negation of the sign as value; the attack on totalization and metanarratives; the opening up to difference and the "other"; the substantive attention to media and popular culture as affective and revealing locations for the production of hyperreality; and the search for tactical and strategic niches rather than universal programs for emancipatory social action. All spring, in one way or another, from the discovery that "reality" is no longer what it used to be, and that our old ways of knowing need to be significantly restructured.

Baudrillard's third phase, wherein the image masks the growing *absence* of a basic reality as a prime referential, can be interpreted as the inaugural moment of contemporary postmodernity and the first step toward the denouement of his fourth phase, when all images become their own pure simulacra, bearing no relation to any reality whatsoever. Whether Baudrillard believes we have reached this final moment of complete hypersimulation is not of consequence, nor should we blame the messenger for all that has gone wrong in the still-evolving postmodern world, as so many persistent modernists have been prone to do. We need not run in the directions Baudrillard has taken since his initial conceptualization of the "precession of simulacra," but we must respect and wrestle seriously with his provocative achievement and epistemological challenge.

Splitting Heirs and Taking Sides

A tentative typology can be constructed to illustrate (and summarize) the arguments implied in the preceding reassessments of modernity and postmodernity. It is offered here not as a definitive classification but as a suggestive sketchmap or snapshot of the contemporary terrain of debate and explicitly political positioning with regard to what now has become widely described as the "postmodern condition."

The side-splitting begins with the original (Enlightenment) division between the "ancients" and the "moderns," the former emphasizing continuity against change (it ain't broken so there is no need to fix it; let us learn only from the past), the latter emphasizing change against continuity (the present has become significantly different from the past so we must try to do something different to construct a better future). This broad division persists to the present, but within the region of the moderns several different positions can be identified among those actively engaged in contemporary debates on what's new and what should be done about it now.

Antimodernists today are the devoted celebrants of the end of the old Modernity in its dominant (capitalized) form. Satisfied with endemic annihilation as the best strategy for the future, they are the smiling morticians who attend to the figurative deaths of the subject, of the author, of ideology, of communism, of liberalism, of history, of feminism, of the progressive project, of practically everything associated with the major modern movements of the twentieth century. They frequently appear under the guise of being postmodern (or occasionally ancients), but are more often short-sighted opportunists intent only on quickly proclaiming a New Age in their premature eulogies.

Late modernists or neomodernists, in contrast, cling to the continuities of the Modern project and adjust to what's new through innovative reforms rather than radical deconstruction and reconstitution. The most agile and insightful of this group (Jürgen Habermas? David Harvey? Anthony Giddens?) edge very close to postmodernism, but refuse to step over the border for fear that too much would be lost. While making occasional and often insightful forays into enemy territory, they ultimately retreat behind the epistemological borderlands to reinforce their defenses in the belief that crossing over into the postmodern camp would bring with it the end of their progressive Modernist projects.

The avowed postmodernists are not so fearful of cooptation. They accept the need for a radically new and different response to what now is to be done, and insist on a much more unsettling process of deconstruction and reconstitution, without necessarily abandoning the emancipatory projects of modernity-in-general. Rather than insistently unmasking what lies behind the invasive sphere of hyperreality or attempting earnestly to understand it through the methods of modern science (still the characteristic methodologies of the late modernists left, right, and center), the postmodernists take as given the precession of simulacra and respond directly to its immanence and immediacy with strategic simulations and adaptively flexible epistemologies of their own.

The postmodernists are a diverse lot, but they can be further differentiated into at least three clusters that as yet have no widely accepted names but can be roughly described for now as leaning left, leaning right, and refusing to lean at all, at least for the moment. The group leaning left is the smallest, for many of its potential allies (especially radical late modernists) refuse to accept that it can exist at all. Ascribing to what is sometimes called a "postmodernism of resistance," this cluster maintains the most progressive intentions of modernity-in-general but sees these intentions as achievable only through contextual strategies that accept the precession of simulacra, reject totalizing visions, search for new combinations and alliances, and engage directly with the instrumental production of hyperreality, that is, with the significantly altered conditions of an increasingly post-Modern contemporary world.

The postmodern left, in which I now obviously position myself, must struggle on at least three fronts: to resist the rising power of right-leaning postmodernism, to awaken those sitting on the fence of the political implications of their immobility, and to convince their insufficiently deconstructed late-modern allies not only to accept their existence but to join them in the first two struggles. They must also deal sympathetically and constructively with parochialisms and exclusive localisms within, for a primary political challenge to radical postmodernism is to gain strength (rather than despair) from the fragmentation of progressive political projects that the Modern left has traditionally seen as one of its major sources of weakness.[10]

The opposing cluster leaning right helps to define and provoke this postmodernism of resistance through its remarkable success in shifting contemporary political discourse to its own spin-doctored simulations and dissimulations. One of the defining moments of its rise to hegemonic political power was Ronald Reagan's sincere announcement that the stagflation and unemployment crisis of the early 1980s was only a state of mind, a pessimistic and unpatriotic image of American reality that needed reengineering (resimulation?) as the primary means of resolving the problems. This and a host of other official suspensions of facticity reaffirmed the meaning of the citation from *Ecclesiastes* that begins Baudrillard's English translation of *Simulations*: "The simulacrum is never that which conceals the truth—it is the truth which conceals that there is none. . . . The simulacrum is true." Ever since, and more than ever before, American foreign and domestic policy and politics has hinged upon such "truthful" simulacra (the Persian Gulf War as CNN special comes to mind).

The hypersimulations of the right have come to monopolize the popular definition of the progressive projects of modernity in an increasing proportion of the contemporary world. This reactionary postmodernism is often termed "neoconservative" but it has thus far been the most radically successful form of postmodernism. Its greatest successes in the United States have revolved around the substitution of strategic simulations of the real for the real itself, especially with respect to all opposing, left-leaning definitions of the progressive projects of modernity. To a remarkable degree, socialism has become imaginatively transformed in public discourse into a synonym for totalitarianism or sadly antiquated idealism, radical feminism has been made to look biologically aberrant and inherently destructive of the most cherished features of the human family, radical environmentalists and antinuclear activists are represented as foolish or demented Luddites, the American liberal democrat is made into an anachronistic oaf fumbling away the country's wealth, postcolonial liberation movements are reduced to the lunacy of primitive despots selfishly enraged at their backwardness, affirmative action becomes reverse racism hidden behind the veils of left-wing political correctness, poverty is equated with laziness, and so on. These are no longer simply deceptions to be factually or logically falsified or unmasked, for a "hard" and powerful reality (if we continue to assume one exists at all) is in them rather than hidden behind them. These hypersimulations increasingly define "what's new" and shape the postmodern answers to what now is to be done.

More than anything else, the need to resist and contravene this expansive reactionary postmodernism makes the third cluster a significant target of attention. Whereas some form of political commitment marks the first two groups, the third sits on the fence and refuses to takes sides, hence my inclination to name them "Humpty Dumpty" postmodernists. They respond to the reality of hyperreality in many different ways. The "pastiche-makers," for example, take hyperreality as a license for whimsical play with the postmodern condition, piecing together the dislocated fragments of contemporary spatiality, historicity, and sociality to build a new and reenchanting "sandbox" culture of space and time, filled with recombinations that are stylistically pleasing and usually eminently marketable. Much of what has been described as postmodern architecture and most of the popularly defined postmodern commodities (from music videos to ice cream) fall into this category

In their rejection of all dogma and any kind of totalizing discourse (except perhaps the historical narrative), the "hyperrelativists" seek primarily to maximize the celebration of differences. Their paradoxical motto seems to be: "If you think you are absolutely certain about anything, you are absolutely and certainly wrong." Often drawing upon the postmodernized philosophy of Richard Rorty, François Lyotard, and others, the hyperrelativists make fence-sitting their most public display and "it depends" (if not "anything goes") their substitute for epistemology. With great agility, they accept (and also reject) everyone's progressive projects and by leaning in all directions at once, nimbly manage to stay on the fence.

The stationary equilibrium of the "Baudrillardistes" is quite different in origin. Radical inaction marks their response to hyperreality's embrace. They are not really fence-sitters, for they have strategically disappeared to engage alone in the ecstatic bovine immobility that is suggested in their inspirational master's recent writings. They may know something we don't know, but they aren't going to tell us. And it is hard to identify them by name or example, for it is no longer possible to see or hear them.

Much more visible are the "pure deconstructivists," who edge close to antimodernism in their reverence for decomposition for decomposition's sake, and to hyperrelativism in their often paralytic refusal to reconstruct or reconstitute. Obsessed with product-less process, they too become easily coopted by reactionary postmodernism, especially when they present themselves leaning to the left. Inspired by Derridean methods, the pure deconstructivists are particularly common in contemporary avant-garde architecture and American literary criticism, where they have unwittingly become key symbolic targets for the attacks on political correctness and its presumed responsibility for the (hypersimulated) decline of Western Civilization.

There are other cultivators of the postmodern middle ground to be identified, but the typological exercise has gone far enough to serve its summative, illustrative, and provocative purposes. After using half of this chapter to specify and clarify my position within the contemporary reassessment of modernity and postmodernity, I can now turn to the central theme announced in the title.

Postmodern Geographies and the Critique of Historicism

Postmodern geographies are definable both as empirical texts and as critical discourses that have arisen in conjunction with what I earlier called the "fourth restructuring" of post-Enlightenment modernity. As texts, they are the products of a concatenation of contemporary restructuring processes that have introduced new forms and functions to the *spatiality* of social life at many different scales, from the design of buildings and the built environment, to the economic patterning of cities and regions, to the organizational structure of the international (spatial) division of labor. Captured in this geographical restructuring are the concretized connections between the political economy and cultural logic of postmodernity, between what is often summarized as the rise of a post-Fordist regime of "flexible accumulation" and the imprint of what I have described as the "rush to the post," the multiplication of post-Modern movements or postmodernisms aimed at constructing a new culture of space and time.[11]

As a mode of critical discourse, postmodern geographies arise from a similar restructuring, from what I have called the "reassertion of space in critical social theory." In part, this reassertion has been stimulated by the practical and theoretical insights derived from analysis of the empirical texts and contexts, a "merit-based" achievement that has brought more widespread attention to interpretive geographies of the contemporary world than at any other time in this century. Even more significant, however, and more central to the argument I am about to develop, has been an "affirmative action" program of sorts that has not just added a useful spatial dimension to critical theory but, in addition, is aggressively demanding a more comprehensive deconstruction and reconstitution of (Modern) critical theory itself.

Some almost forgotten words of Michel Foucault encapsulate the argument most effectively. "Did it start with Bergson or before?" he asks. "Space was treated as the dead, the fixed, the undialectical, the immobile. Time, on the contrary, was richness, fecundity, life, dialectic."[12] In "Of Other Spaces," derived from some lecture notes prepared in 1967 but not published until 1986, Foucault goes on to elaborate a brief manifesto for the reassertion of space in critical social thought.

> The great obsession of the nineteenth century was, as we know, history: with its themes of development and of suspension, of crisis and cycle, themes of the ever-accumulating past, with its great preponderance of dead men and the menacing glaciation of the world . . . . The present epoch will perhaps be above all the epoch of space. We are in the epoch of simultaneity: we are in the epoch of juxtaposition, the epoch of the near and far, of the side-by-side, of the dispersed. We are at a moment, I believe, when our experience of the world is less that of a long line developing through time than that of a network that connects points and intersects with its own skein. One could perhaps say that certain ideolog-

ical conflicts animating present-day polemics oppose the pious descendants of time and the determined inhabitants of space.[13]

Everything that follows (and has come before) in this chapter is an
elaboration upon these prefigurative observations.

Retheorizing Spatiality

I have defined spatiality as part of an encompassing trialectic of relationships that together form the existential macroparameters of human
life. This ontological assumption is not as bold or as idiosyncratic as it
might at first sound, for it is little more than an extension and explicitly
social specification of the conventional ontological triad of the physical
world: space, time, and matter. For matter I substitute social being and
then socially activate the existential trialectic into a triple ontology of
Becoming, defined as the consciousness-shaping social construction (or
"making" if you prefer) of history (as historicity), geography (as spatiality), and society (as sociality).

I have also argued that social theory derives most broadly from the
interconnections within and between the making of histories, geographies, and societies, a premise that echoes in many ways Anthony
Giddens's theorization of the spatiotemporal structuration of social practices. One may be inclined to theorize primarily around one or the other
of these social constructions, but none is inherently privileged—or at
least should not be. This brings us back to the "first positioning" I took
on modernity and postmodernity at the start of the chapter, to the words
of Foucault in the middle, and now to the paragraphs in Chapter 1 of my
Postmodern Geographies that follow immediately after the Foucauldian
invocation.

> The nineteenth-century obsession with history, as Foucault described it,
> did not die in the *fin de siècle*. Nor has it been fully replaced by a spatial-
> ization of thought and experience. An essentially historical epistemology
> continues to pervade the critical consciousness of modern social theory.
> It still comprehends the world primarily through the dynamics arising
> from the emplacement of social being and becoming in the interpretive
> contexts of time: in what Kant called *nacheinander* and Marx defined so
> tranfiguratively as the contingently constrained "making of history".
> This enduring epistemological presence has preserved a privileged place
> for the "historical imagination" in defining the very nature of critical
> insight and interpretation.

So unbudgeably hegemonic has been this historicism of theoretical consciousness that it has tended to occlude a comparable critical sensibility
to the spatiality of social life, a practical theoretical consciousness that
sees the lifeworld of being creatively located not only in the making of
history but also in the construction of human geographies, the social production of space and the restless formation and reformation of geographical landscapes: social being actively emplaced in space *and* time in an
explicitly historical *and* geographical contextualization.[14]

The spatiality being reasserted here (as a dialectical counterpart to
historicity and sociality rather than an antihistory or antisociology) does
not fit either of the two conventional modes of theorizing space that have
dominated the philosophy of science, social science, and scientific socialism over at least the past century. The first of these modes characteristi-
cally externalizes spatiality into an environment of material forms, a
physically fixed container or stage on which is played out the making of
histories and societal development. This exceedingly materialist interpretation of spatiality, the traditional theoretical focus for such explicitly
spatial disciplines as architecture and human geography, typically
reduces theoretical inquiry to the accurate description of forms and patterns, to quantitative geometrics, shape grammars, and social physics, to
the spatiality Foucault described as "the dead, the fixed, the undialectical, the immobile."

This externalized spatiality is rarely seen as socially problematic in
itself. It is empowered theoretically primarily as a naively given environment that impinges upon history and society either as a constraint (Marx
called it an "unnecessary complication") or as a usefully reflective mirror
or screen upon which social relations and historical events are revealingly
projected (a view that can be associated with the Durkheimian compro-
mise with French human geography). Occasionally, however, material
spatiality in either its natural or built forms has been asserted as a determinant force in human life. Significantly for the present argument, pro-
mulgators of such environmental determinisms were particularly vigorous in the nineteenth century and were among the primary triggers for
the *fin de siècle* restructuring of critical social theory. In both the formation
of the social sciences and the development of historical materialism, the
environmental determination of social life as well as more subtle forms of
Kantian and Hegelian spatialism were aggressively rejected in a battle to
free social will and human consciousness from all external (i.e., nonso-
cial) constraints. Sociality and historicity were assertively privileged as
emancipatory fields of inquiry, while spatiality, with very few exceptions,
was shunted further into the environmental background, drained of its
richness, life, fecundity, dialectic.[15]

This first mode of theorizing and, indeed, defining spatiality continues to dominate orthodox and most critical variants of contemporary
Marxism, social science, and historiography. Historically, however, a second mode has frequently attracted adherents to a more internalized and
subjective view of spatiality, emphasizing cognitive processes and phenomenological ideation. Spatiality is theorized here as a mental construct, as subjective "representations of space" rather than as objective
descriptions of the material "space of representations," to borrow from
Henri Lefebvre's brilliant conceptualization of the social production of
space.[16] At its best, as in Bachelard's poetics of space or Jameson's more
contemporary notion of "cognitive mapping," this subjective theorization
edges toward a critical semiology with revealing applications in aesthetics, geographical analysis, and political practice. But even at its best, it
tends to accept as a reflective signifier the same fixed, dead, objective
world of externalized material forms that defines the first mode of theorization.

There are, however, *des espaces autres*, other spaces, another spatiality
to be theorized, a different way of seeing space that combines its subjec-
tification and objectification, the interpretability of its material and cognitive forms, in a critical and emancipatory perspective that problematizes the making of geographies in much the same way critical theorists
have problematized the making of history and the production and reproduction of the social order. In his discussion of the commodity form as a
"concrete abstraction" and a "social hieroglyphic" subject to reification
as a thing only (what Lefebvre would describe as the illusion of opaqueness), or to fetishization as pure ideology (Lefebvre's illusion of transparency), Marx provided an epistemological framework from which to
identify and explore this third spatiality. But his ontology and political
economy assiduously excluded the problematization of space, even when
he came so close to seeing it, as in his discussions of the city-countryside
antagonism. A problematic spatiality was even less likely to be discovered in twentieth-century social science and philosophy, for space was
either ignored entirely (as in most of neoclassical economics) or peripher-
ally attached to the categorical dualisms (subject–object, materialism–idealism, agency–structure, individual–collective, nature–nurture,
micro–macro, and so many more) that defined the intellectual trajectory
of even such spatial disciplines as geography, architecture, and urban
sociology.

In a remarkable coincidence that has yet to be effectively explored
and understood, this third spatiality was most insightfully "discovered"
almost simultaneously by Henri Lefebvre and Michel Foucault in the
late 1960s. Both had been confronting the structuralist and existentialist

alternatives that had polarized French philosophical thought in the post-war period, rejecting each in their most extreme forms yet drawing upon both in a creative and combinatorial revision. Lefebvre had moved from the "first approximation" of his philosophical project in the study of everyday life in the modern world, through a second round focused on the urbanization of consciousness, to an explanation of the survival of capitalism (a question closely tied to the debate on modernity) that was rooted directly in a theory of the social production of space. Socially produced spatiality, he argued, is where the reproduction of the social relations of production takes place, where the relations of exploitation and domination are made concrete, where political consciousness is mystified and manipulated, and where "capitalism has found itself able to attenuate (if not resolve) its internal contradictions for a century."[17] The costs of this survival are incalculable, he observes, but the means are made clear: capitalism has survived by producing and reproducing a specific spatiality of its own making, a problematic spatiality filled with conflict and competition, exploitation and domination, politics and ideology.

In *La Production de l'espace*, written after the 1968 events in Paris that were so deeply influenced by his earlier works, Lefebvre theorized space more broadly in what still remains the most extensive and systematic treatment of what I have described as the third spatiality. It revolves around the assertion of *spatial praxis* as political intervention into the production and reproduction of capitalist (and other repressive forms of) spatiality, from the local to the global, an argument that permeated Paris in 1968, sparked the ideas of Guy Debord and the Situationists, and has subsequently been imbricated in the works of a whole generation of spatializers, including Poulantzas, Ledrut, Baudrillard, Deleuze, Guattari, Castells, Harvey, Giddens, and Jameson.

In a presumably independent discovery (they make little or no mention of each other in their writings), Michel Foucault during the same period developed his own conceptualization of spatiality and located it in the interrogative nexus of space/knowledge/power that would filter through all his works. Unlike Lefebvre, Foucault never explicitly theorized spatiality in any substantial or systematic way, nor would he admit that space was as central to his philosophical discourse and his politics as it was for Lefebvre. Nevertheless, there is a rich conceptualization to be gleaned from Foucault's occasional explicitly spatial salvos. In "Of Other Spaces," in particular, he articulates the search for another spatiality, more revealing than the brilliant illuminations of Bachelard or the empirical geometries of the spatial scientists. More pointedly, he sees the constraints imposed upon this search by an obsessive historicism, an argument never directly made with such force by Lefebvre. He invents a new term, *heterotopology*, for the knowledge of these "other spaces" and fills his "heterotopias" with the disciplinary technologies of power and surveillance, with illusion and transparency, with richness and life. Here is "the space in which we live, which draws us out of ourselves, in which the erosion of our lives, our time and our history occurs, the space that claws and gnaws at us."[18]

This third spatiality is presuppositional, "formed in the very founding of society." It is composed of "something like countersites, a kind of effectively enacted utopia in which the real sites, all the other real sites that can be found within the culture, are simultaneously represented, contested, and inverted." Returning to this spatiality in "The Eye of Power," a preface to the French translation of Bentham's *Panopticon*, Foucault states that "a whole history remains to be written of *spaces*—which would at the same time be the history of *powers* (both these terms in the plural)—from the great strategies of geopolitics to the little tactics of the habitat," a vivid reminder of the scale of this spatiotemporal project.

The retheorized spatiality illuminated by the writings of Lefebvre and Foucault helps to explain what is being "reasserted" in the contemporary critical-theoretical discourse, how it obtains the discursive label "postmodern," and why it calls for a foundational restructuring of critical theory as it is presently constituted. What remains to be done here is to explore in more detail the critique of historicism that must accompany the reassertion of this third spatiality.

Spatializing Historicity

As I have repeatedly stated, the spatialization of historicity and of critical historiography is not an antihistory, a dismissal of the significant critical insights to be gained from an understanding of historical consciousness, the historicity of social life, and the collective making of history. The intent is not one of substitution or even of addition, but of sympathetic deconstruction and reconstitution that aims to combine the interpretive powers of the geographical, historical, and sociological imaginations. Since the critical geographical or spatial imagination has atrophied most over the past century, the current effort can be described as an assertive *spatialization*, a temporarily useful critical stance whose urgency will necessarily disappear once the project is successfully completed.

Spatialization involves a critique of *historicism* for similarly tactical reasons. The historicism defined here is specifically that form that silences and/or subsumes the critical spatial imagination, whether inadvertently or intentionally. This silencing has come from many sources and there is no reason to place all of the blame on historians and historiography, or even on historicism as it has been more conventionally interpreted, that is, as a narrow teleological evolutionism or historical determinism. Geographers and other spatial thinkers have also contributed to the peripheralization of the critical geographical imagination, but this part of the process is not my focus here.

Defined through the provocative juxtapositioning of historicity and spatiality as critical theoretical perspectives, however, historicism becomes a particularly useful trope: a means of configuring an argument indirectly, through nonobvious or nonliteral referencing. This disruptive and unconventional indirectness helps to focus attention on the degree to which narrative discourse and historical representation have dominated the content and form of critical thinking in the twentieth century. The intent again is not to attack and destroy the powerful insights of the historical imagination but to break down its hegemonic exclusivity and open it up to an informative and potentially transformative spatialization.

In *The Content of the Form: Narrative Discourse and Historical Representation*, Hayden White brilliantly exposes both the lasting strengths and the persistent weaknesses of historicism as I have defined it.[19] It is a wonderfully creative defense and reassertion of the power and scope of the historical imagination. In his calculated embrace of the contemporary poststructuralist discourse and such figurative influentials as Michel Foucault and Fredric Jameson, as well as in his inspirational and flexible recomposition of Paul Ricouer's theory of narrativity, White has produced an astutely postmodernized text, so much so that I am tempted to retitle it *Postmodern Historiographies: The Reassertion of Historicity in Contemporary Critical Theory*! In this retitling lies the crux of my argument.

White, as effectively as any contemporary critical thinker, argues for the necessity to historicize via a deconstruction and reconstitution of the narrative form and a rethinking of "the value of narrativity in the representation of reality" and "the politics of historical interpretation" (to draw from the titles of two of his essays). In his retheorization of narrativity, White dissolves the dichotomy between "realistic" and imaginary or "fictional" narratives, between "scientific" and "poetic" historiography, seeking instead a recombinant third way of looking at history that "returns to the narrative as one of its enabling presuppositions," a commitment which he laterally attaches in the preface to "a whole cultural movement in the arts, generally gathered under the name post-modernism."[20] The content of the narrative form is not merely discursive, White asserts, but involves epistemic and ontological choices, with significant political and ideological implications.

There are many other ways in which *The Content of the Form* parallels my *Postmodern Geographies* and exemplifies for historicization and a critical theory of narrativity what I am arguing for spatialization and a critical theory of spatiality. Unfortunately, parallels do not meet. Despite the comparability of the texts and discourses, there is no recognition of the intersection of spatiality and historicity, no spatial content to White's narrative form even when its presupposition stares him in the face, as in the double-coded, spatial and temporal meaning of such key concepts as *plot*, *emplotment*, *configuration*, *context*, and *trope*, not to mention *content* and *form*. The forceful spatializations of Foucault and Jameson, who are discussed extensively by White, are similarly made invisible; and, of course, Lefebvre is nowhere to be seen.

Why is there no attention to space and spatiality in *The Content of the Form*? The easiest answer is that White is a historian and every cobbler prefers his or her own leather. The subject, after all, was narrative discourse and historical representation, certainly not postmodern geographies; and, in any case, critical historiography is itself currently in crisis and needs to be vigorously defended against its attackers. But there is more to this omission than meets the eye of the specialist. It is symptomatic of the persistence and power of a fundamentally unspatialized historicism in contemporary critical theory. That even the most far-reaching, open-minded, and imaginative theoretician of historicity should be blind to the need to spatialize, especially given his presentist attachment to cultural self-understanding, the practical relevance of the contemporary, and the configurative tropics of discourse, is the strongest argument I can find to continue the call for a deeper spatialization of critical social theory.

There is still another answer that can be given by those Foucault described as the "pious descendants of time" to the "determined inhabitants of space." It is that good historians are always good geographers too, that they are inherently spatial in their historiography, that they as much as anyone "love maps" and agree that "geography matters." I hope that by now the reader will recognize that the "synchronic" geography and spatiality implied in these attachments is not what is meant by a critical spatialization of the historical narrative.[21] There is always an incidental geography in every historical analysis and, I might add, an incidental history to every good geographical analysis. This much is implied in the very nature of being-in-the-world. The spatialization of historicity, however, demands much more than this incidental recognition.

It also requires more than the "additive" spatialization that characterizes the exemplary historiography of Fernand Braudel and the *Annales* school, often presented as being about as geographical as historians can get. The Braudelian model advances the spatializing project significantly ahead of the sympathetic silence of Hayden White, but such spatialization by adjacency remains theoretically unproblematic and supplemental. It represents no major challenge to the historian's task other than the accumulation of more and more geographical information and insight. Moreover, the spatiality it addresses is either that of an externalized environment of material forms frozen into the background of the *longue durée* or else an incidental tableau of geographical sites and situations that impinge upon historical *évènements* and *mentalités*.

Another level of spatialization and "other spaces" must be reached for and explored, a critical spatialization which problematizes the combination of spatiality and historicity and sees in this problematic juxtapositioning the necessity to rethink them as co-equal modes of representation, inquiry, and theorization. There are significant precedents for this project in the writings of Neitzsche, Hegel, Heidegger, Sartre, Baudelaire, the surrealists, Georg Simmel, and especially Walter Benjamin, who once urged that the alluring "narcotic of the narrative" required a withdrawal strategy that involved "blasting" the embedded historical object out of its temporal matrix and into a more visual, imagistic, and spatial contextualization.[22]

These earlier attempts to connect the theorization of historicity and spatiality are currently being revived after a long period of invisibility and neglect, in itself further testimony to the power of historicism to block an appropriate conceptualization of spatiality throughout most of the twentieth century. In most cases, the revival has been spurred by the more recent insights of such key figures as Foucault and Lefebvre, but the larger project of spatializing historiography and narrativity has only just begun and still attracts minimal attention and curiosity from even the best contemporary critical historians and social scientists.

What is still missing, I suggest in closing, is a wider engagement in the critique of historicism and the reassertion of spatiality as defining moments in the contemporary reassessment of modernity and postmodernity. This wider engagement is not only an invitation for more attention from critical scholars but also an announcement that the scope and impact of the project extends across the production of all forms of knowledge, from ontology and epistemology through theory formation into modes of empirical analysis and political practice. At each of these levels of knowledge production there is a spatial struggle to be fought against the residual powers of historicism.

Notes

1. I refer, in particular, to those now familiar tabular exercises that reduce modernity and postmodernity to a simplistic dichotomy and list endless presumptions of their polar opposition. While appearing to be a convenient means of clarifying differences, these exercises fundamentally obscure the complexity, interrelatedness, and heterogeneity of the two concepts.

2. Stephen Kern, *The Culture of Time and Space 1880–1918* (Cambridge: Harvard University Press, 1983); Marshall Berman, *All That Is Solid Melts into Air* (New York: Simon and Schuster, 1982).

3. I have posed these arguments before, in *Postmodern Geographies: The Reassertion of Space in Critical Social Theory* (London: Verso, 1989). This chapter is both a summary and a clarifying extension of my earlier arguments.

4. The roots of the word "modern" are probably in the Latin modo, or "just now."

5. I adopt the broad definitions of modernity, modernism, and modernization used by Berman, *All That Is Solid*. Modernisms, or modern movements, are the diverse cultural, ideological, and reflective responses to the more concrete processes of modernization and to the generative question of what now is to be done given that the context of the contemporary has changed significantly. Modernity-in-general is thus produced and reproduced by the specific interaction between modernization and modernism.

6. I do not wish to imply that there were no significant changes in the development of modernity-as-Enlightenment before the end of the eighteenth century. What I am arguing, however, is that none were as profound, as deep, and as widespread, as the transformations associated with the Age of Revolution, from the late eighteenth century to 1848–49.

7. For further discussion, see Soja *Postmodern Geographies*, Kern *Culture of Time and Space*, and Berman *All That Is Solid*, and E. J. Hobsbawm, *The Age of Revolution 1789–1848* (New York: New American Library, 1962), *The Age of Capital 1848–1875* (New York: Charles Scribner's Sons, 1975), and *The Age of Empire 1875–1914* (New York: Pantheon, 1987). A comprehensive and detailed discussion of the periodization and regionalization of modernity as an adjunct to the "long wave" development of capitalism can be found in Ernest Mandel, *Late Capitalism* (London: Verso, 1975), and *Long Waves in Capitalist Development: The Marxist Interpretation* (Cambridge: Cambridge University Press, 1980). Mandel never refers specifically to the debates on modernity and postmodernity, but the periods of transformative restructuring he describes for the development of capitalism reflect directly upon the succession of modernities I have outlined here.

8. See, for example, Raymond Williams, *Marxism and Literature* (London: Verso, 1977), and *Problems in Materialism and Culture* (London: Verso, 1980).

9. Jean Baudrillard, *Simulations* (New York: Semiotext(e), 1983), a translation by Paul Foss, Paul Patton, and Philip Beitchman of two articles, "The Precession of Simulacra" and "The Orders of Simulacra."

10. I refer specifically to the need to find ways to build alliances among the

many separate and typically modernist polycentric movements based on class, gender, race, ethnicity, colonial liberation, environmental politics, sexual practice, and other mobilizations of the oppressed. For a particularly geographical approach to this challenge, see Edward W. Soja and Barbara Hooper, "The Spaces That Difference Makes: Some Notes on the Geographical Margins of the New Cultural Politics," forthcoming in *Spaces of Resistance: Geography and the New Politics of Identity*, ed. M. Keith and S. Pyle (London: Routledge).

11. My preferred empirical text over the past decade has been the greater Los Angeles urban region, where the postmodernization of the human landscape has proceeded with particular vividness and intensity. The last two chapters in *Postmodern Geographies* summarize my earliest (con)textual readings. For more recent examples, see "Heterotopologies: A Remembrance of Other Spaces in the Citadel—LA," *Strategies* 3 (1990): 6–39; "Inside Exopolis: Scenes from Orange County," in *Variations on a Theme Park: The New American City and the End of Public Space*, ed. M. Sorkin (New York: Hill and Wang, 1992), 94–122; and "The Stimulus of a Little Confusion: A Contemporary Comparison of Amsterdam and Los Angeles," in *After Modernism: Global Restructuring and the Changing Boundaries of City Life*, ed. M. P. Smith (Sage, Comparative Urban and Community Research Series, vol. 4, 1992), 17–38.

12. From "Questions on Geography," in *Power/Knowledge: Selected Interviews and Other Writings 1972–1977*, ed. C. Gordon (New York: Pantheon, 1980).

13. M. Foucault, "Of Other Spaces," *Diacritics* (Spring 1986), 22–27; translated from the French, "Des Espaces Autres," by Jay Miskiewic.

14. "History: Geography: Modernity," chapter 1 in *Postmodern Geographies*, 10–11.

15. Still one of the best descriptions of this restructuring of theoretical consciousness, although with little direct reference to spatiality or geography, is H. S. Hughes, *Consciousness and Society: The Reconstruction of European Social Thought 1890–1930* (New York: Knopf, 1958).

16. At long last, there is an English translation of Lefebvre's key text, *La Production de l'espace* (Paris: Anthropos, 1974), see Henri Lefebvre, *The Production of Space*, trans. Donald Nicholson-Smith (Cambridge, Mass.: Blackwell, 1991).

17. Henri Lefebvre, *The Survival of Capitalism* (London: Allison and Busby, 1976), 21. The original text, *La Survie du Capitalisme*, was published in Paris in 1972.

18. See Soja, "Heterotopologies", for this and all subsequent quotations from Foucault.

19. H. White, *The Content of the Form: Narrative Discourse and Historical Representation* (Baltimore: The Johns Hopkins University Press, 1987).

20. The full quote from p. xi is: "Philosophers have sought to justify narrative as a mode of explanation different from, but not less important than, the nomological-deductive mode favored in the physical sciences. Theologians and moralists have recognized the relation between a specifically narrativistic view of reality and the social vitality of any ethical system. Anthropologists, sociologists, psychologists, and psychoanalysts have begun to re-examine the function of narrative representation in the preliminary description of their objects of study. And

cultural critics, Marxist and non-Marxist alike, have commented on the death of the great 'master narratives' that formerly provided precognitive bases of belief in the higher civilizations and sustained even in the early phases of industrial society, utopic impulses to social transformation. And indeed, a whole cultural movement in the arts, generally gathered under the name post-modernism, is informed by a programmatic, if ironic, commitment to the return to the narrative as one of its enabling assumptions."

21. The term "synchronic" (from *chronos*, time) is itself a subsumption of the spatial, especially in the absence of an equivalent concept of the "synchoric" (from *choros*, space).

22. W. Benjamin, "N [Theoretics of Knowledge, Theory of Progress]," *Philosophical Forum* 15 (1983–4): 1–40. My thanks to Beverley Pitman for bringing this work, and her own ideas about spatializing the narrative, to my attention.

7

Social Contexts
of Postmodern
Cultural Analysis

CATHERINE LUTZ

Postmodernism as Serious Language Game

Anthropology is just beginning to suffer from the PMS of Postmodern syndrome. Like premenstrual syndrome, postmodernism is a category of recent invention, highly contested, and—depending on the diagnostician—either a badge of weakness or of courage in those who have it, and either rampant in the population at risk or exceedingly rare. Both are also susceptible to feminist analysis, given that the social construction of each involves a gender politics.

In this chapter I will discuss the social processes that have given impetus to the writing and canon establishment of the postmodern in anthropology. My emphasis is on the social construction of the category "postmodern" and the questions of power and pragmatics its use raises. My goal, then, is not to say what postmodernism is or ought to be as a cultural formation, aesthetic style, or social science movement; rather, it is to trace some of the ways the term is deployed by anthropologists to talk about themselves or others. Explicitly, this labeling work covers forms of ethnographic writing, cultural style, and historical periodization. Implicitly, to use, accept, reject, or redefine the category of the postmodern for one's own or others' work is to engage in a complex round of politics, particularly a politics of gender. This argument follows several feminist analyses that are deeply suspicious of postmodernism as practiced by

137

those already canonized as *the* postmodernists, even while being sympathetic to significant aspects of this discourse.

This chapter has several parts. In the first, I describe my sense of what features have commonly been said to distinguish postmodern cultural analyses from other such analyses, focusing particularly on the question of reflexivity. Next, I discuss some of the social contexts—both local academic and global—that have helped produce the impulse to postmodern ethnography. In two final sections, I address more directly the question of the relationship between feminism and postmodernism in anthropology. Here I examine some recent explicit conflicts over the marginalization of feminism in this movement, and also show how, despite or rather because of this exclusion of the female, a cultural analysis of the categories of modern/postmodern in the academic literature reveals that postmodernism is a woman, or rather a man in woman's clothing.

What Is Postmodern Cultural Analysis?

The postmodern has been defined in a bewildering number of ways and used to point to many features of cultural, social, or artistic formations.[1] Most broadly, it has been used to refer to a set of cultural features that are seen as a function of changes in capitalism as a mode of production, in particular its shift from an emphasis on production to consumption and the expansion of felt consumer needs. The associated cultural features include a focus on appearances as opposed to underlying meanings or essences—a concern with style, surfaces, and spectacle rather than essence, depth models, and the really real. They encompass a concern with texts rather than experience, seen in the ascendance, as cultural icons, of Donald Trump and Marla Maples (or rather of glossy magazine coverage of the couple) over the Benny Goodman recording or the best-seller. The postmodern is supposed to be evident in an erosion of the boundaries between high and low cultures, with academic film criticism subjecting *Rambo: First Blood Part II* to an analysis as "serious" as that once reserved for the films of Ingmar Bergman; a lack of interest in or reformulation of the meaning of history, such that Victorian gingerbread and Grecian columns will be attached to a California contemporary-style house and Ronald Reagan and David Duke could more easily rewrite their personal histories than public figures of an earlier era; the rejection of the search for unity or closure via linear or totalizing thought, and a converse interest in difference and contradiction; and a critique of dominant forms of rationality, which includes placing a value on play and on the sensual in academic discourse. Some of these features are said to characterize only the avant-garde in the arts and academia, while others are said to aptly characterize trends in mass or popular culture (advertisers and advertising take a place between these two groups). Interestingly enough, the more positively evaluated of these features (e.g., the critique of logocentrism) tend to be cultural features assigned to the intellectual community, while the relatively negative (e.g., life lived as spectacle) are more often ascribed to mass culture.[2]

How do these features relate to trends in contemporary ethnography? One can use at least four more-or-less narrow boundary conditions on what constitutes postmodernist work in anthropology. From the most restricted view, one should include only those works that (1) systematically engage in a writing practice that appears to exhibit a good number of those tendencies, with citation of the core texts most commonly associated with postmodernism. By this criteria, postmodernism is a kind of work done by only a handful of anthropologists. Throwing a somewhat broader net, (2) postmodernism in anthropology might also be identified with works that find and deploy postmodernism as a useful category to periodize recent history, identify a cultural system, or focus on a problematic such as tourism or television experience, sometimes appearing to remain ambivalent (or only vaguely sympathetic) to some of the fundamental premises of one or more postmodern theories.[3] Taking a still broader view, (3) an observer could claim to find at least some of the features of postmodernism listed above in the majority of contemporary ethnographies, and judge this evidence sufficient to characterize postmodernism as the dominant movement in anthropology, or at least as a key to characterizing the contemporary situation; I will explore some of these affinities between contemporary ethnography and some features of postmodernist attitudes in a moment.[4] This third view is based on the notion that "postmodernism" is a very broad and ideal typical concept, and as such will never simply or exhaustively characterize any one work or works. Instead, like other American cultural artifacts, most contemporary ethnographies might be seen as "a contradictory amalgam" of modern and postmodern elements.[5]

Finally, (4) one could locate postmodernism within a purely pragmatic or social field, identifying postmodernism wherever the term is deployed, whether "inaccurately" or not. Readers of anthropological texts make their own diverse judgments, and in their discussions (in hallway and conference conversations as much as in print), "postmodernism" is often a catch-all term, left undefined, used in a variety of ways, and often without clear relationship to the above features of postmodern thought as commonly accepted in the humanities. While these uses might be thought mistakes not worth examining, they are important indicators of the impact of the term, a topic I will explore below. For now, I should point out that untangling the domain of "kinds of anthropologists" in which the postmodernist is taken to be one type is, in this context, a pragmatic rather than a referential job. It involves not the matching of anthropologists to ideas (one person's postmodernist is another's retrograde neo-Weberian) so much as an examination of how the meaning of the term "postmodern" emerges and is evident in its use by particular people pursuing various goals.

For readers unfamiliar with movements in anthropological thinking over the last two decades, I will attempt a brief summary of those changes which at least some people have seen as related to the erosion of modernist assumptions about truth and social life. After looking at what could be considered very loose signs of the postmodern (in sense 3 above), I will contrast two recent ethnographies, examining them in terms of the more restricted views of the postmodern that others would prefer.

Much anthropological writing since the late 1960s has expressed doubts (although sometimes quite limited ones) about its author's ability to describe and explain social processes once and for all, free of the bias of history or social location. Those doubts have taken several forms. One involves questioning the role of theory and explanation in ethnography, that is, questioning the traditional ways in which representations and realities have been dichotomized and re-related. Rejected is the notion that one collects data (reality) in the field and then later tries to attach a representation to it. For some observers, this postpositivist mood constitutes postmodernism. It has meant an increased interest in practice and discourse approaches, and less interest in depth models like the Freudian, Marxist, or Chomskyan, these latter theorists having, in postmodernist views, "a pathological itch to scratch surfaces,"[6] and reveal the nonvisible worlds below. While linguistic models continue to be popular, there is a move from use of the *emic/etic* distinction (local representations vs. the real reality to which science gives access) to attention to speech or performance rather than competence. The tendency is to follow Barthes in the premise that sociocultural "reality is not destroyed [or necessarily buried under] but inflated by speech."[7]

Ethnographers have become uneasy with generalized talk about "The Japanese" or "The Ifaluk." This unease emerges from, among other things, a long-standing critique of views of culture as homogeneous and from a concern with the borders between cultures rather than with a single culture presented as a unit for analysis. Culture has been redefined. Once seen as a stable, received, and traditional code of meanings, it has been viewed anew as a negotiated, contested, emergent process, or as a concept to be written against.[8] These moves are consistent with the general view of postmodernism as involved with the breakup of master narratives, the introduction of analytic indeterminacy, and a crisis of representation.[9] The political dimension of this is crucial. Where a colonial and neocolonial anthropology saw secure units of meaning which the ethnographer had merely to observe and describe, the postcolonial ethnographer more and more frequently has had his or her ethnographies read by "informants" who can and do contest the description. The anthropological theorist's hand has been forced by history, in a sense, and as a result there emerge destabilized ethnographies, cultures as contests.[10] The increasing numbers of people of color who have entered the field of anthropology in the United States and the growth of other national anthropologies have had a similar effect (although not always in the ways one might hope for).[11] Western anthropology has had its self-image—as writer of the world as it is—shaken. Instead it is seen as writing descriptions that are partial, positioned, and political.

A few contemporary anthropologists have tried to write ethnography that rejects the goal of representing others and simply tries to evoke other cultural realities. This includes Stoller's ethnographic attempts to use other senses besides the visual, which has had, in his view, an imperial hold controlling the deployment of other sense modalities.[12] When Geertz radically reconceptualized the ethnographic project, he said people are not data for our law-building but texts for our reading. More recently, and in rejection of the dehumanizing qualities of the text model, others say informants are friends for the making or breaking, partners in a cross-cultural dialogue; these anthropologists claim that ethnography ought to reflect the several different voices/perspectives involved in the field encounter. The move is from talk of the discovery of cultural patterns to that of (in some limited sense) the invention of them, and from talk of the rigors of fieldwork to the notion of the anthropologist at play in a field of symbols.[13]

Attention has been drawn to how ethnographies traditionally have been written. The literary conventions (realism, for example, and predominately third-person narrative) guiding ethnographic construction are seen as both facilitating and limiting certain modes of thinking about other societies. A rise in "experimental" writing has been noted. In other words, one central point being made by many who examine anthropological writing as a genre is that how something is written cannot be separated from what is written about.[14] Even if writing is seen as a matter of style independent of substance, the focus on the way ethnographic authors make their texts has shown that the ethnographer who styles his text in the new pompadour fashion is no more a stylist than the one who produces the standard crewcut text, for that latter narrative involves no less culturally shaped and evaluated tastes. Postmodernism has been identified with this textualist emphasis in anthropology in part because the latter draws attention to the culturally constructed nature of ethnographic science; because the experiments are often made and evaluated with some eye to the degree to which they avoid telling simple, coherent tales; and because it draws attention to the "surfaces" of the anthropological enterprise, which are the pages of its books.

The contemporary mood in ethnographic writing is also frequently identified by the use of reflexive analysis. Anthropology has always had a special genre, the fieldwork confessional, often a second, companion volume to the first volume given over to data presentation. In some exceptional early cases, there was no such separation, as with Hurston's 1935 *Mules and Men*, and even more thoroughly in 1970 with Briggs's *Never in Anger*. They, as well as Allen, Crapanzano, Dwyer, Kondo, Lavie, and Trawick—to take just a few examples of the dozens of such works—all show us the fieldworker at work, presenting interpretations of those field relationships from which ethnographic understandings were developed.[15] Reflexive analysis is used in a variety of ways.[16] In some cases, it is intensively practiced only in an initial chapter or two of the monograph, while in others, the ethnographer appears frequently throughout the text. Its operation in the text also varies. In some, the goal is simply to allow both the writer and the reader to evaluate "the instrument of observation," to know what the ethnographer's position in the field and his or her preconceptions were.[17] Alternatively, the ethnographer's self-reflections are used to present theory (in the form of thoughts prompted in him or her by particular field experiences) or as a narrative device to promote reader interest. In yet other instances (and it is perhaps only these that, in a strict sense, one could take as a sign of the postmodern), some ethnographers have used these self-descriptions to undermine the authority of the author, and to demonstrate the nature, not of their positioned certainties, but of their self-doubt, undigested observations, confusions, and quandaries—to present "the field" as made rather than discovered, as having an indeterminate description, a contingent, inessential nature.

Here is an example of one style of reflexive analysis. Narayan begins her recent, eloquent ethnography of a Hindu guru and religious storytelling practices—*Storytellers, Saints, and Scoundrels*—with the following account.[18] We find the guru, Swamiji, sitting on a deck chair talking to a group of visitors who came daily for his wisdom. The ethnographer sat listening, together with a group on the women's side of the room, when he began to describe the difference between educated and uneducated people, a difference that would be revealed when each accidentally stepped into some feces in the road. The uneducated person would notice, wipe off his or her foot with a stick, and go on.

> "But educated people have doubts about everything. You say, 'What's this?!' and you rub your foot against the other. . . . Then you reach down to feel what it could be." . . . A grin was breaking over his face. "Something sticky! You lift some up and sniff it. Then you say, 'Oh! This is *shit.*'" . . . Everyone present in the room was laughing uncontrollably. I managed an uncomfortable smile. . . . "Educated people always doubt everything. They lie awake at night thinking, 'What was that? Why did it happen?' . . . Uneducated people pass judgement and walk on."

This episode does not dissuade her, indeed she is careful to include the Swamiji's later proviso that "it's not that you shouldn't study. . . . You should gain wisdom. But you should realize that in the end, this means nothing." On this self-deprecating and anxious note, Narayan begins an ethnography that is explicitly framed as a partial, problematic, nonomniscient account, though it is intended as a contribution to knowledge, and could not have been written without field research.

Narayan's opening description usefully serves to do a number of things. It introduces us to the guru's worldview; it suggests that some of the religious stories Narayan collected may have been told with her in mind, and so may have influenced the nature of the corpus she examines; and it signals that the ethnographer's commitments are dual and sometimes contradictory—both to a (humanistic) science and to the principles of her friend, the Swamiji. These reflexive analyses run throughout the book, including its photographs: the opening one presents the Swamiji gazing at and acknowledging the camera/ethnographer/reader. It remains otherwise a traditional account of the role of the story in Hindu religious teaching, situated in Western academic theories of language, including sociolinguistics and so on.

A contrasting example is John Dorst's *The Written Suburb*.[19] This ethnography is a postmodern account of a postmodern setting, the wealthy Pennsylvania town of Chadd's Ford, an area of historical farm buildings and home of the artist Andrew Wyeth. Dorst focuses on the ways in which the town can be seen as engaged in making a spectacle of itself, constantly rewriting its history, preserving buildings and building new "authentically" historic ones. The town's residents sell its image through such means as an annual Chadd's Ford Days and local museums, in all of which we increasingly see the construction of an image of an image of an image of the area. Dorst illustrates this thesis with a gallery of three photographs that show Andrew Wyeth's representation of a local farm, another local artist's re-representation of a Wyeth-style farm picture, and a photograph of a farm, evocative of the former artistic forms, which is also a public relations pitch to potential tourists.

Dorst reflects on whether his ethnography becomes superfluous or at least disrupted in a place like this, where people are constantly engaged in their own self-inscription. Like Jameson's description of the emotional tone of postmodern culture, Dorst likens his ethnographic practice to "a four wheel skid on the highway." By this analogy he means to question his ability to find a solid descriptive hold on a society that traffics in images of images of images. The overwhelmed, disempowered ethnographer could be describing his own work when he quotes Eagleton's description of the postmodern as focused on "the depthless, styleless, dehistoricized, decathected" surface.[20] Dorst's ethnography is also nearly devoid of individuals, something evident in his pictures as well as the book's text. We have photographs of the town's main intersection with no people and a shot from an arts and crafts festival in which we see only anonymous legs through the low opening in a false-front country-kitchen display. The fragmented subject of postmodern theory is not just described but reproduced here, and that provides a radical contrast with Narayan's work; Dorst's approach accepts that these cultural forces of postmodernism will simply have their way with him, the ethnographer, as well as with the town.

Reflexivity is taken a step further—into consideration of anthropology as a social institution—in a distinct minority of ethnographies. These works often find their origin in Vietnam era questions about American society and its relation to the rest of the world. A series of books and articles in the early 1970s began to ask how anthropologists' work articulated with powerful Western institutions, including patriarchy, racism, and colonialism.[21] People began to ask how anthropologists' questions or frames of reference reflect local Western cultural concepts, including, for example, ideas about gender and white anthropologists' "discomforts" around race, or emerge out of preexisting regional stereotypes.[22] These questions also led to an increasing number of ethnographic treatments of communities in the United States. Feminism's extensive development of the notion that the "personal is political" was a key influence on the emerging body of reflexive analysis, although it has been noted that women's ethnographic self-reflection has been consistently ignored, both pre- and post-second-wave feminism.[23]

It is striking, however, that the text that has been most influential in identifying postmodernist anthropology for a wide audience—*Writing Culture*—is primarily about reflection on how ethnographers behave at the typewriter or word processor, not in the field. Anthropologists are advised to change their writing practices, not their actual social relations with others (which would include their field methods). These social relations are treated as simply there (unlike culture in the new views), immutable and waiting for description. Of the two chapters in *Writing Culture* that consider field relations or methods, one (written by Rosaldo) looks deep into the past, and the other (by Pratt), which examines contemporary field behavior, is by a nonanthropologist.

Despite the unevenness with which the literature frequently identified with reflexivity and/or postmodernism explicitly takes up issues of contemporary politics, it is the political element of the new ethnography that seems to have generated the most nervousness. What appears to be most at issue here is not whether anthropologists have culture too, but *how* much they've got, whether that culture is also a politics, who's got more of those cultural politics (e.g., the feminists, the nonfeminists, the positivists?), and whether these latter facts are sordid and best worked on in private or a reality that requires intellectual analysis and public discussion. The politics of postmodernism may appear to be centered on whether and how the *other* should be represented but in fact appear more crucially focused on how the *we* of Western anthropologists should be represented—whether as guilty First Worlders or not, as individual bourgeois selves or as members of a social group or class, as having a particular view of gender, and so on. When the ethnographic lens is focused squarely on someone construed as other, a self is still being described by implicit contrast. But it is more obvious, when ethnographers turn explicitly to an American self, that these are descriptions into which American politics can percolate, particularly those politics of the Reagan-Bush era in which American self-definitions have been openly central (as a nation of families or as people already kind and gentle and becoming more so, a nation without class and quickly erasing race.) In sum, the political subtext to discussions of reflexivity bears close examination.

The Social Contexts of Postmodern Ethnography

There are at least three social arenas surrounding the coming of post-modernity to anthropology and affecting postmodern cultural descriptions. The first one includes the political economic conditions that Harvey and others have noted.[24] They include the economic instability and cultural changes that accompany shifts in strategies of capital investment from the rigidities of Fordism to "flexible accumulation," the latter characterized by global mobility and rapid shifts in the use of labor, markets, and products. This regime, which Harvey dates from about 1973, is also symptomatized by such things as increased "time-space compression" (due to lowered transportation costs and communication barriers), the declining power of organized labor, the increasingly wild fluctuations in currency exchange rates, the explosion of U.S. bank failures, and the sharp rise in the concentration of wealth in the hands of the richest 1 percent of the U.S. population, as well as, "on the consumption side . . . by a much greater attention to quick-changing fashions and the mobilization of all the artifices of need inducement and cultural transformation that this implies."[25] The cultural changes include an emphasis on "the new, the fleeting, the ephemeral, the fugitive, and the contingent in modern life."[26]

This instability—some of which reaches into the lives of academics—may have helped introduce the kinds of authorial hedges and uncertainties described above, and may well fuel the lack of faith in our ability to find universal laws, stable truths. While the 1930s were also a period of economic and political insecurity, the 1980s differ, of course, not only in the underlying political economic structures of that insecurity, but in the intervening decline of American international power in the wake of Vietnam. Another difference is the changed public view and social role of the intellectual and scientist. Over that half century, faith eroded in the unequivocal promise of progress directed by experts: nuclear weapons, the fruits of the labors of "the best and the brightest" in Vietnam, and the more recently recognized environmental degradation can all be laid at their doorsteps. Even less than natural scientists do social scientists now find people looking to them for solutions to their problems.[27]

The change in capitalism from a producer to a consumer orientation is something commonly identified with postmodern cultural currents. The consumer mentality that facilitated rapid generation of new, advertising-induced product needs also amplified the spectacularization of social life. While this shift in orientation began in earnest between the world wars, the 1950s saw the explosion of advertising images, televisual experience, and related cultural trends. The post–World War II generation, coming into the academy in the 1970s, might be most likely to find sense in aspects of postmodern writing. The influence of consumer and entertainment culture might be found in the shift from a notion of fieldwork as involved in the backbreaking labor of data collection—as in putting rocks into a basket—to an emphasis on the service-sector end of the anthropological enterprise—the writing of ethnography at the computer for an audience of readers about whose "boredom" (read pleasure) we ought to be concerned (see also Stoller's call for more "delicious prose" in ethnography).[28] Ethnography has become a consumer item, a more spectacular kind of book than in the past. From ethnography as representation of the real we come to ethnography as a narrative somewhat untethered from its base, from a concentration on the Marxian mode of production of ethnography in fieldwork to one on Baudrillard's code of production, the ethnographic sign and its relationship to other signs (including previous ethnographies and other cultural texts such as the novel).[29]

The second social context for anthropological postmodernism is the academic institutional one in which the term is deployed and audiences for its announcement and denouncement garnered, and resources allocated toward those ends. One of the first factors to note is how the extremely vituperative debate over postmodernism in anthropology has been subsumed within the terms of the long-standing debates between the humanists and the scientists. It has reenergized this dichotomy and those conflicts and placed many anthropologists as uneasy or sometimes unwanted bedfellows on the other side from the positive scientists. Several astute observers have objected to the reinforcement of a chasm between the sciences and humanities, arguing that it is a cultural dualism that artificially separates facts from values, hierarchizes facts over values, and, in this instance, splits anthropology into political camps that should only exist if the goal is to produce factless value statements or valueless facts.[30]

For the many within anthropology who still model themselves as scientists in the classical sense, the postmodernist is anyone who questions the possibility of objectivity. The postmodernist category for them includes everyone from Geertz and his interpretive tradition, to all versions of critical anthropology (including those influenced by Marxism, feminism, antiracist scholarship, or various French poststructuralisms), to confessional fieldwork accounts. The postmodern category includes all those who serve as the *other* to the self of positive science, and serves as a convenient way of wrapping these others up. This strategy of boundary maintenance would give us, in the language of recent national political campaigns, a mainstream anthropology and a special-interest anthropology.[31] Nonetheless, this latter group includes large numbers of people, most of whom are in fact very concerned with their differences vis-à-vis the other groups.

Another institutional factor is the sheer volume of cultural analysis being done. It has been estimated that 90 percent of all the scientists who ever lived are at work today. As more and more people do academic anthropology, write books and articles, and attempt to differentiate themselves in a culture of competitive individualism (something Harvey sees as on the rise, throughout culture, along with flexible accumulation[32]), we have hit what has been called "the exhaustion of theoretical proliferation." Postmodernism's rejection of any kind of grand synthesis can be seen as one response to this reality.

Moreover, anthropologists find themselves in a different position in the academy than the literary critics from whom much of the theoretical apparatus of postmodern thought has filtered into anthropology. As the authority anthropologists once garnered from their overseas field experiences becomes less convincing in a postcolonial and already-been-televised world, they have had to turn somewhat more earnestly to other disciplines for methodological or theoretical power. Given anthropology's traditional position somewhere between science and the humanities, this has meant a turning either to quantification and other aspects of a scientific self-image or to current theory in the humanities. To the extent that postmodernism is a powerful ongoing discourse in those latter circles, it is a language many humanistic anthropologists may have felt constrained to learn in order to participate in interdisciplinary networks of intellectual stimulation and prestige (the small number of anthropologists in increasingly financially strapped academic institutions makes this a pragmatic as well as an intellectually defensible strategy).[33] On the other hand, the term "science" is still claimed by anthropologists as thoroughly postmodern and humanistic in orientation as Stoller.[34] Few want to give up the rhetoric of science, still the primary means by which knowledge has its authoritative effects, and the dominant discourse within the granting agencies providing much of the money for anthropological research.

Many anthropologists would date the official arrival of postmodernity to the discipline to George Marcus and Dick Cushman's 1982 article in the prestigious *Annual Review of Anthropology*, titled "Ethnographies as Texts." In that article, they treat ethnography as a literary genre with particular characteristics; describe its classic, realist form, and review a number of ethnographies of the 1970s that experiment with changing some of those conventions.[35] Marcus and Cushman's article reached a wider audience than any one of the ethnographies mentioned, identified intellectual trends surrounding a crisis in anthropological representation, and began to theorize about the sources and nature of what they called "ethnographic experimentation" (something Marcus developed later in his books with Fischer and Clifford). Although Marcus and Fisher in fact refer to much of the latter work as modernist in order to draw formal parallels between it and the turn-of-the-century literary reaction against realism, both that work and the *Annual Review* piece have been widely identified with postmodernism through their focus on textualism, and their identification of the problem of interpretive authority as central to much of the new experimentation.[36]

This article was followed by a conference on the same topic at the School of American Research in 1984. This conference resulted in 1986 in the publication of *Writing Culture*, a book whose sales have been phenomenal by academic anthropological publishing standards. The conference and the book emerged from the center of the institutional apparatus of anthropology. They both also excluded feminists and female anthropologists, as has been frequently noted since. The significance and critiques of this fact will be reviewed in a moment, but for now I want simply to point out that this process of canon formation has been a nearly exclusively male one.[37] More generally, one can say that nothing has been more central to the institutional nexus of postmodernism than the entrance of white women and people of color into the academy in larger numbers as both students and faculty, something which might lead those who are socially advantaged by gender and/or race to begin "questioning the basis of the truths that they are losing the privilege to define."[38]

The third arena in which postmodernity has emerged is at the global border between North and South. Anthropologists have been defined by the position they take, via fieldwork, on that border. When historical processes alter that relationship, as they have in significant ways in the post–World War II period, anthropologists are necessarily affected.[39] The Vietnam War, which crystallized and brought home the struggle between American imperial ambitions and decolonization and self-determination movements, led many anthropologists, as I just noted, to a critique of the role of the discipline in both the colonial and the postcolonial periods. They looked both at how anthropologists have directly served colonial regimes and at the resonances between, for example, equilibrium models of social systems and state ideologies about the pathological nature of social conflict. The reflexive mode of contemporary ethnography is in part a result of the fact that the southern subjects of ethnography and Third World anthropologists have turned around and begun a critical ethnography of anthropology,[40] which it may be unfair to say was simply appropriated and turned to disciplinary advantage as a "newer and better" brand of ethnography.

Rosaldo, in his book *Truth and Culture*, has described the increased significance of cultural borders in this context, noting,

Despite the intensification of North American imperialism, the "Third World" has imploded into the metropolis. Even the conservative national politics of containment, designed to shield "us" from "them," betray the impossibility of maintaining hermetically sealed cultures. Consider a series of efforts: police fight cocaine dealers, border guards detain undocumented workers, tariffs try to keep out Japanese imports, and celestial canopies promise to fend off Soviet missiles.[41]

A preoccupation with the boundaries between things (the body and the world, classes, nations) has been identified as something that is intensified during periods of social conflict,[42] and here the anthropological debate about the nature of culture takes shape in the context of this broader social phenomenon. One feature of contemporary ethnography is its attempt to see culture not as a timeless essence but, in Clifford's apt phrase, as "contested, temporal, and emergent."[43] The enforced stability of the immediate post–World War II period was reflected in the prevalent definition of culture as a bounded unit, operating with equilibrium and holding essential meanings. The regional wars and resultant mass of international refugees, the second great wave of immigration to the United States, and the internationalization of mass media have all played a role in the anthropological construction of a new, more fragmented, and highly politicized view of culture.

This view of culture can, however, coexist with textual moves that depoliticize the author's voice.[44] The escape from politics has been achieved through the erosion of some aspects of ethnographic authority, a move similar to that which Pratt finds in some postmodern literary criticism. There "what is being sought . . . is not something totalitarian, not power without responsibility, [but] a space to be an expert in (an ____ist) without being The Boss." She traces this process, quoting Fish, to "the wish to deny that its activities have any consequences."[45] In anthropology, this wish might be strong indeed, given the documented but well-repressed cases of ethnographies used to build counterinsurgency tactics in Southeast Asia, ethnographies whose subjects are deeply offended by them, and ethnographies whose details show up in distorted form in mass media arguments against the value or interests of the people described.

The argument, then, is that the relationship between ethnographies and their social contexts is substantially similar to that between other cultural artifacts and the histories surrounding them. To demonstrate some of the ways this may work, I will briefly examine the relationship of decolonization to three instances of what can be called "cross-cultural encounter artifacts," including travel literature, *National Geographic* photographs of the "non-Western" world, and ethnography.

Decolonization produced important changes in the way travel literature portrays the landscapes of the Third World, as shown by Pratt.[46] From the colonial viewpoint, atop a hill, the countrysides "discovered" in Africa and elsewhere constituted a rich plentitude. They were evaluated and found good, as in the following quote from Sir Richard Burton, on his view of Lake Tanganyika:

Villages, cultivated lands, the frequent canoes of the fishermen on the waters, and on a nearer approach the murmurs of the waves breaking upon the shore. . . . the landscape . . . wants but little of the neatness and finish of Art . . . [and] rival[s] if not excel[s], the most admired scenery of the classic regions. . . . Truly it was a revel for soul and sight![47]

The postcolonial landscape, after the emergence of the African states and the defeat of American forces in Vietnam, looks very different. The world traveler still frequently describes the landscape from atop some height, and still claims what Pratt calls the-lord-of-all-I-survey stance, or the right to evaluate what is seen. What he or she sees, however, is a world used up and degraded, a world which, because of this has little worth taking, as in the following example from best-selling author Paul Theroux's less appealing descriptions of two Third World cities:

> From the balcony of my room I had a panoramic view over Accra, capital of Ghana. Beneath a sky of hazy blue, filled with mists and ragged yellow and grey clouds, the town looked like a huge pan of thick, dark cabbage soup in which numerous pieces of white pasta were on the boil.

> Guatemala City, an extremely horizontal place, is like a city on its back. Its ugliness, which is a threatened look (the low morose houses have earthquake cracks in their facades; the buildings wince at you with bright lines) is ugliest on those streets where, just past the last toppling house, a blue volcano's cone bulges.[48]

This rejecting stance protects that observer from the painful frustration of seeing something valuable but out of reach, the latter made more likely since independence came to much of the once colonial world.

Pratt's insights can be applied to other cultural artifacts, as in the following examples from the photography of *National Geographic* magazine. In these we can see an analogous shift from a colonial to a postcolonial view of the South, as in a photo taken in 1956 in Mauritius in the Indian Ocean. A white hiker looks out over a bright and lush valley. The sun is shining, and the landscape looks rich and unspoiled. Come forward to 1982 and a photograph taken from a rooftop in Khartoum, Africa. This is Pratt's postcolonial landscape view, with its muddy, dark colors, its depiction of low urban sprawl, its lack of a focal point. In the thirty-year space between these pictures, the white observer, while still at a height, has disappeared, the sun has gone in, resources have been used up. Compare also two articles on Micronesia, one published in 1968 and the other in 1986,[49] in which occur two pictures with strikingly similar content and composition. Both show a Micronesian atoll beachfront. Both are large-format pictures running across two pages of their respective issues, and both show a lagoon with small wading figures to the left, beach to the right, and the rusting metal brought by colonial powers in the lower right foreground. But the meaning of the rusted metal and thus of the whole scene is fundamentally different in each picture. The airplane carcass, the 1967 caption informs us, is a boon to the Micronesians, for "scrap metal provides the Territory's 2nd most valuable export." The rusted metal on Ebeye in 1986 is "pollution in paradise, junk overwhelm[ing] a beach." Neither the scale of the trash in 1986 nor the captions are needed, however, to send the pictures' intended messages. The lyrical curve of the beach in 1967 gives way to the harsh straight line of the 1986 shoreline; the bright, sunlit, optimistic colors of the former to the muddy forbidding tones of the latter; the small parent-child group of one to the anomic individuals of the latter. The expansive sky of an earlier period is squashed years later, while neither the graceful palm frond nor any touch of greenery remains in 1986. From a view of a cultural and physical landscape which is often beautiful, a place of many resources, we come to a view of the region as degraded, polluted, used up (although the mention of "paradise" in the caption suggests that it is still feasible to think of cleaning up the beach and that by so doing one could produce an ideal tourist destination).[50]

Changes in these two aspects of popular culture, travel literature and popular photography, have their corollaries in the postmodern turn in ethnography. Anthropologists too have responded to changed conditions in the countries where they have typically done fieldwork and in a variety of ways, as I have already noted. To give one last example of this shift in ethnography, we can look at the opening to Margaret Mead's 1930 classic ethnography of Melanesian cultural socialization, *Growing Up in New Guinea*, and compare it with Narayan's 1989 ethnography of Hindu religious teaching. After her introduction, Mead plunges directly into the Manus world: "To the Manus native the world is a great platter, curving upwards on all sides, from his flat lagoon village where the pile houses stand like long-legged birds, placid and unstirred by the changing tides." She goes on in this graceful style to describe their canoes, their ethnic neighbors and the stereotypes they associate with them, and so on. Contrast this with the opening to Narayan's book described above. Note, however, that what is used up here is not the world outside the observer itself (Narayan's guru is portrayed as a warm and wise individual), but the deference of locals toward the ethnographer or the ethnographer's ability to ignore the politics of the ethnographic encounter. Fieldwork does not always or even usually reveal a soiled world, so much as a more vulnerable, less omniscient ethnographer.[51] Narayan inherits anthropology's critical tradition which has meant that the response to a postcolonial world is somewhat different than that found in travel literature, photography, and perhaps some other academic disciplines; the other is still to be defended by anthropology, not diagnosed or at least not diagnosed any more than is usual.

A number of ethnographers who have looked at American society, however, see both ethnographer and ethnographic setting as fundamentally degraded or dehumanized. Dorst's description of Chadd's Ford is ominously empty of people as subjects become so fragmented that they cannot even speak but simply bedeck themselves with artifacts that communicate for them. Another example is found in Dan Rose's work where everyone, ethnographer and subject alike, seems anesthetized, perhaps even aestheticized, against the pain of American racism and class distinctions.[52]

Feminist Critique and Postmodern Anthropology

Feminist anthropologists are both skeptical about and sympathetic to many of the themes of postmodern ethnography (in the second, loose sense described above).[53] Gordon began the discussion with her critique of the problematic response to feminism in the book *Writing Culture*; in her words, "an important problem with 'experimental' ethnographic authority is its grounding in a masculine subjectivity which encourages feminists to identify with new modes of ethnography, claiming to be decolonial, while simultaneously relegating feminism to a strained position of servitude."[54] She identifies a variety of theoretical confusions around "experimental ethnography" that follow from that response. These include a continued use of a form/content split in which feminism is then falsely characterized as concerned only with the content. This corresponds to a dichotomizing of conventional and avant-garde ethnographic writing and the masculinization of the latter. In their assessment of the relations between the two fields, Mascia-Lees, Sharpe, and Cohen see many affinities in method and focus, including the view of culture as contested, the notion that the language of both social science and everyday life is imbued with a political charge, and the idea that the construction/description of an "other" (whether Woman or Ethnic/Primitive/Non-White) can replicate relations of dominance between writer and subject. They correctly point out, however, that these insights, declared original in *Writing Culture*, were first developed within feminist thinking decades ago (they cite, for example, Simone de Beauvoir's 1949 *The Second Sex*). "Like European explorers discovering the New World," they write, "Clifford and his colleagues perceive a new and uninhabited space where, in fact, feminists have long been at work."[55] They are worried, moreover, about postmodernism's cooptation of the oppositional impulse or what they call "anthropologists' traditional moral imperative [to] question and expand Western definitions of the human."[56] Postmodernism, they argue, unlike feminism, does not "know its politics."[57]

Many feminists have noted that the death of the author, proclaimed by postmodernism, promotes "an indifference to who's speaking" and so the social position and politics of the observer can go nearly as undercover as they do in positivism. They are skeptical of the move to declare the death of the author and the death of truth just at the moment, as Hartsock and others have noted, when women and people of color have first been able to insert their voices into the academy, and to claim the right to speak in the world at large.[58] As Modleski notes, following Nancy Miller, "Only those who have it [authority] can play with not having it."[59] It is not just play, however, as these moribund authors continue to build departments, win journal editorships and other symbolic capital, and so on.[60]

Postmodern anthropological writing outside of feminism has been no better than other types of anthropology in challenging how the canon works to erase the voices of women and feminism. In their summation of the most important recent work in anthropology, Marcus and Fischer focus on work of the previous ten years. In their review, feminism is nowhere to be found, and women ethnographers scarce (10 percent of their citation list is to female authors).[61] While constituting significant numbers of those in the field, women and feminists continue to be marginalized and relatively excluded from those arenas of intellectual culture and society deemed most significant.[62] The vigorous critique of *Writing Culture*'s treatment of issues of gender has also been marginalized, circulating to far smaller numbers of anthropologists than the original volume.[63] Marcus and Fisher are but one example of a more widespread process of failure to recognize the voice of men's academic Other: their women colleagues. The dialogical ideal in postmodern anthropology is here, perhaps as in the field, a dialogue which carefully picks (unchallenging) partners, and a dialogue for which the script continues to be written by those in power.

Postmodernism is said to be the stance that follows the death of the belief in progress. This death, however, like the death of the authoritative ethnographer, is more apparent than real. Postmodern ethnographers often at least implicitly claim that their views represent substantial progress over previous views. At one conference I attended several years ago, a distinguished and innovative critical/interpretive ethnographer was giving his presentation when I heard, behind me, one of the leading self-identified postmodernist anthropologists muttering his dissatisfaction with some lingering foundationalism in the talk: "Stone Age. Stone Age."

So too Clifford's explanation for the absence of feminism in the volume *Writing Culture* is, despite the care with which he phrases his exclusion, that feminism has not progressed to the point of attention to narrative strategy, having been waylaid by the task of correcting androcentric gaps and distortions in previous ethnographies. In an ironic twist, feminist anthropology is placed in the role of cultural conservative. One can easily imagine, in Clifford's rhetoric, the women at home tidying up the errors in the edifice of anthropology, while the postmodern men are out hunting for a new and more satisfying narrative strategy for ethnography. But this move of Clifford's demonstrates the contradiction of women's position in which, as Modleski says, they are "first assigned a restricted place in patriarchy and then condemned for occupying it."[64]

Is Postmodernism a Man in Woman's Clothing?

In concluding, I would like to step back from the anthropological discipline to ask whether a sociocultural analysis of the category of the postmodern as used more generally might throw light on the gender politics of the conflicts just noted in anthropology. Some of the main contrasts between modernism and postmodernism as diagnosed historical types correspond to Western ideologies of gender differences (see Table 7.1). The association of postmodernism with consumer culture, for example, is paralleled by the popular culture assignment of the task of shopping to women (as well as its denigration, as when Blondie, Lucy, and the "Shop Till You Drop" T-shirt wearer announce their shopping behaviors' comic-shameful character). Several feminist observers have noted the implicit association drawn between mass culture and the feminine, with the two linked through the ascription to both of passivity, emotionality, and mystifying qualities.[65]

These analogies between postmodernism and the female and between modernism and the male are so numerous that one might say that postmodernism is a woman. However, given the dominance of men among its explicit or canonized practitioners across the disciplines, this would have to be amended to say that the postmodernist is a man in woman's clothing. In fact, the problem looks like one analyzed elsewhere in which a masculine identification with the feminine is an underlying psychocultural dynamic producing a discourse. Modleski finds it in Hitch-

Table 7.1. Postmodernism and Gender Ideologies

Modernity	Postmodernity
Gender as Usual:	
Production (man as breadwinner)	Consumption (woman as shopper)
Sharp self-other distinction (man as individualist)	Absence of self (woman as lacking ego boundaries)
Depth models (man as deep thinker, inner directed)	Surface as all there is (woman as appearance, fashion-oriented, outer-directed, shallow)
Universalistic (man as operating with universal principles of market)	Particularistic (woman as operating with particularistic criteria of family)
Heyday of positive science (man as objective)	Critique of science, use of reflexivity (woman as subjective)
Some wholeness (man as whole person)	Fragments (woman as a face, a breast, a womb)
Cultural hierarchy maintained (men as involved in dominance displays, competition, power brokering)	Cultural hierarchy collapsed (woman as noncompetitive, not interested in power)
Gender hierarchy intact	Gender hierarchy erased (equality achieved, affirmative action no longer needed)
Gender Reversals:	
Mood of alienation and angst (woman as emotional)	Absence of feeling (man as emotionless, stoic)
Neurosis as model (woman's emotional disease)	Schizophrenia as model (man's cognitive disease)
Essentialism tolerated (woman as nature/born)	Essentialism rejected (man as culture/constructed)

cock's films, in which men are often both threatened and fascinated by the notion of their own and women's bisexuality.[66] The violence done or threatened to women in these films—from Janet Leigh in the *Psycho* shower scene to Grace Kelly in *Rear Window*—is the price women pay for this male ambivalence. Modleski finds in his movies "an oscillation between attraction to the feminine and a corresponding need to erect, sometimes brutally, a barrier to the femininity which is perceived as all-absorbing."[67] Huyssen has identified the same process in the modern novel, as when Flaubert says of his most famous heroine, "Madame Bovary, c'est moi." This identification is likely in the novelist who is situated in the "increasingly marginal position of literature and the arts in a society in which masculinity is identified with action, enterprise, and progress."[68]

So too with postmodernism in anthropology, a movement which, in its association with literary criticism and its antiscience reputation, is itself associated with the female. This is in contrast with the thoroughgoing masculine self-presentation of someone like Napolean Chagnon, intrepid scientist among "the fierce people," whose account of fieldwork stresses his exploits in heroic, dangerous pursuit of the facts.[69] What Huyssen says of the novelist can also apply to writers such as Marcus and Clifford, which is that "the imaginary femininity of male authors, which often grounds their oppositional stance vis-à-vis bourgeois society, can easily go hand in hand with the exclusion of real women from the [literary] enterprise."[70] While the feminine attributes of the postmodern may appear to be simply a function of the way the postmodern, as oppositional practice, is peripheralized, one has to question why the official postmodernists have not taken feminist writing into the canon, or acknowledged its role in the rise of postpositivist ethnography and theory.

In sum, debates about postmodernity in anthropology reveal much about the social contexts that produce them. These include anthropology's institutional context in which gender politics are prominent, as is a legacy of racism and imperial assumptions both ongoing and contested. The debates seem to me useful primarily to the extent that they reintroduce questions of the social/political context of ethnographic work, both in the "field" and in the academy, reenergizing the question of the relationship between what have traditionally been known as science, politics, power, and social history. This is true even though a focus on the ethnographic text—the expunging of its objectivizing and the enhancing of its pleasures—has not infrequently avoided a focus on aspects of the world that are papered over by theory or glossed over by spectacle. The reasons why can be elucidated by attention to the pragmatics of postmodernism, and the category's relationship to both global and gender politics.

Notes

1. The description to follow draws on a number of characterizations, including especially Terry Eagleton, "Capitalism, Modernism and Postmodernism," *New Left Review* 152 (1985):60–73; Todd Gitlin, "Postmodernism: Roots and Politics," in *Cultural Politics in Contemporary America*, ed. I. Angus and S. Jhally (London: Routledge and Kegan Paul, 1989); David Harvey, *The Condition of Postmodernity* (Oxford, England: Blackwell, 1989); Frederic Jameson, "Post-Modernism, or the Cultural Logic of Late Capitalism," *New Left Review* 146 (1984):53–92; and Linda J. Nicholson, *Feminism/Postmodernism* (New York: Routledge, 1990).

2. This distinction is, of course, not absolute. Even as Jameson, in "Post-Modernism," defines the postmodern as a reflex of capitalism's consumer form, he treats it more as an interesting symptom than a pernicious ideology or political challenge. The disease model is explicit in his metaphors, and here the metaphorically schizophrenic postmodern is, like the nineteenth-century tubercular (see Susan Sontag, *Illness as Metaphor* [New York: Farrar, Straus, Giroux, 1978] or the twentieth-century depressive, seen in some lights as a romantic figure, the hero or antihero of the age, the one whose sensitivity, perhaps more keen than most, picks up on and reflects the vibes of an era.

3. Examples of the first, strict type include Stephen Tyler, *The Unspeakable: Discourse, Dialogue, and Rhetoric in the Postmodern World* (Madison: University of Wisconsin Press, 1987), and John Dorst, *The Written Suburb: An American Site, an Ethnographic Dilemma* (Philadelphia: University of Pennsylvania Press, 1989). The second type might be exemplified by Marilyn Ivy, "Critical Texts, Mass Artifacts: The Consumption of Knowledge in Postmodern Japan," *South Atlantic Quarterly* 87, no. 3 (1988):419–44; George Marcus and Michael Fischer, *Anthropology as Cultural Critique: An Experimental Moment in the Human Sciences* (Chicago: University of Chicago Press, 1986); and James Clifford and George Marcus, *Writing Culture: The Poetics and Politics of Ethnography* (Berkeley: University of California Press, 1986).

4. Marcus and Fischer take the latter stance when they note that "To still pose one paradigm against the other [in anthropology, for example, interpretivism vs. positivism] is to miss the essential characteristic of the moment as an exhaustion with a paradigmatic style of discourse . . . a suspicion of all totalizing styles of knowledge" (*Anthropology as Cultural Critique*, x, xi).

5. The quote is from Terry Eagleton, "Capitalism, Modernism and Postmodernism," 71. On the amalgam in anthropology, see also Marilyn Strathern, "Out of Context: The Persuasive Fictions of Anthropology," *Current Anthropology* 28, no. 3 (1987):251–70. For other, more detailed attempts to characterize the contemporary changes in anthropology around questions of ethnographic authority, see James Clifford, *The Predicament of Culture: Twentieth-Century Ethnography, Literature, and Art* (Cambridge: Harvard University Press, 1988); Faye Harrison, "Anthropology as an agent of transformation: Introductory Comments and Queries," in *Decolonizing Anthropology* (Washington, D.C.: American Anthropological Association, 1991); Marcus and Fischer, *Anthropology as*

Cultural Critique; and Renato Rosaldo, *Culture and Truth: The Remaking of Social Analysis* (Boston: Beacon Press, 1989).

6. Eagleton, "Capitalism, Modernism and Postmodernism," 70.

7. John Murphy, *Postmodern Social Analysis and Criticism* (New York: Greenwood Press, 1989), 45.

8. For important reformulations of the concept of culture, see Lila Abu-Lughod, "Writing against Culture," in *Recapturing Anthropology: Working in the Present*, ed. Richard Fox (Seattle: University of Washington Press, 1991); Clifford, *The Predicament of Culture*; Smadar Lavie, *The Poetics of Military Occupation: Mzeina Allegories of Bedouin Identity under Israeli and Egyptian Rule* (Berkeley: University of California Press, 1990); Rosaldo, *Culture and Truth*; Lawrence Rosen, *Bargaining for Reality*, (Chicago: University of Chicago Press, 1984).

9. Marcus and Fischer, *Anthropology as Cultural Critique*.

10. There have, of course, long been conflict models of social systems that focus on struggles between groups within a social unit, but the postmodern move expands that sense of conflict to include the anthropologists' attempts to represent another's culture. See also Clifford, *The Predicament of Culture*.

11. Per Harrison, "Anthropology as an Agent of Transformation."

12. Paul Stoller, *The Taste of Ethnographic Things: The Senses in Anthropology* (Philadelphia: University of Pennsylvania Press, 1989). See also Tyler, *The Unspeakable*.

13. On the question of dialogical anthropology, see Kevin Dwyer, *Moroccan Dialogues: Anthropology in Question* (Baltimore: Johns Hopkins University Press, 1982). For the main source of the notion of cultural invention, see Roy Wagner, *The Invention of Culture* (Chicago: University of Chicago Press, 1981). It should be noted that Geertzian interpretive anthropology can be associated with postmodernism only in the loosest sense: its critique of positivism undermines the notion of the possibility of a single authoritative and timeless knowledge.

14. George Marcus and Dick Cushman, "Ethnographies as Texts," *Annual Review of Anthropology* 11 (1982):25–69, and Marcus and Fischer, *Anthropology as Cultural Critique*. Rosaldo, *Culture and Truth*, gives some important examples of the connection between experimental writing styles and the new forms of social analysis (see p. 38).

15. Zora Neale Hurston, *Mules and Men* (Philadelphia: J. B. Lippincott, 1935); Jean Briggs, *Never in Anger* (Cambridge: Harvard University Press, 1970); Catherine Allen, *The Hold Life Has* (Washington, D.C.: Smithsonian Institution Press, 1988); Vincent Crapanzano, *Tuhami: Portrait of a Moroccan* (Chicago: University of Chicago Press, 1980); Dwyer, *Moroccan Dialogues*; Dorinne Kondo, *Crafting Selves* (Chicago: University of Chicago Press, 1990); Lavie, *Poetics of Military Occupation*; and Margaret Trawick, *Notes on Love in a Tamil Family* (Berkeley: University of California Press, 1990). For lists of other examples, see Lila Abu-Lughod, "Can There be a Feminist Anthropology?," *Women and Performance* 9, no. 1 (1990):1–24; and Frances E. Mascia-Lees, Patricia Sharpe, and Colleen Ballerino Cohen, "The Postmodernist Turn in Anthropology: Cautions from a Feminist Perspective," *Signs* 15, no. 1 (1989):7–33.

16. I am very grateful to an anonymous reviewer of this chapter for pointing out this diversity to me in some detail.

17. In writing an ethnography of the atoll of Ifaluk in Micronesia (Catherine Lutz, *Unnatural Emotions: Everyday Sentiments on a Micronesian Atoll and their Challenge to Western Theory* [Chicago: University of Chicago Press, 1988]), I intended to make clear that my descriptions of their emotional qua social lives were created by someone who was looking as a feminist, an American coming of age during the Vietnam War and race conflicts of the 1960s, an American entering a place where the U.S. has been the colonial power for decades. I also tried to describe the position from which I was able to view people (for example, as a woman in a gender-segregated society, both pressured and motivated to spend time primarily with women), and the ideologies of emotion and gender that structure the academic discourse in which I participated.

18. Kirin Narayan, *Storytellers, Saints, and Scoundrels: Folk Narrative in Hindu Religious Teaching* (Philadelphia: University of Pennsylvania Press, 1989).

19. Dorst, *Written Suburb*.

20. Eagleton cited in Dorst, *Written Suburb*, 105.

21. Central texts included Michelle Rosaldo and Louise Lamphere, *Woman, Culture and Society* (Stanford: Stanford University Press, 1974) on patriarchy; John F. Szwed, "An American Anthropological Dilemma: The Politics of Afro-American Culture," in *Reinventing Anthropology*, ed. Dell Hymes (New York: Vintage Books, 1974 [1969]) on racism; and Talal Asad, *Anthropology and the Colonial Encounter* (London: Ithaca Press, 1973) on colonialism.

22. Carol MacCormack and Marilyn Strathern, *Nature, Culture, and Gender* (Cambridge: Cambridge University Press, 1980); Carol Mukhopadhyay and Patricia Higgins, "Anthropological Studies of Women's Status Revisited: 1977–1987," *Annual Review of Anthropology* 17 (1988):461–95; Faye Harrison, "Introduction: An African Diaspora Perspective for Urban Anthropology," *Urban Anthropology* 17, nos. 2–3 (1988):111–41; Lila Abu-Lughod, "Zones of Theory in the Anthropology of the Arab World," *Annual Review of Anthropology* 18 (1989):267–306; Arjun Appadurai, "Theory in Anthropology: Center and Periphery," *Comparative Studies in Society and History* 28 (1986):356–61.

23. Abu-Lughod, "Can There Be a Feminist Anthropology?," and Mascia-Lees, Sharpe, and Cohen, "The Postmodernist Turn." Also see below.

24. Harvey, *Condition of Postmodernity*. See also Marcus and Fischer, *Anthropology as Cultural Critique*; and Mascia-Lees, Sharpe, and Cohen, "The Postmodernist Turn".

25. Harvey, *Condition of Postmodernity*, 156.

26. Ibid., 171.

27. This is not an argument that attempts to universalize these postmodern processes. For many people, the faith in science and master narratives continues unabated, and is perhaps even solidified by these same political economic and cultural experiences.

28. For statements of this concern, see Rosaldo, *Culture and Truth*, 40; Barbara Tedlock, "Fiction, Faction, and Fieldwork" (Paper presented at the Annual Meetings of the American Anthropological Association, 1989); and Stoller, *Taste of Ethnographic Things*.

29. See Guy Debord, *Society of the Spectacle* (Detroit, Mich.: Black and Red,

1983), for an original statement on the notion of spectacle in postmodern society, and Douglas Kellner, *Jean Baudrillard: From Marxism to Postmodernism and Beyond* (Stanford, Calif.: Stanford University Press, 1989), for a lucid explication of the wildly shifting but suggestive ideas of Baudrillard. Beyond these general cultural influences, ethnographic writing may have experienced pressures in a changed publishing market. It is plausible that academic publishers have altered their expectations for writing, elevating the importance of the criteria of sales potential and therefore placing a premium on entertaining appeal in a book.

30. Sangren (Stephen Sangren, "Rhetoric and the Authority of Ethnography," *Current Anthropology* 29, no 3 [1988]: 405–24) critiques this dualism cogently, noting that in it "science is essential, humanities a welcomed escape. Within the university, science commands a much larger budget, the humanities are a kind of luxury of conspicuous consumption (although perhaps necessary for validation of class status)" (420). In his rejoinder to Sangren, Rabinow points out that many postmodernists would agree with Sangren "that drawing an overly sharp line between science and the humanities is a dangerous game" (429).

31. In her analysis of canon-formation processes surrounding the question of race, Harrison, in "Introduction: An African Diaspora Perspective," uses the language of "center and periphery" literatures, drawing attention to the replication of global race relations in academic writing.

32. Harvey, *Condition of Postmodernity*, 170–71.

33. One could also argue that a generation of anthropology graduate students has thought and written in ways that reflect their relatively poor job prospects in the academy. If innovative thinking comes in part from a breakdown in paradigm commitments among "extruded" intellectuals, alienated from their social context, then the tight job market for academic anthropologists through the late 1970s and into the 1980s contributes some of the personpower for postmodern and other nonnormative approaches. I am grateful to Eytan Bercovitch for suggesting this idea to me.

34. Stoller, *Taste of Ethnographic Things*, 9.

35. Marcus and Cushman, "Ethnographies as Texts". Anthropologists have not yet really come to examine the issue of the reading of ethnographies in the way that literary critics have done with other genres (but see David E. Sutton, "Is Anybody Out There? Anthropology and the Question of Audience," *Critique of Anthropology* 11 [1991]: 91–104). The one issue of readership that has emerged is that of the subjects of ethnography for whom, according to Rosaldo, *Culture and Truth*, the classic ethnography often sounds like so much parody. See, however, Stephen Feld, *Sound and Sentiment: Birds, Weeping, Poetics, and Song in Kaluli Expression*, 2d ed. (Philadelphia: University of Pennsylvania Press, 1990).

36. Marcus and Fisher, *Anthropology as Cultural Critique*, 67–73; cf. Sangren, "Rhetoric and the Authority of Ethnography."

37. For commentary on Clifford and Marcus, see Deborah Gordon, "Writing Culture, Writing Feminism: The Poetics and Politics of Experimental Ethnography," *Inscriptions*, nos. 3–4 (1988):7–24; Mascia-Lees, Sharpe, and Cohen, "The Postmodern Turn"; and Abu-Lughod, "Can There Be a Feminist Ethnography?" The process was also evident at the lecture series at the University of Kentucky

in which this chapter first emerged as an invited lecture. The lecturers and pre-pared reading lists associated with them were overwhelmingly male (and appar-ently also white). As another example, Jameson, in "Post-Modernism," cites no women in his definition of postmodernism as either postmodernists *or* mod-ernists.

38. Mascia-Lees, Sharpe, and Cohen, "The Postmodern Turn," 15; see also Harrison, "Anthropology as an Agent of Transformation," and Sangren, "Rhetoric and the Authority of Ethnography."

39. Marcus and Fischer, *Anthropology as Cultural Critique.*

40. For example, Valerie Amos and Pratibha Parmar, "Challenging Imperial Feminism," *Feminist Review* 17 (1984):3–19; Bernard Magubane and James Faris, "On the Political Relevance of Anthropology," *Dialectical Anthropology* 9 (1985):91–104; and Maxwell Owusu, "Colonial and Postcolonial Anthropology of Africa: Scholarship or Sentiment?, in *The Politics of Anthropology*, ed. G. Huizer and B. Mannheim (The Hague: Mouton, 1979); cf. Harrison, "Anthropology as an Agent of Transformation."

41. Rosaldo, *Culture and Truth*, 44–45.

42. For example, Emily Martin, *The Woman in the Body* (Boston: Beacon Press, 1987).

43. Clifford, in Clifford and Marcus, *Writing Culture*, 19.

44. Patricia Sharpe, and Frances Mascia-Lees, "Culture, Power, and Text: Anthropology and Literature Confront Each 'Other'" (Manuscript in possession of authors, n.d.).

45. Mary Pratt, "Interpretive Strategies/Strategic Interpretations: On Anglo-American Reader Response Criticism," in *Postmodernism and Politics*, ed. J. Arac (Minneapolis: University of Minnesota Press, 1986), 47.

46. Mary Pratt, "Conventions of Representation: Where Discourse and Ideology Meet," in *Contemporary Perceptions of Language: Interdisciplinary Dimensions*, ed. H. Byrnes (Washington, D.C.: Georgetown University Press, 1982).

47. Burton, quoted in Pratt, "Conventions of Representation," 145–46.

48. Theroux, quoted ibid., 148–49.

49. A significant time lag occurs between the historical processes I am talking about and *National Geographic* and American public response to them. Otherwise, we would have expected the 1968 article to look more like the 1986 article.

50. I am grateful to Gerald Thomas for this latter insight.

51. The loss of confident high ground in anthropology certainly accompanies the development of all nonpositivist approaches since the 1960s. The point is that postmodern assertions about the death of the author or the futility of master narratives produces speakers with even less confidence, at least on the surface, than standard interpretive ones.

52. Dan Rose, *Black American Street Life: South Philadelphia, 1969–71* (Philadelphia: University of Pennsylvania Press, 1987), and *Patterns of American Culture: Ethnography and Estrangement* (Philadelphia: University of Pennsylvania Press, 1989).

53. On feminism and postmodernism more generally, see also Sandra

Harding, "The Instability of the Analytical Categories of Feminist Theory," in *Sex and Scientific Inquiry*, ed. S. Harding and J. O'Barr (Chicago: University of Chicago Press, 1987); Nicholson, *Feminism/Postmodernism*; Bell Hooks, *Yearning: Race, Gender and Cultural Politics* (Boston: South End Press, 1990); and Jacqueline Rose, "The Man Who Mistook His Wife for a Hat, or a Wife is Like an Umbrella—Fantasies of the Modern and Postmodern," *Social Text* 7, no. 3 (1989):237–250. What is said here about feminism's relationship to postmodernism bears important affinities to what can be said about the ambivalent relationship between postmodernism and long-standing minority, oppositional critiques of business-as-usual in the disciplines (e.g., Raymond Rocco, "The Theoretical Construction of the 'Other' in Postmodernist Thought: Latinos in the New Urban Political Economy," *Cultural Studies* 4, no. 3 [1990]:321–330). Feminist and minority scholars have both pointed out that many postmodernists have trafficked in an abstracted, dehistoricized subordinant, ignoring real cases, and excluding the marginal even as attention is paid to it (although this appears to be less often the case in anthropology in comparison with other fields).

54. Gordon, "Writing Culture, Writing Feminism," 8.

55. Mascia-Lees, Sharpe, and Cohen, "The Postmodern Turn," 14.

56. Ibid., 9.

57. Ibid., 8. But see Rosaldo, *Culture and Truth*, and Michael Taussig, "Culture of Terror—Space of Death. Roger Casement's Putumayo Report and the Explanation of Torture," *Comparative Studies in Society and History* 26 (1984): 467–97, for some contradiction of this statement. Mascia-Lees, Sharpe, and Cohen, in "The Postmodern Turn," 14, accept the view, articulated by others as well, that the cultural helplessness that permeates some postmodernism is the result of postmodernism's having emerged from outside the politics of the late 1960s. Contrast this theory with Rosaldo's claim that "the political turbulence of the late 1960's and 1970's began a process" leading to the postmodern social analysis he espouses. The problem is that postmodernism is not a unitary category, and both can be right in different cases.

58. Nancy Hartsock, "Rethinking Modernism," *Cultural Critique* 7 (1987): 187–206.

59. Tania Modleski, "Femininity as Mas(s)querade: A Feminist Approach to Mass Culture," in *High Theory/Low Culture*, ed. C. MacCabe (Manchester, England: University of Manchester Press, 1986), 50.

60. Mascia-Lees, Sharpe and Cohen, "The Postmodern Turn," and Sangren, "Rhetoric and the Authority of Ethnography."

61. Marcus and Fisher, *Anthropology as Cultural Critique*.

62. Catherine Lutz, "The Erasure of Women's Writing in Sociocultural Anthropology," *American Ethnologist* 17 (1990): 611–25, and Catherine Lutz, "The Gender of Theory," *Women Writing Culture*, ed. R. Behar and D. Gordon, forthcoming.

63. For example, Abu-Lughod, "Can There Be a Feminist Ethnography?" and Gordon, "Writing Culture, Writing Feminism."

64. Tania Modleski, *The Women Who Knew Too Much: Hitchcock and Feminist Theory* (New York: Methuen, 1988), 77. Ross makes this kind of move when he

claims that feminists are seen as high on "affectivity" and therefore "historically effective" but nonetheless "politically [in]consistent" (Andrew Ross, ed., *Universal Abandon: The Politics of Postmodernism* [Minneapolis: University of Minnesota Press, 1989], xiii). Feminists are also pigeonholed as essentialists and then the claim is made that essentialism is (subsumed as) one of the "subject positions" of postmodernism's "radical pluralism".

65. Patrice Petro, "Mass Culture and the Feminine: The 'Place' of Television in Film Studies," *Cinema Journal* 25, no. 3 (1986):5–21. For expansion on this point and further details on Table 1, see Lutz, "The Gender of Theory." The table demonstrates that the analytic categories of modernism and postmodernism are no different than other such categories insofar as they show their roots in the cultural and historical context of their users. This does not constitute an argument against the continued use or validity of the terms but suggests an important caution and some additional questions. For example, is the response to postmodernism entirely pregnant with attitudes toward women? Does this category system receive continual replenishment from a view of contemporary American history as involving the ascendency of affirmative-action-category peoples and especially white women (about whom the version of the feminine catalogued in the table appears most applicable) and/or the demasculinization and decline of "the" culture?

66. Modleski, *The Women Who Knew Too Much*.

67. Ibid., 42.

68. Andreas Huyssen, "Mass Culture as Woman: Modernism's Other," in *Studies in Entertainment*, ed. T. Modleski (Bloomington: Indiana University Press, 1986), 189.

69. As discussed in J. Okely, "The Self and Scientism," *Journal of the Anthropological Society of Oxford* 6, no. 3 (1975):171–88.

70. Huyssen, "Mass Culture as Woman," 189.

8

Signposts toward a Poststructuralist Geography

WOLFGANG NATTER
JOHN PAUL JONES III

We are writing as social theorists housed in two disciplines that, on the surface, would seem to share little apart from the first letter of their institutional designation, namely, German and geography. Ours would seem to be a model case of different disciplines lacking direct connections, or even knowledge of one another's methods, objects, and interests. The apparent impossibility of confluent understandings, which we take as our point of departure, is partly the product of an institutional setting that *disciplines* the organization of knowledge by creating oppositions not only between the humanities and science, but also between history and space, understanding and explanation, writing and mapping, and theory and practice. Yet one feature of the current discussion over postmodernism is the rethinking of any number of imposed oppositions that resound with and have been resolved by universalizing truth value. Of all the multiaccentual meanings attaching themselves to "the postmodern," one of the few that unites its usage among scholars who feel sufficient inclination to answer its uncertain call is the sense that the foundational ontology inscribing such oppositions has exhausted its currency, as well as its capacity to render meaningful the social world.

Postmodernism, as an umbrella term, is a way of thinking ourselves out of this impasse, and as such, is tied to efforts seeking to form alternative understandings which do not rely upon the oppositional thinking

165

that continues to organize the academy and its products. Such thinking, however, does make for an uneasy grounding of disciplinary identities, as not only their "natural" objects of inquiry, but also their methods for rendering them, become ever less self-evident. As Sam Weber notes:

> The widespread "identity crisis" that is affecting a variety of different disciplines today is only the most obvious indication of a process of rethinking, the implications of which extend to the academic division of labor itself. As the binary, oppositional logic that has traditionally organized scientific inquiry ceases simply to be taken for granted, its institutional corollary, the procedures by which the disciplines and divisions of "scholarship" have demarcated their domains and consolidated their authority, is being subjected to renewed scrutiny.[1]

A critical question posed under the aegis of postmodernism is how we shall react to such a scrutiny that moves past conceptions both of disciplinary boundaries as hermetically sealed, and of the entities contained within as self-referential objects subject to independent laws, principles, or rules. As the argumentation that follows will hopefully elucidate, our answer to this question is not a nihilistic postmodernism content to unground the possibility of all understanding, but rather one that takes its impulses from poststructuralism in attempting to provide a direction for a critical dialogue between the humanities and social sciences.

In this vein, one boundary urgently requiring reassessment is the one separating the domains that consider representation and space as their principle objects of inquiry. Largely in isolation from each other, thinkers of space and thinkers of representation have developed profound critiques of extant social thought. Geographers have taught us that space "matters," that space is implicated not only in any concrete understanding of the conditions of social life, but also that without a perspective inclusive of the horizontality of social life, any theoretical pronouncement is imminently suspect.[2] Literary theorists, meanwhile, have generated an extensive critique of representation and language that fruitfully problematizes the questions of context, narration, and communication, and all that is thereby implicated.

Both literary theory and geography, meanwhile, find a commonality in the critique of positivist/empiricist/objectivist history, which not only relegated space to the periphery of social investigation, but which also viewed the imminence of the social world and its re-presentability in language and thought in an oversimplified manner.[3] Peter Novick's characterization of the "matter-of-fact, antitheoretical and antiphilosophical objectivist empiricism which had always been the dominant stance of

American historians,"[4] aptly summarizes the continued influence of Ranke's charge to historians to "give an account of the past as it actually was." Ultimately, "modernist" history (in contrast to modernist literature) assumes, if not an intelligibility of events in the world, at least a confidence in the sovereign subject's ability to find (rather than construct) the pertinent facts, to master these fragments of social life, and to present a coherent if not omniscient account of them.

This neglect of representation, problematized by intellectual historians such as Hayden White, Dominick LaCapra, and Mark Poster, is paralleled by history's relegation of space to an inert horizontality which, according to one of historicism's most persistent critics, Ed Soja, "actively submerges and peripheralizes the geographical or spatial imagination."[5] Historicism's method freezes space: with the possible exception of the *Annales* school, empiricist history deploys geography not as a dialectical part of the process by which history is made and places "become," but rather as a device that supplements the explanation of events in terms of climatic or topographical features. It is, as Soja suggests, as if "an already-made geography sets the stage, while the willful making of history dictates the action and defines the story line."[6]

The post-Enlightenment era has accorded the historical imagination a privileged place in critical social theory. Modernist history, or "historical thinking," suggests not just stories and histories; it implies an all-pervasive subjugation of human affairs to the signifying power of history. History *is* the horizon of signification in this sense. Yet, as Nägele, following Szondi, has commented, history "does not need much of the historical gaze, directed at itself, to recognize that historical thinking in an emphatic sense is a relatively modern phenomena, emerging specifically in eighteenth-century Europe."[7] Nonetheless, to be charged with thinking "ahistorically" today means that one is missing the true significance of things. To "deny history" would seem to deny the emancipatory project itself. Thus, spatial thinking, when it has entered the domain of social theory at all, has been charged as manifesting a conservative ahistoricism, instead of being viewed, for example, "as an attempt to deal with history in a different way, as a spatio-temporal configuration, simultaneously and interactively synchronic and diachronic."[8] Likewise, the rigorous questioning of context that illuminates the indeterminacy, nonreferentiality, and instability of language has often been taken to imply a nihilistic denial of historical knowledge, rather than seen as an effort to overcome the ideological and epistemological limits of its Rankean version.

As our argument here will demonstrate, however, space and language make social investigation much more complicated than "modernist" history presumes. Societies, as Michael Mann has written, "are much *messier* than our theories of them."[9] This is, as Derek Gregory suggests, partly due to their inherent spatiality,[10] yet it is also because writing about societies and their histories is not as simple as the modernist historian's mirror paradigm assumed. To us, the messiness of social life which surfeits "our theory of it," challenges the capability of any theory to make universalizing pronouncements irrespective of differentiations of space and contexts of reception.

In what follows, a sketch of the disciplinary histories of literary theory and geography provides an initial framework for mutual understandings of space and representation. Our narrative registers the conceptual, methodological, and theoretical transformations characterizing each discipline's stances toward their object of inquiry. The commonalities displayed by our montage suggests a position from which one can write a prolegomena toward both a spatialized poststructuralist critique of representation and a poststructural geography. We hope to encourage and foster this mutual understanding by permeating the boundaries of these two disciplines. We do so from positions which themselves are spatially, temporally, and intellectually situated, namely, a literary theory critically embedded in the German cultural tradition, and North American human geography. Our narrative unfolds from these two positions.

Submerged Affinities

Any mapping of intellectual affinities, especially when charted, as ours is, over time, runs the dual risks of creating the appearance of a universal *Geist* moving through space/time and informing all thought, or of creating an empty identity where, as Hegel wrote, all cows are black in the night. This is certainly not our intent. For while the disciplinary self-reflexivity that we associate with the "postmodern" enables our inquiry, we do not take the term to indicate a force whose emergence has annihilated its precursor. The tendencies associated with both modernity and postmodernity have been present as "political positions in the century-long struggle between art and technology" since the start of industrial culture.[11] Just as there is no single "postmodernity"—as any catalogue of its symptoms demonstrates—there are many more "modernist" projects, geographical or narrational, than any uniaccentual fixing of this referent would suggest. We are thus compelled to begin our portrait with a caution: the internal dynamics of disciplinary development display their own logic and cannot be too easily collapsed one unto the other. Doing so would subsume the voices of authors and their positions under a totalized account of theoretical currents. Yet at the same time, it is quite clear that no person writes outside of the existent social world, and that knowledge, consequently, is socially constructed; herein lies one explanation for the affinities we shall mark.

The embeddedness of thought provides the basis for a second caution, namely, that one should not be too surprised that both literary theory and geography have been profoundly affected by events such as the two world wars of this century, and the rise of class, race, and gender as central moments in social investigation. Yet to be content with such commonalities would impose on our account an all-too-ready affinity of empty identities, however significant may be their subject matter. Instead, the selective (but how could it be otherwise?) signposts we shall identify are located in confluent, but not necessarily identical nor even simultaneous, methodological and theoretical developments in these disciplines.

Inasmuch as literary theory has thought little about space (at least in forms recognizable to geographers), and geography has thought little about representation (beyond that of the mirror paradigm), the metonymic relationship each has demarcated between its objects of inquiry and the social world has of necessity been differently construed. Nevertheless, each of their objects, being as they are, "in the world," necessarily provides a perspectival account of that world, and thus at the same time offers at least partial traces of the other.

We proceed with the understanding that the text exists materially. A text must be written, printed, or electronically displayed for it to enter social life. Books, for example, have a substance and materiality without which their message cannot enter circulation. Writers and their intentions form only one part of this social process. It is essential to remember that no text exists outside of the support that enables it to be read; any comprehension of a writing, no matter what it is, depends upon the forms in which it reaches its reader.[12] Implicated in this understanding of literature as a social process are publishing houses, booksellers, the academy, and the state, all of which promote and inhibit the parameters of the iterable in any given space and time.

While it might seem self-evident to assert that "space" is likewise a material product, it is worth bearing in mind that some geographers have gone so far in reifying their object of inquiry as to reduce the understanding of social life in space to little more than geometry. Space, we now know, is, like the text, both produced by and constitutive of society and embedded in a system of social practices. The materiality of texts and space provides the basis for an examination of the historical affinities to be discussed below.

We should also note that as observers who would have suspected no disciplinary commonalities, we were surprised to discover affinities after all; not so much in their objects of inquiry *per se*, but rather in the way in which these have been constituted and approached both methodologically and theoretically. On a fundamental level, the transposition of "texts" for "space" reveals analogies in the efforts of disciplinary practitioners to imbue meaning onto their objects by theorizing them in terms that have at various times privileged authorship, the object itself, or its interpreter.

These affinities may be conceived via literary criticism's traditional point of departure:

Author ——→ Text ——→ Literary Critic

As hierarchically conceived by this traditional rendering of the relationship, the author, as addresser, communicates a message, the text, to the literary critic, the addressee. In contrast, a simple version relying on a "space" for "text" transposition would appear in geography as:

Agent ——→ Space ——→ Geographer

In elaborating this metaphor between literary theory and geography, we must develop a parallelism between "text" and "space." The multiplicity of meanings the latter term evokes in geography—for example, objective space, relative space, landscape, the built environment, place, locality—corresponds to the contemporary literary theorist's understanding of "text," which designates not only the printed word, both fiction and nonfiction, but also pictorial images, political discourse, electronic systems of information, and indeed any form of communication that can be read as a product of historically variable discourse formations.[13] Such broad views of textuality have recently been applied to traditional objects of geographic analysis such as maps, landscapes, and architecture.[14] Space, following Soja and the theorists whose work his position amplifies, is here taken to be a material product of a wide range of social relations which themselves are reproduced and mediated by it. Place, or its variant "locality," are the terms we attach to specific spaces. Places result from a spatial "framing" of a particular scale, from the nation-state, to regions, communities, and neighborhoods, and even to the microsettings within a house. (Here we distance ourselves from the oppositional use of "space" and "place" that align, respectively, with the scientific and humanistic traditions in geography.) Thus, just as the term "text" explicitly challenges the boundaries delineating the roles for the author, reader, and "work" in a particular economy of reading, thereby opening reading to a variety of phenomena such as advertising and film (as well as episte-mological stances toward these objects), so also does space carry with it a great number of possible objects of analysis and positions toward them.

Continuing with the above triad, "agent" marks those who create and modify spaces. In literary criticism, authors have traditionally been desig-nated as the agents who produce the "work." Importantly, just as the term "author" for more recent theorists not only refers to the individual who writes the book, but also and more pertinently to the social, politi-cal, and linguistic processes and institutions that produce texts to be read and categorized, so too can "agent" implicate both the individual who builds the fence and the collective, institutionally embedded actions of those who create massive suburban developments. Thus both contempo-rary literary theory and geography have come to view each of their objects in terms of a matrix of social powers that give rise to them. Finally, the right-hand side of the triadic model positions the geographer as the professional analogue to the text's critic. Like literary theory's crit-ic, the geographer's *raison d'être* is the study (reading) of spaces (texts).

We begin our historical account of both literary theory and geography with modes of interpretation whose referent is the left-hand side of each of the above diagrams. We note first that traditional authorial explana-tions of literary works stress the intentionality of the individual who crafts an imaginative world based upon his or her life experience. In its classical, Enlightenment, and romantic versions, genius authorizes the poetic mission of the author. Language is the medium, the poetic work the result. The author is variously a vehicle through which *Geist* or a cul-ture expresses itself or a Promethean forger of the unknown or new, through whom the cultural life of a nation is rejuvenated. In either case, what stands out in this mode of understanding is the central role of the author and the univocal relationship between his or her words and the intentions they express. For the reader as professional critic, the work's identity as an object to be read and understood has depended upon this constitutive understanding of the Author as the source and defining prin-ciple of the Work.

For example, literary critics who ground meaning through authorial intentionality might say the following: If you want to know what *The Magic Mountain* means or is about, ask Thomas Mann, its author, who meant what he said. Even after the empirical death of the author, what grounds the work's meaning is authorial intentionality; the task of the lit-erary critic is to ferret out those significant aspects of the author's life and ancillary writings that can account for the particular form his writings assumed. Problems arise, however, as proponents of other modes of explanation have since argued, when, to begin with, overlapping intentions on the part of the author reveal themselves. Thomas Mann, to stay with the above example, saw his own novel, first published in 1924, very differently depending upon the period or context in which he was questioned. His text was made different, even for himself, by the events of 1933, by World War II, and so forth. In short, authorial intention is itself embedded in a temporal matrix, which to foreshadow a later discussion, has everything to do with difference. In addition, seeing all writings as embedded in the social world—the starting point of our discussion of the materiality of the text—likewise undermines the type of analysis that thinks of the author as an autonomous subject.

Questions of autonomy, moreover, may be raised when we examine how geographers have considered the "authorship" of space. Intentionality arises inasmuch as space is viewed as being the result of actions of sovereign individuals through whose agency landscapes are composed and transformed. The effort to locate the causal underpinnings of human landscapes in human agency arose in the early twentieth century with the discipline's rejection of environmental determinism. Authors such as Semple and Davis had interpreted variations in ways of living as a one-to-one mapping of an ever-present physical environment onto social life.[15] When this mode of thinking lost credibility in the 1920s, geographers either eschewed the search for human intentionality, focusing, as it were, on the places themselves, or they turned to a transcendental view of culture, regarding it as an already given template, but one through which intentional agents shaped the landscape. In the latter case, humans stood at the precipice of various choices, though what choices were conceived and how they reacted to them ultimately depended upon their culture. According to Sauer, whose works defined cultural geography, "Culture is the agent, the natural area is the medium, the cultural landscape is the result."[16] The concurrent literary critic's concept of authorial intentionality likewise recognized the importance of the author's lived experience and culture in shaping the text, making him or her the conveyer or medium of *Geist* (or *Zeitgeist*) whose reflection could be found in the Work.

Concerns over the intentionality of the place-makers were by no means resolved during the 1920s. Questions of autonomy arose again in the 1960s under the heading "behavioral" geography, a paradigm which argued that to understand space one had to research those whose activities shaped it. Indeed, few behavioral geographers would fail to recognize the impulse prompting the literary critic's interrogation of Thomas Mann.

An early turn away from understanding the meaning of texts in terms of author-centered realist accounts was undertaken by the Russian formalists, whose efforts to overturn previous interpretive strategies were tied to parallel efforts to restructure the public sphere following the Russian Revolution. Above all, the formalists were keenly aware of the literary work as foremost a particular organization of language. Rather than privileging authorial intentions, the formalists focused on the complex nature of language and poetic utterance itself, which in turn were viewed as intimately connected to the social and economic sphere. Formalists concentrated on the mechanistic structures, devices, and laws governing the operation of the literary work. The text was seen not as the incarnation of some transcendental truth or as the expression of an author's mind, nor, finally, as an organic unity or a symbolic whole, but rather as a collection of effects, to be dissected by the critic.[17]

If language was to be seen as a socially constructed sign system, it needed itself to be metonymically understood as both a social product and constitutive of the larger social world. Moreover, these signs were no longer to be viewed as the expression of a univocal relationship between signifier and signified, word and object. Language is many things, but it was certainly not natural. Language is a social construct, the result of a highly contentious process. Russian formalism marks a shift in emphasis, continued by structural criticism, away from authorial intentionality and toward an understanding of its object based upon a system of rules. All of this left the author and those critics who would derive meaning from authorial intentionality in a much more tenuous position *vis-à-vis* the interpretation of writing.

For Bakhtin, perhaps the most unabashedly Marxist of the Russian formalists, the medium within which thought is presented—the verbal sign—is itself an arena of continuous struggle. Words, to say nothing of assemblages of words, such as poems or novels, are inherently multiaccentual, even though a perusal of literary histories demonstrates that the ruling class will always try to reduce their polymorphous nature to a uniaccentuality so as to support the dominant order. In sum, language is seen as a site of contestation, a battleground for control of the social world.[18]

While Russian formalism was decentering author-based readings of texts, spatial theory in the United States was being transformed by the human ecologists of the Chicago school of sociology, in particular Park, Burgess, and McKenzie, who became influential in shaping the subsequent rise of urban geography.[19] Their analyses of the communities of 1920s Chicago bear two parallels of note with the Russian formalists as described above. These include a rejection of the explanation of their objects of inquiry based upon intentionality in favor of a focus on internally constituted mechanisms governing the objects, and a view of places, like texts, as sites of social contestation. As regards intentionality, these social scientists conceived of places not as expressions of symbolic wholes, "authored" by intentional agents, but instead as entities constructed through the interplay of systems of ecological relationships whose underlying mechanisms governed the spatial distribution of human activity.

In constructing their account, the human ecologists analyzed the city in much the same way that biologists treated living organisms. Burgess's model of urban form documented spatially "the way in which the city was the playground of competition between social groups and economic forces, believed by the early Chicago School to be propelled by biogenic drives."[20] Although the biological analogy and its deterministic underpinning distinguish it sharply from the theoretical and political orientation of Russian formalism, both shared a methodological stance focusing on effect-creating mechanisms that viewed the city (or alternatively, the text), not as given, but as a site of social contestation and struggle. In the Chicago school's language, "dominance," "invasion and succession," and "impersonal competition" were the governing mechanisms giving rise to spatial difference. Viewing the social outcomes of spatial competition as the product of contestation marked a shift from earlier studies which—if they carried any theoretical framework at all—located the causal forces within individuals, who, via intentionality or embodied culture, shaped places. In human ecology, places were no longer authored by intentional agents, but rather were written by the mechanisms that structure them. The human ecologists viewed the city as a social organism, with individual behavior and social organization governed by a struggle for existence.[21]

Russian formalism, meanwhile, silenced by Stalin's policies, was replaced by social realism, the Soviet Union's state-sanctioned aesthetic. The only other place where concerns similar to those espoused by the formalists occurred, the early work of the Frankfurt school and Brecht's creation of a theater of *Verfremdung* during the 1920s in Germany, was likewise repressed with Hitler's rise to power in 1933. National Socialism restored an aesthetic that gave prominence to authorial intentionality, along with such notions as genius, heroic creation, and eternal (and immutable) value, as Walter Benjamin was able to observe before he died while attempting to flee a Nazified Europe.[22]

While formalism was not to be rediscovered until the late 1960s, at which time it exercised considerable effect on Marxist criticism in the United States, another critical movement gained widespread currency at American and English universities between the 1930s and 1950s. Like formalism before it, the so-called New Criticism continued to mark a shift away from authorial intentionality as the grounding concept in defining literary criticism's object of inquiry. Two leading proponents of the school boldly announced that "critical inquiries are not settled by consulting the oracle."[23] Thus authorial intentionality, even if it could be recovered, was of no relevance for an interpretation of the work's meaning. A poem was a self-sufficient object, which meant what it meant. Yet as we shall see below, on a more subtle level, the "author-function" continued to provide the enabling limits determining its method. For New Critics, the literary work retained a measure of autonomy in New Criticism such that no social context, not even the possible intentions of its author, could be held accountable in a causal way for the meaning to be "found" in a poem by the critic. The poem was that "which could not be paraphrased, expressed in any language other than itself: each of its parts was folded in on the others in a complex organic unity which it would be a kind of blasphemy to violate."[24]

The New Critic's text was approached much like the geographer's region of the same period, wherein coherence and integration were the to-be-discovered characteristics of the poem/place. The task of the literary critic, to whom was now transferred the authority of interpretation, was to celebrate the uniqueness and particularity of each great literary work. The contemplative stance of the critic was one of reverence before the work's beauty. The method of analysis associated with this school was that of "close reading," through which the harmonious interactions of the elements comprising the poem's uniqueness could be discerned. Whereas the formalists saw language's multiaccentual character as the basis for reading in terms of conflict and contestation, the New Critics saw harmony and wholeness in the great works. Social conflict was, along with the author's intentions, irrelevant to "the work itself," which was simply given, not made. Needless to say, this understanding of the "text itself" found merely trivial assertions that the text needed to be understood as "itself" produced and embedded in the social world.

This celebration of the unique was not without a critical method. New Criticism inherited from the formalists a desire to understand the formal laws governing the structure of the poem. Through their close readings, however, what appeared on a manifest level to involve paradoxes and tensions could be resolved by a New Critic into a harmonious and beautiful identity that respected the autonomous integrity of the work. Any given poem could thus be understood by virtue of its own (to-be-discerned) inherent system, and not as bearing relationships to transcontextual laws. Indeed, a New Critic's insistence upon the uniqueness of the individual work, the belief that each work could be adequately studied and understood in isolation from others, must be seen as an effort to prevent language's materialization as mere instances of general, or "scientific," laws. While scientific rationalism was stripping human experience of its sensuous particularity, poetry presented a possible aesthetic alternative. As Hayden White has summarized its impulse, the New Critics were engaged in a defense of autotelism for the artwork. Toward this end, "They progressively sheared away, as interpretatively trivial, the relations which the literary artifact bore to its historical context, its author, and its audience(s), leaving the ideal critical situation to be conceived as that in which a single sensitive reader, which usually turned out to be a New Critic, studied a single literary work in the effort to determine the inner dynamics of the work's intrinsic irony."[25]

New Criticism has been accused of ahistoricism, by White, Terry Eagleton, and many others, but the grounds for such a critique are themselves most illuminating. Eagleton, for example, is right in condemning the New Critics for converting the poem into a fetish, and in characterizing New Criticism's valorization of literature as being "a solution to social problems, not part of them; the poem must be plucked free of the wreckage of history and hoisted into a sublime space above it."[26] The category of space, which seems to have only metaphorical meaning here, is reiterated when Eagleton likewise remarks that for New Criticism, "The poem became a spatial figure rather than a temporal process."[27] What is remarkable in his otherwise admirable characterization is Eagleton's understanding of space here as an empty, nondialectical concept. For to be ahistorical (really he means acontextual, or divorced from any general laws governing social life) relegates thinking to a realm best expressed by the spatial. This observation pointedly amplifies Soja's claims regarding the subordination of spatial thinking in critical social theory.

From our perspective, New Criticism contains many parallels to its geographic contemporary, regional geography. As a paradigm dominating the North American scene from the 1930s to 1950s, regional geography was equally prone to celebrating the uniqueness of its objects, and to see in them not the operation of transcontextual laws but instances of distinctive interrelations. Like New Criticism's turn from authorial intentionality, regional geographers rejected analyses centered on agental forces, focusing instead on places as self-sufficient objects of inquiry. Moreover, the region (like the text) was seen to embody a complex unity that the geographer (like the critic) examined in terms of coherence/integration/harmony/wholeness. Regional geographers took as their core problematic the description and analysis of specific places, defining them in terms of surface homogeneity and directing attention to the varied interrelations they contained. As the leading spokesperson for regional geography, Richard Hartshorne, notes, geographers study phenomena:

[N]ot in themselves nor in their separate variations over the earth but in the areal variation of the phenomena as interrelated with each other, either in relatively simple integrations or in more complex but still partial integrations, in order to approach the total integration of interrelated phenomena which form the varying character of the earth as the home of man.[28]

Folding the parts into one another permits the geographer to achieve a gestalt-like unity, culminating in Hart's description of the discipline's highest art: "evocative descriptions that facilitate an understanding and an appreciation of places, areas, and regions."[29] Such sentimentalism was not without a critical method, however. Regional geography required equally a careful mapping and description of spatial variations, a classification of the phenomena under investigation, and a decoding of their interrelations. Thus at the same time literary critics were enjoined to emphasize the organic unity of the work through a "careful reading," geographers were encouraged to carefully map and analyze the varied features of regions such that an appreciation of their unique character and identity emerged.

Regional geography suffered from a number of contradictions, not the least of which was its attempt to bound the limits of its object. Consider the following comment by Hartshorne: "The purpose in dividing up the area is to secure areal sections, or 'regions,' such that within each region the elements . . . under study will demonstrate nearly constant interrelations."[30] Paradoxically, regional geographers have to know the "what" and "how" of interrelations before they can identify the object of analysis, yet the "what" and "how" of these interrelations also constitute their goals. Yet even if we are to disregard this theoretical circularity, it is evident that the process of defining the spatial limits of interrelations would do no less than sever the region from its larger context. No wonder, then, that regional geographers were content to theorize their objects outside of their position in global systems of capitalism, colonialism, or militarism. Nor were they overly concerned with history, that is, with the processes whereby places become. As Hartshorne again writes: "Explanatory description of individual relationships may require analysis of process relationships considerably farther back in time, but the purpose of such dips into the past is not to trace developments or seek origins but to facilitate comprehension of the present."[31] Thus we see that, just as the poem hovered outside of the domain of history for the New Critics, so too did the geographer's region. Finally, regions were divorced from the agency that gave rise to them, lest geographers be accused of doing so much sociology. The region was not unreflective of the intentionality of those who lived in them, but the place itself, and not the place-makers, focused the paradigm.

Second, regional geographies adopted an unusually straightforward narrative form, typically beginning with a description of the physical environment (e.g., climate, landforms, soils, etc.), followed by a brief history of the sequence of man's (usually white European) occupance and a lengthy discussion of the distribution of various social and economic features (population location and growth, agricultural production, industry, and cities). Such descriptions might conclude with instrumental commentary on the region's "political situation."[32] Once regional geography established its own paradigmatic narrative strategy, it disciplined what could be conceived and written, which elements counted in understanding a region and which did not. Thus, the confluence of regional geography's content and its narrative form is, to foreshadow a later discussion, an exemplary case of what Hayden White recognized in the context of narrative theory as the "content of the form."[33] As a consequence, regional geography failed to live up to its promise of understanding, in any theoretical sense, its objects of inquiry. The accusation, "mere" description, was a common critique leveled against the appearance of volume after volume of detailed, but theoretically unreflective, idiography.

Third, regional geography accepted as unproblematic a "mirror-of-reality" paradigm, in which the geographer could claim to have captured the essence of regions *via* cartographic representation and careful scientific description. Left uninterrogated was both the status of the observing subject, that is, the geographer as a "reader" of places, and the process of depiction, that is, the geographer as an author re-presenting places. Regional geography assumed that an objective observer with a thorough knowledge of the region being described could unproblematically render an understanding and explanation of the place in his or her writing. As Richard Hartshorne defined it, the discipline is "a science that interprets the realities of areal differentiation of the world *as they are found.*"[34] This perspective assumes that the realities or facts of the world exist independent of the observer, that is, that there exists a realm of the Real in which "facts speak for themselves" prior to and independent of interpretation. Moreover, Hartshorne continues, understanding and explanation of this reality requires "accurate, orderly, and rational description and interpretation."[35] This additionally assumes that the representation of that which is given or present can be communicated without distortion and with its full presence. The problem of geographic description extends no further than the question of one's knowledge and honesty; in essence, geographic description posits an autonomous author who writes about, but as if outside, the social world.

In the 1960s regional geography and New Criticism began to lose their power of persuasion to other schools, spatial science and literary structuralism, respectively, each of which promised more rigor in relating particular instances to universal laws. Literary structuralism, like spatial science, continued impulses from earlier schools (formalism and the Chicago school) by conceptualizing their objects not as self-contained entities but rather as the realization of transcontextual processes. In discarding the celebration of uniqueness practiced by the New Critics and regional geography, literary structuralism and spatial science interrogated their objects with the aim of establishing a system of universal laws operating throughout diverse texts and places. Both schools have been attacked (and praised) for being antihumanist, which in the case of literary structuralism marked its difference from any approach for which the human subject is the source and origin of literary meaning. Similarly, spatial science has been accused of erasing the "human" from human geography through its overly abstract emphasis on spatial laws, its use of models, and its reliance upon quantitative analysis.

The proper object of structuralist analysis is, following Saussurean linguistics, the system that underlies any particular signifying practice, not the individual utterance. The elements of any language or grammar—be it spoken or written—acquire meaning not as the result of some connection between words and things, but only as parts of a system of relations.[36] Whether applied to a literary work or to other cultural practices—fashion, architecture, myths—structuralism looks for the system of differences through which meaning is conveyed.[37]

Structuralism tacitly assumes a universal man and mind, a point which our later discussion of poststructuralism will consider further. While cultures may express themselves in different words or concepts, structuralism assumes a fundamental unity of laws governing these differences, once one has indeed discovered these central laws. Identifying and subsuming particulars under these universal laws became the task that structuralism, as a scientific enterprise, posed for itself. Phrased linguistically, structuralism sought to understand the nature of and the relationship between any given *parole* and the underlying structure of *langue*. It was attractive to literary critics, whose appetite had been whetted but not satisfied by New Criticism, because it promised to make the study of literature scientific by introducing rigor, objective universal laws, and hence, objectivity, into analysis. To do so, structuralists continued the formalist stress on form, and downplayed the actual content of any particular story. One can replace the particular nouns of any given plot—boy and man, daughter and woman—or its verbs, and still have the same story. Not the particular items, but the structure of the relations between the units is what is important.

The parallel to the rise of structuralism in literary theory is found in geography's turn toward spatial science, which employed geometric representations of space coupled with quantitative methodologies to identify laws governing the spatial organization of society. As Schaefer writes, "To explain the phenomena one has described means always to recognize them as instances of laws." Hence, he goes on, "geography has to be conceived as the science concerned with the formulation of the laws governing the spatial distribution of certain features on the surface of the earth."[38]

Within this paradigm, the most theoretically grounded approach is a deductive form of inquiry that homogenizes the diversity of places. The *tabula rasa* of location theory, upon which spatial laws are set into motion, reduces diversity to either an unnecessary complication or understands it as the outcome of manifestly complicated laws that we have only begun to identify. What is lost in this impulse toward the general is the heterogeneity posed by the unique, the specific, and the particular. Alternatively, variation over space can be analyzed inductively, by estimating functional relations between covarying spatial distributions. In either case, the goal is to establish general causal relationships between that which is under investigation and that to which it is presumed to be causally related.

Spatial science has been rightly accused of being profoundly antihumanist. It reduces all spatial organization of society to a set of discoverable principles outside of the control of the active agents who shape it. Moreover, its space is objective, physical, even Euclidean, rather than dialectically related to society or lived and meaningful to individuals. The antihumanist orientation of this paradigm is dramatically marked in the words of Stewart, an early spatial scientist who, with William Warntz, gave rise to a subparadigm known as social physics: "There is no longer any excuse for anyone to ignore the fact that human beings, on the average and at least in certain circumstances, obey mathematical rules resembling in a general way some of the primitive 'laws' of physics."[39] The reduction of agency to the neoclassical economist's world populated by persons with identical tastes, capacities, and incomes, enabled the universal application of models. One might just as easily apply Christaller's central place theory to southern Germany, as he did, or to China, Iowa, or Sweden, as was done by others.[40]

Importantly, representations of the spatial scientists' objects of inquiry (e.g., regions, cities, transportation networks, etc.) detached geography from the lived world. People, as well as the neighborhoods, cities, and regions in which they live, were analyzed, represented, and ultimately, universalized, as points, observational "units," or binary matrices.

The erasure of agency in both literary structuralism and spatial science prompted nearly simultaneous critiques in the early 1970s. In literary theory's version, agency was returned to textual interpretation by stressing the role that readers play in activating the meaning that resides in the individual work. Reader response theory, as it came to be known, can be understood as an effort to relocate agency, in the wake of the death of the humanist subject, not on the part of the author, but rather, on the part of the reader or communities of readers. Meaning, though not indifferent to authorial intentionality, could not be limited to it.

Roland Barthes, who profoundly influenced the turns toward reader response criticism and poststructuralism, discerned in the "death of the author" a reopening of the "text" against the closure of signification that the concept of the author had imposed upon the work. "The reader," he wrote, "is the space on which all the quotations that make up a writing are inscribed without any of them being lost; a text's unity lies not in its origin but in its destination."[41] Thus, the author, like her or his contemporary audience, was only one of a potentially unlimited number of readers, each with their own horizon of expectations that prefigured the way the text would acquire meaning for them.

Strongly influenced by phenomenology and Gadamer's hermeneutics, reader response criticism rejects the conception of textual meaning that assumes the fixity of a work, whether by appeal to authorial intention or to linguistic structures. It furthermore marks a breakdown of the separation presumed to exist between knowing subjects, on the one hand, and their objects of inquiry, on the other. The separation of thought from its object and the priority of the latter over the former no longer are assumed. Moreover, as in Gadamer's hermeneutics, the historical (not necessarily social) embeddedness of interpretation is presupposed. Meaning depends upon the historical situation of the interpreter who will produce varying results depending upon his or her place in this ongoing historicity. As the work passes from one cultural or historical context to another, new meanings may be culled from it that were never anticipated by either its author or its original audience.[42]

Thus for Gadamer, reading is essentially a dialogue, the effort at fusion between the present and the past. Neither Plato nor Shakespeare should be read as if they were present in the classroom with us or given to us in an unmediated way. While the reader cannot expect simply to transcend what separates the present from the past, she or he can engage the tradition of reading through which any present reading also occurs. The work is not fixed forever, like a tombstone, nor is its meaning universal. In the thought of Jauss and Iser, close study of literature reveals gaps that actively solicit the reader's participation. Jauss refers to the criteria readers use to judge literary texts in any given period as their "horizon of expectations."[43] As described by Iser, the competent reader recognizes literary conventions, genre laws, and so forth, which thus frame the manner in which the reader approaches the text.[44] In one sense, such approaches not only make understanding a matter of the observer's position, but in their more radical and literalist vein understand the printed word as being, after all, nothing more than the black marks on a page that await the interpreter's signifying desire to imbue them with meaning.

In its impulse, reader response theory can be extremely democratic: imagine a theory that assumes that actual readers, including but not limited to professional critics, *count* in the discerning of meaning. Works are not simply given, nor are the intentions of the author the measure of the work. The text is not a fixed entity, indifferent to those who choose to engage it. The irreducibly polymorphous nature of the work can never be contained by any single reader for all times. By activating not *the* reader in the process of interpretation (which unproblematically assumed the sameness of readers regardless of differentiations, for example, of place and time), but by instead seeing the work as something read by a plenitude of readers, questions of class, gender, and other social differentiations may also come into play. On the other hand, the notion of tradition that ultimately contains or limits the danger of a mere solipsism in the hermeneutics of Gadamer, is not without its problems. For Gadamer, the many transformations wrought over time unto the work are still unified by tradition, which as a continuing chain, has all the characteristics of "a club of the like-minded."[45] History, and the history of reading, is not for Gadamer a place of struggle, discontinuity, or exclusion.

Stanley Fish, meanwhile, is quite content to acknowledge that there is no "objective" work of literature to be interpreted. Specific readings occur based upon interpretive predilections, themselves the basis for the schooling of readers into communities. The work is what it does for "us" as Marxists, New Critics, feminists, and so on. The "danger" manifested by the acknowledged heterogeneity of the work is contained by reference to such interpretative communities, a redefinition of the concept of horizons of expectation such that distinct groups of competent readers are shown to share the same assumptions authorizing their interpretations.[46] The institutional framework in which interpretation proceeds is thus acknowledged by Fish, yet the institution is in no way thought of as interfering in the free choices of "disciplined" readers. The competent reader may, after all, choose which paradigm he or she will take to inform reading. Yet, as Marxist critics influenced by reception theory have shown, all of this leaves the reader in an oddly uncontextual frame. Readers too are constituted—by educational practices, class, race, and gender—and to transfer interpretative authority to the reader is not to resolve the problem of autonomy, but merely to displace it upon the reader.[47]

Geography's turn from the "text"-centered analyses of the regional and spatial science schools began in the 1970s with the emergence of phenomenological perspectives. Early writers such as Buttimer, Tuan, and Relph launched an attack against the pervasive objectification of space practiced by spatial science. To the phenomenologists, space was nongeometric, "a space of human concern and involvement."[48] The impossibility of an objective reading of space independent of the reader resonates in the words of Relph, who wrote: "Man's relationship with the world is understood not merely as a cognitive relationship, but as something which permeates man's whole being. Similarly the world is permeated by man. Man and the world thus constitute a unity through their mutual implication."[49] Seamon likewise emphasized the inseparability of text and reader, space and geographer, when he noted that: "we are the world—we are subsumed in the world like a fish is joined with water . . . we do not experience the world as an object. . . Rather, we interpenetrate that world, are fused with it through an invisible, web-like presence woven of the threads of body and feeling."[50] Phenomenology thus complicates the subject-object distinction that had previously dominated human geography. Whereas regional geographers and spatial scientists were able to disconnect themselves from their objects of inquiry, phenomenologists rejected the notion that interpretation could be divorced from one's experiences, including one's actions, memories, fantasies, and perceptions.[51] If knowledge cannot exist independently of experience, then projects such as regional geography, which presumes to interpret places objectively, and spatial science, which aspires for transcontextual generality, become highly suspect.

Like reader response criticism in literary theory, phenomenology in geography challenged the knowing-subject/known-object dichotomy that heretofore had permitted geographers to view themselves and their works as independent of their interactions with the world. In practice, most phenomenologists were content to interpret their own spatial experiences, though some employed humanistic methods to understand the place readings of others.[52] Yet the approach threatened to undermine decades of research previously insulated from external criticism, and consequently phenomenologists witnessed a twofold reaction to what was seen as their overly perspectival form of social investigation. First, the *person* recovered in a phenomenological geography was most often the individual geographer, that is, the geographer as interpreter, rather than the agents who create and modify places, ostensibly the discipline's object of inquiry. While some humanistic geographers would allow for a sensitive reading of other's intentions in creating places, under a strict Husserlian interpretation—the one providing the impulse to most early authors—the only recovery possible lies in the interiority of the individual writer, that is, as that space exists *for me*. Some geographers were sympathetic to the critique of positivism's conception of space, but few were willing to purchase a humanistic geography that focused attention on the geographer herself and which thereby seemed to eliminate the possibility of scientific verification.[53] A second critique of phenomenology, arising out of Marxism, claimed that phenomenology presupposes a causal structure in which individual meanings and intentions take precedence over social relations and culture. From a Marxist perspective, volunteerism and the rhetoric of choice mar phenomenology's humanistic turn. Such autonomistic interpretations belie the fact that one does not chose one's race, class, and gender nor the social structures that prefigure them. Marxist geographers, in response, echoed the critique of Marxist reader-response theorists, whose analyses stressed the social structures underpinning reading and interpretation.

The lacunas permeating humanistic geography's self-reflective accounts of the meaning of places were, in the 1970s and 1980s, countered by Marxist theorists who sought to relocate analyses on the processes creating and transforming space. In contrast to earlier culture-based accounts such as Sauer's, however, Marxists chose to examine the ways in which capitalism "scrawls its ugly hand across the landscape." In their analyses of capitalist space, Marxists focused attention on the processes of inter- and intra-class competition and the ensuing contradictions which structure spatial change. To Harvey, for example:

> Capital thus comes to represent itself in the form of a physical landscape created in its own image, created as use values to enhance the progressive accumulation of capital on an expanding scale. The geographical landscape which fixed and immobile capital comprises is both a crowning glory of past capital development and a prison which inhibits the further progress of accumulation.[54]

Though Harvey was quick to emphasize capitalism as an ongoing social process, to many geographers writing in the 1980s what had emerged was an overly deterministic form of Marxism that not only bore the trappings of economism, but that also neglected the dialectical relationship between human agency and social structures.[55] In turning to writers such as Giddens, therefore, geographers attempted to "relocate human agency" in their explanations of spatiality. Agency, as theorized by Giddens, has little to do with the autonomous subjectivity of authorial intentionality encountered earlier, but rather must be understood in terms of situated practices emergent from large-scale social structures which are seen to both constrain and enable human activity and which in turn may be reproduced or transformed by it. In this sense, structuration theory can be seen as bridging Marxist geography's structuralist account of the processes by which space is produced and humanistic geography's individualistic rendering of its meanings to intentional human actors.

Toward a Poststructuralist Understanding

The above account has marked many of the major positions taken by geographers and literary critics *vis-à-vis* their objects of inquiry, alternatively privileging one or another moment of the triad, author (agent), text (space), or critic (geographer). Central to a poststructuralist epistemology are the problems that result once the object of inquiry is stabilized by reference to any one of these moments. The remainder of this chapter will, we hope, not only suggest what poststructuralism can contribute to social inquiry, but also provide an impulse toward a poststructuralist episteme for geography. Key features of this episteme include the implications that derive from the critique of representation; a stance toward objectivity that takes into account both its use-value and its production as a social process; and a perspective in which both the knowing subject and its object are no longer pregiven and bounded, nor separated according to disciplinary or institutional demarcations. Parallel to our introductory remarks, however, we wish to raise a note of caution. The poststructural impulse animating our analysis is not one that characterizes or justifies the theoretical fence-sitting permeating so much of what is taken to be the postmodern sensibility (Humpty Dumpty-ism, as Ed Soja refers to it).[56] Nor do we believe that poststructuralism leaves one incapable of writing with any possibility of assuredness, objectivity (properly conceived), or political commitment. It does, however, rigorously question the operating assumptions of those epistemes that have too easily rendered as unproblematic the relations among writing, truth, and politics. Poststructuralism should not be equated with an inability to speak, though it does alert us to the potential indignity of professing to speak for the other. That some would offer the former interpretation makes it all the more important to steer the debate at this time.

Second, we do not accept the view that poststructuralism can be reduced to a position that elevates language to the status of an independent variable, which is to say, makes a fetish of its object of analysis. Instead, the currents of poststructuralism that focus on the indeterminan-

cy of language may precisely be understood as efforts to grasp more fully
the "messiness" of social life which earlier epistemes either submerged
under universal modes of explanation or set aside as anomalous. Poststructuralism's reconsideration of representation holds as untenable the
assumption of a correspondence, natural or otherwise, between the word
and the thing it represents. Its critique of representation undermines the
possibility of a fixed and stable relation between the object and that
which signifies it. Various poststructuralisms have problematized the
assumption that objects are given, extant, and that we then can find
words to express, or represent, them in their full presence. This critique
of representation, which discerns numerous antecedents in literary modernism, stands in contrast to the epistemologies of verisimilitude that
continue to underwrite most social science. As we suggest below, a poststructuralist understanding of representation has important implications
for the writing of geography and history, as well as for the yet- uncompleted project of reasserting space into critical social theory.

    A poststructuralist conception of representation breaks with a pre-
sentation-representation model, and with all the safety and security that
worldview provided. One casualty of this critique is the assumption that
there exist acontextual things, objects, or facts already given or present
that may merely be represented in our accounts of them. Another casualty is the scientific theology that is anchored by the promise of full,
though necessarily deferred, presence, whose teleological guarantee at
the same time warrants the positing of its claims as more than provisional. Neither knowing subject nor its objects are as plainly distinct or transparent as modernist social science writings have assumed. If one takes
Derrida's questioning of identity seriously, then the givenness of the
thing and of the knowing subject is all importantly a matter of context,
whether linguistic, epistemic, social, or political.

    In language, as scholars have known since Aristotle's definition of
metaphor, one transports the presumed object from one context to
another. This transport, for Derrida, cannot leave the object identical to
itself. Rather, the object has been reproduced with a difference. Repetition necessarily entails alterity, transcontextual nonidentity. The stability and identity of intentional actions are thus unsettled when communication is understood as a vehicle of transport.[57] In short, both time and
space "matter" in this understanding of representation. This characterization has force for all communication in written form. Not only this, but
the implicit separation between oral and written speech upon which the
degradation of the written as mere representation is based, cannot be
sustained following Derrida's critique of phonocentrism.[58] The problem
of difference, of a repetition of the message that is not a repetition of the

same, but rather one characterized by alterity, holds no less true for oral communication. Anchoring this privileging of the oral is at heart (so to speak) a postulation of a face-to-face presence guaranteed by the identity and intentionality of the utterer. Yet, if it can be demonstrated, as Derrida has undertaken to do in his critique of speech act theory,[59] that this notion of presence relies upon a complete transparency of context, then the presumed difference between written and oral communication collapses, and with it the linchpin of logocentrism. Also rendered problematic thereby are the presumed boundaries that ground the identities of intentions, events, and contexts.

We can view such analysis, far from being esoterically philosophical, as a sensitive characterization of the obstacles that are always the precondition for communication, whether face-to-face, or in the textual forms of poetry, philosophy, or electronic images. Difference is, moreover, particularly appropriate for understanding the consequences of the accelerated transport of communications made possible by the electronic age, which readily gives language the appearance of generating meaning self-referentially and of acquiring the force of a thing itself.[60]

All of this makes universalizing theoretical statements that act as if neither space nor time (context) matter more than suspect. As regards context, Derrida has recently characterized "what is called deconstruction" as the "effort to take this limitless context into account, to pay the sharpest and broadest attention possible to context, and thus to an incessant movement of recontextualization."[61] Thus understood, "context" does not mean simply the recovery of topologically similar forms, but rather the generation of transformative meanings and effects. The "ceaseless recontextualization of context" does not imply the end of all meaning, as some would characterize deconstruction or poststructuralism. Deconstruction does, however, in its task of disarming the force that has rendered its critique "merely" aesthetic, require interrogation of the powers that render interpretations and their settings as static, universal, and beyond ideology. As Derrida notes, objectivity itself must be understood as thoroughly contextual:

> What is called "objectivity," scientific for instance (in which I firmly believe in a given situation), imposes itself only within a context which is extremely vast, old, powerfully established, stabilized or rooted in a network of conventions (for instance, those of language) and yet which still remains a context. And the emergence of the value of objectivity (and hence of so many others) also belongs to a context.[62]

For Derrida, finally, the university itself is one such context: never neutral or independent, it is an indispensable but also inevitably problematic part of the articulation of meaning. Both moments, the university's problematic organization of knowledge production (as in what sanctions the divide between the social sciences and the humanities, for example) and its indispensability (political, social, economic, etc.), underscore the complexity of the issues faced by all academics who profess in the name of either "science" or the "people."

Signposts for Space

In charting the signposts for a poststructuralist geography, it is useful to reiterate an understanding of the relationship between power and representation that has been a dominant concern in most contemporary literary theory. As the discussion above has suggested synoptically, poststructuralist literary theory should be taken as an orientation toward the social world that considers the ways in which power undergirds the origins, deployments, and effects of representations. Any attempt to stabilize or naturalize the text in terms of the object itself, its author, or its contexts of reception is thereby rendered suspect. The geographic corollary would be to equally recognize that irrespective of the naturalizing impulses brought to bear on spatial thinking through the Cartesian and Euclidean paradigms, space, like the text, is anything but static, universal, and beyond ideology. Space, to use Henri Lefebvre's favorite modifier, is always "social," and anything social can never be stable, transcontextual, or apolitical.

To break through to an understanding of the complexity imposed by space, it is necessary to overcome the "illusion of opaqueness"[63] which hides the social production of space behind an opacity of surface appearances that reduces it to a mere setting upon which the fecundity of social life unfolds. Opacity veils the interpenetration of social life and space, displacing space as a "natural thing" (object, fact), independent of politics, conflict, and agency. Lefebvre has devoted years and pages to arguing the impossibility of this view:

> Space is not a scientific object removed from ideology and politics; it has always been political and strategic. If space has an air of neutrality and indifference with regard to its contents and thus seems to be "purely" formal, the epitome of rational abstraction, it is precisely because it has been occupied and used, and has already been the focus of past processes whose traces are not always evident on the landscape. Space has been shaped and molded from historical and natural elements, but this has been a political process. Space is political and ideological. It is a product literally filled with ideologies.[64]

Not only is society constitutive of space—in the authorial sense of underlying its production—but space and society must also be conceived dialectically, in the sense that (social) space reproduces social relations, framing reception contexts for the activities of social life. As Lefebvre puts it, "Space and the political organization of space express social relationships but also react back upon them."[65] Thus spaces, no less than commodities or language (and by extension, our understandings of them), cannot exist independently of social relations. In the same way that commodities and language are not natural but are produced socially and in turn reconstitute the network of social powers that give rise to them, so too is space dialectically embedded.

This dialectic works at many scales, from the power/space that produces the panoptican and the power of surveillance that results from it, to the differentiated space of regions produced by capital through processes of development and underdevelopment, which in turn create new opportunities for reproducing capital by virtue of its uneven development.[66] At the microlevel, as in Bentham's prison, the panopticon operates as a spatially organized power relation "testing" an emerging social relation, while also establishing, at the macrolevel, surveillance as the basis of social relationships more generally, as in the control exercised over territory by the police state. Panoptocism disciplines through the techniques it provides to assure the ordering of human multiplicities. Discipline "fixes; it arrests or regulates movements; it clears up confusion; it dissipates compact groupings of individuals wandering about the country in unpredictable ways; it establishes calculated distributions."[67] The spatial organization of society—the creation of calculated distributions in space—gives chaotic multiplicity an order that is the precondition for the exercise of power. Power sheers space of its illusion of opacity; poised between the natural, the social, and the political, space is thus revealed to be both product and producer of social organization. As de Certeau argues while amplifying Foucault's point, "'the often tiny ploys of discipline,' the 'minor but flawless' machinery that has colonized and made uniform the institutions of the state, derive their effectiveness from a relationship between *procedures* and the *space* they redistribute to create an 'operator.'"[68] The relationship suggested between user and space by Foucault and de Certeau is, of course, commensurate with her or his social positioning. De Certeau's point, whose theoretical goal parallels reader response criticism, is the empowerment of "operators." Nevertheless, like readers, operators are never simply "born," yet neither are they entirely reducible to the position of mere functional subjects.

A denaturalized understanding of the origins, form and content, and reception contexts of space is, therefore, one highly pertinent goal for a poststructuralist understanding of geography. A further imperative arises from our discussion of representation/power, namely, how this juxtaposition can be complicated by an understanding of space/power. A metonymic interpretation of space and representation, one in which being "in the social world" entails seeing each object of interest as constituted by social relations and in turn constitutive of them, has implications for both the author→text→critic and the agent→space→geographer models. Our argumentation suggests two propositions, that the author→text→critic model must be problematized in terms of space, as one element of its contextualization, and that the agent→space→geographer model must be problematized in terms of representation.

To fully appreciate the geographic significance of this project, it is worth recalling that traditional analyses of regions, spatial structures, and landscapes have ignored the critique of representation, obfuscated the extent to which representational processes mediate objects of geographic analysis, and overlooked the very representational status of these objects. This is so because the discipline of geography has tended to focus its attention on the material conditions purported to constitute "real life," to the exclusion of issues that arise from the critique of representation. Overcoming the rigid distinction between that which is thought of as "representational" and that which is thought of as "material" requires a recognition of their mutual determination as well as the development of a theoretical frame that problematizes the setting that has naturalized this divide. It is not suggesting too much to insist that the representation of social life and social life as lived spatially would be better conceived dialectically.[69] For a start, this implies that the conditions of material life are shaped through their representation as objects of recognition, contestation, and indifference, just as representations are shaped by materially situated powers. Thus what is regarded as material has almost certainly been made possible by some previous form of representation. Representations, in turn, emerge out of the signifying chain to frame, discipline, and transform the thinking and action of individuals and ultimately to shape future sociospatial powers.

In analyzing these connections, users of both models, textual and spatial, would do well to integrate alterity in their efforts to account for the differences wrought by incessant recontextualization. The poststructuralist critique of representation and the sociospatial dialectic together enjoin us to reject any type of analysis, no matter how internally complex, that seeks to center itself on any one of the key elements of either model, irrespective of the others or of social relations. Understanding the social world requires a theoretically critical stance characterized by greater complexity, and thus truer to Mann's thesis regarding the "messiness" of social life, than has heretofore been adopted by our disciplines. As a corollary to these considerations, a model of history that situates the historian as the renderer of the past (in the same way that the geographer renders places), cannot sweep aside fundamental consideration of the critique of representation and the inherent spatiality of social life.

Narratology: Writing and Mapping

These comments have profound implications for how geographers and other social investigators narrate accounts of the social world. Since the early days of exploration—a startling, yet enabling limit of geographical thinking—geographic writing and mapping have adhered to a mirror model of reality. Geography, or *geo-graph*, means inscribing the world— "as it is found," Hartshorne would insist. Let us separate for a moment the world from the writing and mapping of it, analogous to the duality signaled by the German word for history, *Geschichte*, which entails in equal measure history and the writing of it (narration). In both instances, attention is directed to the principle role narration plays for its subject matter. Our consideration of geographic narration begins by asking what assumptions have traditionally guided the writing of geographical stories. We later turn to cartography as a special form of geographic narration.

The social sciences have come to adopt a natural science laboratory model in which the results of experiments are assumed to obtain equivalent outcomes across all contexts. The traditional form of narration used to describe the social world reflects this model of stability: we write as we believe, namely, that the results from my laboratory will, under the same conditions, give the same results in yours, regardless of temporal or spatial differentiation. However, inasmuch as the social world is *messier* than the theories we have to account for it, do we not do a disservice in utilizing a narrative form that presupposes the causality of a linear narration—that is, stories with beginnings, middles and ends—through which all the webs are brought together without significant contradiction, and hence are quotable as "transportable" facts or univocal truths regardless of contexts, temporal or spatial?

The recent work of Hayden White summarizes the evidence that narrative, far from being merely a form of discourse that can be filled with different contents, real or imaginary, "already possesses a content prior to any given actualization of it in speech or writing."[70] Narrative discourse, by providing the assurance that "social reality can be both lived and realistically comprehended as a story," tends to legitimate a dominant social order regardless of the critical intent of the narrative's content. Narrative "strains for the effect of having filled in all the gaps, of having put an image of continuity, coherency, and meaning" onto the events it describes.[71] This legitimating function of narrative must be reckoned with by anyone who writes but who does not intend to affirm the values implied by a conservative ideology.

Moreover, the status of the authority that enables any author to profess an account of (to represent) the world is not irrelevant to the narrative stance of the author. All too often we encounter in social science writing the "disappearance of the I" in favor of a passive voice, the narrative corollary to the disappearance of the subject behind the object for which it speaks. In essence, no one speaks in this kind of scientific writing, for the events seem to tell themselves through the introduction, literature review, model, data, analysis, and conclusion. Such a narrative effaces the *I* behind the story: this was done not by the *I*, for the *I* is irrelevant, as any *I* would achieve the same results, where she or he follow the checklist of steps presented in the article. From such a model results a particular legitimating authority: no mere subjectivity has determined this outcome; rather a collective, presumably self-identical voice of all humanity (were all to follow this checklist) is invoked. Instead, critical social theory should experiment with forms of narration that rupture such invocations of their ideological, authoritarian force. Since we cannot in good faith speak in the voice of divine illumination in which meaning and truth are identical and fully present to themselves and to the reader (for this voice, after all, would have to be reserved for those who can claim to have witnessed the "end of history"), to write as if this were the case violates the very pursuit of truth that these authors hold so dear, or, alternatively, exposes them as voices writing in the mode of prophecy.

What the mutable, unstable contexts we have discussed above make impossible is the writing of any kind of history or geography that assumes identity as its operating principle. Objectivity as conceived in the natural science form is rendered impossible for the social world. But the recognition of the contingent nature of writing-reading (or cause-effect recognition in the scientific model) presents us with a new task, namely, the writing of a history of the mutations that take place, that is, a *contextual* understanding of the already shifting, mutable contexts, which, moreover, are not to be thought of as interfering with an understanding of the "thing itself" but rather are the very condition under which all dialogues occur. What Derrida refers to as "difference" points to this alterity in every repetition. This opens the rigorous questioning of "context" which is no longer to be thought of as the simple repetition of the same. It is for this reason, we offer, that normative history should be unsettled by both

Derrida's analysis of context and the critical reassertion of space. Lest the project sketched above be seen in negative terms, it is important to reiterate that what we do not have to fear is the end of the writing of geography (or history). On the contrary, a great deal of writing needs be undertaken once we are informed by an understanding of the instabilities that intervene on all interpretation and narration. Such writing, whether in geography or history, will prove far more illuminating as regards these disciplines' purported objectives than a history or geography in which facts are presented as given "unto themselves." The facts *do not speak* for themselves: they are *spoken for* by the historian or geographer who fashions fragments into a coherent narrative. In the same way that the unity of the text discovered by the New Critics turns out to have been mostly a reflection of their own intentionality as interpreters, the unity of places discovered by regional geographers can be seen to reflect their own interpretation given coherence by their narrative form.

Geographic representation of a different sort, cartography, is not immune to the type of critique developed above. Like geographic analysis in general, today's cartography is wedded to a model of reality and representation that is reproducible on the one hand via natural scientific understanding, and on the other hand by the age of mechanical reproduction that has given us computer cartography and geographic information systems (GIS). The epistemological assumptions behind both is that the representation of the world is flawless, save for the inherent impossibility posed by scale. Both suggest an identity—mediated but nonetheless topologically equivalent—that collapses any distance between the narrator and the narrated world, between the *graph*-ing and the *geo*. As the reality paradigm has always assumed, the role of the observer is limited to her or him holding a mirror up to the extant world. Moreover, the objection of a mere subjectivity imposing itself upon that world is averted by the precision seemingly afforded by computer cartography and GIS. The thing and its representation have collapsed; computer cartography and GIS suggest presentation without representation, mediation, or displacement. It is through this process that both their social production and effects are utterly veiled.

The symptoms catalogued above have been productively examined with regard to cartography in a recent paper by Brian Harley.[72] In the paragraphs that follow we draw from our own commentary on his article.[73] Cartography, like any field of inquiry "disciplined" by a perceived necessity to claim scientific verisimilitude, faces a potential crisis when it stops to consider its own language of representation and the embeddedness of its products in the social world. Such questioning would seem to threaten the possibility of generalizable objective knowledge. It is an issue that, in the era of the postmodern, has surfaced in many of the social sciences and humanities, and with the publication of Harley's paper, in cartography as well.

Harley's work brings a new perspective to the widely perceived crisis of realism and representation underlying the various "narratives of suspicion" to be found in deconstructive thinking. One such narrative questions the ability of language or any semiotic code to signify its object, as it were, translucently. Russian formalism, reader response theory, and Derridian deconstruction have all, as we have seen, explored the sometimes intersecting problems of representation, reading, and "context" that arise from this fundamental nonidentity of language. Various deconstructive strategies have therefore stressed the fundamental indeterminacy of language—its "messiness"—by stressing the rhetorical, political, and temporal nature of all discourse, and thus force a rethinking of the simple binary opposition between rhetoric (meant pejoratively), on the one hand, and disinterested, objective scientific language, on the other. The mere presence of this dualistic notion only serves to sustain the possibility of the latter. Its implication for cartography—ever-better maps, ever more accurately depicting the world as a result of technological innovation—currently fuels the widely accepted view of cartography as a disinterested science.

Another focus of suspicion, deriving from Foucault, rethinks institutions less as disinterested knowledge gatherers than as centers of power defining agendas and thereby redefining, through that which is produced, the realities of social life.[74] Disciplinary knowledge grows out of struggles of legitimation; when that knowledge, in turn, is imbued with the scientific stamp of "natural order," it imposes rather than mirrors reality. Revealing the implications of these twin processes is tantamount to rewriting the history of the cartographic enterprise and at the same time creating ground for a new praxis of cartography.

In it, cartographers would be urged to think further about the layers of meaning embedded in the "objective" symbols that constitute the discourse of the map as well as those elements that signify precisely by their absence. Any system of signification presupposes notions of what is thought to constitute the significant. Such choices of necessity implicate the map as a socially constructed vehicle of meaning. Likewise, omissions from maps convey that which has been deemed insignificant by its producers or that which has been consciously veiled in a strategy of mystification. Underlying both the present and the omitted iconographies are a complex of historically variable power relations that must be subjected to critical scrutiny. Such scrutiny might first consider the truth-power constructions of class in cartographic discourse, as in, for example, the mapped depictions of central Kentucky as a series of bucolic bluegrass horse farms, or the messages of a single-gendered history transmitted by our maps of military victories, or the social construction of race and ethnicity both legitimated in and reproduced by maps labeling an area as "Chinatown" or "Little Havana," or the ethos of humans as the dominate partner in an exploitative dualism with nature in our maps of resources.

It is not only the cartographer, however, who stands to gain from these understandings, for both literary critics and historians need to overcome their own reliance on maps as disinterested instruments, and instead to see them in light of what Hayden White has called the "fictions of factual representation."[75] Maps are undeniably social products—even the most scientific among us must admit that. Yet to hide behind the guise of objectivity constrains cartographic theory to rigidly scientific boundaries of inquiry that deny both its historically artistic connections and limit that which can be attained from the critical reading of maps. Seen as vessels of social meaning, maps become ever-more revealing of embodied cultural constellations and historical moments. As we emphasized above, what is not at stake is the legitimacy of cartography itself. We can no longer imagine a world without maps, any more than we can imagine a world without language. Nor should we. Yet maps, like language, have been vehicles of domination and the pursuit of power. In recognizing this and developing a critical stance toward the map, we will need to grasp a sense of the ongoing historicity of cartographic discourse and to transcend, rather than hide behind, the time-bound language of objectivity.

Conclusion

Of the many empiricist histories made questionable by poststructuralism, those that have charted the growth of the discipline of geography are of particular importance to us. It should now be clear that a poststructuralist spatiality, one that refuses to accept space as "natural" in either its origin or effects, might also critically reexamine those disciplinary histories whose accounts, in bearing the imprimatur of "progress," have likewise naturalized the discipline's "evolution." As we have shown through the twin mappings of the development of literary theory and geography, both disciplines have been marked by surprising parallels in the constitution of and approach toward their objects of inquiry. This, in spite of the incommensurability so readily acknowledged by those who would separate the domain of each as, for example, science versus aesthetics or explanation versus interpretation. Our collocation leads us to situate both disciplines as themselves texts embedded in a wider sphere of social and academic contexts and power relationships.

Geography's histories, by contrast, have tended to be written from one of two perspectives: either as hagiographies in which the plot is written by monumental figures, or as a series of contradictions and resolutions illustrative of Kuhnian paradigm shifts.[76] In the former case geographic knowledge is not located within a field of power relationships that give it its form and content, but instead unfolds in the minds of the authors whose products provide the discipline's unique story. In the latter case, actors bearing particular paradigms struggle for legitimacy on a scientific battleground where victories are short-lived as new, better paradigms ascend. Both forms of history resound with a sense of "trajectory"—that is, a discipline *soaring above* context and *directed*, even if nonlinearly, *toward* its target, the full and final presence of true knowledge.

Our historiography contrasts the futurist myth of historical progress sustained by such narrations with a disciplinary path much more grounded in the everyday affairs of the academy and society at large. It is one in which, at the institutional level, geographical thinking can be read as being engaged in the attempt to distinguish itself from the practices of geology, anthropology, sociology, economics, and so on. An anxious tone frequently accompanies pronouncements regarding geography's field, and within it its proper objects of analysis. The fear of incorporation, of being dissolved by adjoining disciplines, or of losing its center, has often characterized reflections upon the enabling limits of geography.[77]

A social history of geography likewise remains to be written. Disciplines, geography no less than others, may create the knowledges necessary for continued capital accumulation; they may provide society with individuals inculcated with appropriate, nonrevolutionary ideology that legitimates the status quo; they may service the state by educating technically competent students to assist society in the making of war and in the identification of within-the-system solutions to social problems. Geography, as an historically applied discipline, has often been complicitous in these projects. The works of geographers can be read as having rationalized colonialism through the paradigm of environmental determinism, assisted in militarism through work on geopolitics and terrain analysis, contributed to an instrumentalized view of nature through environmental policy research, and legitimated state planning through the paradigm of efficiency dominating spatial science.

So, yes, geography is a "normal" science, though not in the way that Kuhn meant it. It is normal in the sense that in striving for legitimacy its practitioners have engaged in border wars, honing its tools of analysis so as to provide it with the sharpest edge *vis-à-vis* society and its disciplinary neighbors. As an exemplar of this tendency, consider the following definition of geography offered by Richard Hartshorne, who sought to reinforce distinctions between science and aesthetics, explanation and interpretation. Here we selectively interrupt his account with divergent epistemological signposts, borrowed from a recent commentator on the "postmodern":

> Geography seeks (1) on the basis of empirical observation [*presence vs. absence*] as independent as possible of the person of the observer [*distance vs. participation*], to describe [*narrative vs. antinarrative*] phenomena with the maximum degree of accuracy and certainty [*signified vs. signifier*]; (2) on this basis, to classify [*hierarchy vs. anarchy*] the phenomena, as far as reality permits, in terms of generic concepts or universals [*metaphysics vs. irony*]; (3) through rational consideration of the facts thus secured [*determinancy vs. undeterminancy*] and by logical processes of analysis [*design vs. chance*] and synthesis [*totalization vs. deconstruction*], including the construction [*form vs. antiform*] and use wherever possible of general principles or laws of generic relationships [*master code vs. idiolect*], to attain the maximum comprehension [*depth vs. surface*] of the scientific [*interpretation vs. against interpretation*] interrelationships of phenomena [*metaphor vs. metonymy*]; and (4) to arrange these findings in orderly [*cause vs. trace*] systems so that what is known leads directly to the margin of the unknown [*paranoia vs. schizophrenia*].[78]

Our intent in these interruptions is not simply to expose the limits of Hartshorne's epistemology, but to reveal his model as an affirmation of an objective, orderly, and rational mode of social investigation whose merely provisional knowledge claims are legitimated by the ultimate promise of full presence. What is so remarkable about Hartshorne's definition is his wholesale appropriation of a model of scientific inquiry so shorn of particularity that virtually any "natural" science, whether physics, astronomy, or chemistry, could be readily substituted for "Geography" as its point of departure. In so doing, Hartshorne has legitimated geography's task by appeal to its character as a scientific enterprise.

It is undoubtedly easier to critique what is problematic in a paradigm than it is to predict what will replace it, since, as Sam Weber notes, "the new 'paradigm' can hardly be expected to [nor would we want it to] have the same unity as the old."[79] We thus end here not with a roadmap, for this would require a new language, indeed, a new form of writing that has yet to be *created*. This language, in the intent signaled here, will bespeak both the critique of representation and an understanding of space as a social product and process. Most importantly, our new explorations must reveal the interconnections between both so as to overcome the divisions, institutionalized in the nineteenth century, that separated the domains of literary theory (art) and geography (technology).

A reconstructed literary theory stands to gain by contextualizing its objects of inquiry spatially. In its critique of representation, literary theory has come to understand power as central to the understanding of communication. Yet space in literary theory has been notable mostly for its absence, rather commensurate with its designation as mere metaphor. Space, however, is more than metaphorical, or put differently, "metaphor" is itself spatial. Never empty or nonideological, (social) space undergirds all practices of production and reception, beginning with the materiality of the book itself. A global economy and its forces and relations of production are materially assembled by the paper, ink, and cloth that make it a frame for the communication of ideas. More broadly, but no less materially, the fusion of space and power establishes the conditions under which represented thought may be produced and then transported from one context to another, one receiver to another, in all forms of communication.

Geography too can stand to gain from the poststructuralist critique of representation and the problematization of *its* objects of analysis which thereby ensues. In so doing, the discipline would benefit by adopting a stance toward (social) space that rejects the imperative to frame monolithic interpretations of society, a precondition for the disclosure of new human geographies. Thirty years ago the scientific consensus provided no discourse for, nor understanding of, spatiality that would enable the discipline to encircle a feminist geography, a working-class geography, a gay and lesbian geography, or a postcolonial geography. Today we can envision all of these and more. And as we continue to situate our accounts of the social world *in* the social world, our future disciplinary histories will doubtless bear the marks of it as well.

Finally, just as a reconstructed literary theory should consider space/power as a central moment in its analysis of representations, so too must its geographic counterpart more seriously engage and learn from the former's critique of representation. The powers that transform and are reproduced by space are *transported*, and hence activated, by and through representations. The conditions of space/power are thus equally material and representational. Indeed, the trifold nexus of space/power/ representation brings into question the very distinction between the material and the representational, and with it, the stability of all disciplines demarcated via their separation.

Acknowledgments

It is a pleasure to acknowledge those colleagues who read earlier versions of this chapter and offered many insightful suggestions: Anne Buttimer, Derek Gregory, John Pickles, Ted Schatzki, Ed Soja, and Peter Wissoker.

Notes

1. Samuel Weber, *Institution and Interpretation* (Minneapolis: University of Minnesota Press, 1987), x.

2. Doreen Massey and J. Allen, eds., *Geography Matters!* (Cambridge: Cambridge University Press, 1984).

3. For representation and history, see Hayden White, *Tropics of Discourse* (Baltimore: Johns Hopkins University Press, 1978), and also his *The Content of the Form* (Baltimore: Johns Hopkins University Press, 1987), and Dominick LaCapra, *History and Criticism* (Ithaca, N.Y.: Cornell University Press, 1986). For space and history, see Ed Soja, *Postmodern Geographies* (London: Verso, 1989).

4. Peter Novick, *That Noble Dream: The Objectivity Question in History* (Chicago: University of Chicago Press, 1989), 593–4.

5. Soja, *Postmodern Geographies*, 15.

6. Soja, Ibid., 14.

7. Rainer Nägele, "History after Freud and Lacan," in *Reading after Freud* (New York: Columbia University Press, 1987), 170.

8. Soja, *Postmodern Geographies*, 18.

9. Michael Mann, *Sources of Social Power* (Cambridge: Cambridge University Press, 1986), 4.

10. Derek Gregory, "Areal Differentiation and Post-Modern Human Geography," in *Horizons in Human Geography*, ed. Derek Gregory and Rex Walford (Totowa, N.J.: Barnes and Noble, 1989), 67–96.

11. Susan Buck-Morss, *The Dialectics of Seeing: Walter Benjamin and the Arcades Project* (Cambridge: MIT Press, 1991), 359.

12. Roger Chartier, "Texts, Printings, Readings," in *The New Cultural History*, ed. Lynn Hunt (Berkeley and Los Angeles: University of California Press, 1989), 161.

13. Three fecund texts on these points are Roland Barthes, *Image, Music, Text*, trans. Stephen Heath (New York: Hill and Wang, 1977); Marshall Blonsky, ed., *On Signs* (Baltimore: Johns Hopkins University Press, 1985); and Jacques Derrida, "Afterword," in *Limited Inc*, trans. Samuel Weber (Evanston, Ill.: Northwestern University Press, 1988).

14. See the essays in Denis Cosgrove and Stephen Daniels, eds., *The Iconography of Landscape* (Cambridge: Cambridge University Press, 1988); and Trevor Barnes and James Duncan, eds., *Writing Worlds* (London: Routledge, 1992). Also see Charles Jencks, *The Language of Post-Modern Architecture*, 4th ed. (London: Academy Editions, 1984).

15. See, for example, Ellen Churchill Semple, *Influences of Geographical Environment* (New York: Henry Holt, 1911), 1, who writes: "Man is a product of the earth's surface. This means . . . that the earth has mothered him, set him tasks, directed his thoughts, confronted him with difficulties that have strengthened his body and sharpened his wits, given him his problems of navigation or irrigation, and at the same time whispered hints for their solution. She has entered into his bone and tissue, into his mind and soul. On the mountains she has given him leg muscles of iron to climb the slope; along the coast she has left these weak and flabby, but given him instead vigorous development of chest and arm to handle his paddle or oar. In the river valley she attaches him to the fertile soil, circumscribes his ideas and ambitions by a dull round of calm, exacting duties, narrows his outlook to the cramped horizon of his farm." For a less poetic, but no less deterministic account, see William M. Davis, "An Inductive Study of the Content of Geography," *Bulletin of the American Geographical Society* 38, (1906): 67–84.

16. Carl O. Sauer, "The Morphology of Landscape," *University of California Publications in Geography* 2 (1925): 46.

17. See, for example, the essays in Lee Lemon and Marion Reis, eds. *Russian Formalist Criticism: Four Essays* (Lincoln: University of Nebraska Press, 1965), and Tony Bennett, *Formalism and Marxism* (New York: Methuen, 1979).

18. Mikhail Bakhtin, *The Dialogic Imagination: Four Essays*, ed. Michael Holquist (Austin: University of Texas Press, 1985).

19. R. E. Park, E. W. Burgess, and R. D. McKenzie, eds., *The City* (Chicago: University of Chicago Press, 1925).

20. M. Gottdiener, *The Social Production of Urban Space* (Austin: University of Texas Press, 1985), 33.

21. Paul Knox, *Urban Social Geography* (London: Longman, 1987), 59.

22. Walter Benjamin, preface to "The Work of Art in the Age of Technological Reproducibility," in *Illuminations*, ed. Hannah Arendt (New York: Schocken, 1969).

23. W. K. Wimsatt, Jr., and Monroe Beardsley, "The Intentional Fallacy," in *The Verbal Icon* (New York: Noonday, 1954), 18.

24. Terry Eagleton, *Literary Theory* (Minneapolis: University of Minnesota Press, 1983), 47.

25. Hayden White, "The Absurdist Moment in Contemporary Literary Theory," in *Tropics of Discourse*, 274.

26. Eagleton, *Literary Theory*, 48.

27. Ibid. Also see Eagleton's foreword to Kristen Ross' *The Emergence of Social Space* (Minneapolis: University of Minnesota Press, 1988), vi–xiv.

28. Richard Hartshorne, *Perspective on the Nature of Geography* (Washington, D.C.: Association of American Geographers, 1959), 106.

29. John Fraser Hart, "The Highest Form of a Geographer's Art," *Annals of the Association of American Geographers*, 72 (1982): 2.

30. Hartshorne, *Perspective*, 129.

31. Ibid., 106.

32. See, for example, Preston James, *Latin America* (Indianapolis, Ind.: Bobbs-Merrill, 1975).

33. White, *Content of the Form*, xi.

34. Richard Hartshorne, *The Nature of Geography* (Lancaster, Penn.: Association of American Geographers, 1939), 462; our emphasis.

35. Hartshorne, *Nature of Geography*, 21.

36. Ferdinand de Saussure, *A Course in General Linguistics*, trans. W. Baskin (London: Fontana, 1974).

37. See, for example, Roland Barthes, *Elements of Semiology*, trans. A. Lavers and C. Smith (London: Jonathan Cape, 1967), and Claude Lévi-Strauss, *Structural Anthropology*, trans. C. Jacobson and B. G. Schoepf (London: Allen Lane, 1968).

38. Fred K. Schaefer, "Exceptionalism in Geography: A Methodological Examination," *Annals of the Association of American Geographers* 43 (1953): 227.

39. J. Q. Stewart, "Empirical Mathematical Rules Concerning the Distribution and Equilibrium of Population," *Geographical Review*, 37 (1947): 485.

40. Walter Christaller, *Central Places in Southern Germany*, trans. C. W. Baskin (Englewood Cliffs, N.J.: Prentice-Hall, 1966); see also Brian J. L. Berry, *Geography of Market Centers and Retail Distribution* ((Englewood Cliffs, N.J.: Prentice-Hall, 1967).

41. Barthes, *Image, Music, Text*, 148.

42. Hans-Georg Gadamer, *Truth and Method* (London: Routledge, 1975).

43. Hans Robert Jauss, "Literary History as a Challenge to Literary Theory," in *New Directions in Literary Theory*, ed. Ralph Cohen (London: Routledge, 1974).

44. Wolfgang Iser, *The Act of Reading* (Baltimore: Johns Hopkins University Press, 1978).

45. Eagleton, *Literary Theory*, 73.

46. Stanley Fish, *Is There a Text in This Class?* (Cambridge: Harvard University Press, 1980).

47. Tony Bennett, "Texts in History: The Determinations of Readings and Their Texts," in *Poststructuralism and the Question of History* (Cambridge: Cambridge University Press, 1987), 63–81.

48. J. Nicholas Entrikin, "Contemporary Humanism in Geography," *Annals of the Association of American Geographers*, 66 (1976): 625.

49. Edward Relph, "An Inquiry into the Relations between Phenomenology and Geography," *Canadian Geographer* 14 (1970): 197.

50. David Seamon, *A Geography of the Lifeworld* (New York: St. Martins Press, 1979), 161.

51. Relph, "An Inquiry," 193.

52. See: Yi-Fu Tuan, "Place: An Experiential Perspective," *Geographical Review*, 65 (1975): 151–165; and also *Topophilia* (Englewood Cliffs, N.J.: Prentice-Hall, 1974); Edward Relph, *Place and Placelessness* (London: Pion, 1976); and David Seamon, *A Geography of the Lifeworld*.

53. D. J. Walmsley, "Positivism and Phenomenology in Human Geography," *Canadian Geographer*, 18 (1974): 95–107.

54. David Harvey, "The Geography of Capitalist Accumulation: A Reconstruction of the Marxian Theory," in *Radical Geography*, ed. Richard Peet (Chicago: Maaroufa Press, 1977), 273.

55. For theoretical work attempting to recover agency in human geography, see Derek Gregory, "Human Agency and Human Geography," *Transactions of the Institute of British Geographers*, n.s. 6 (1981): 1–18, and Nigel Thrift, "On the Determination of Social Action in Space and Time," *Environment and Planning D* 1 (1983): 23–57.

56. Ed Soja, "Postmodern Geographies and the Deconstruction of Historicism" (Paper presented at the Committee on Social Theory's Lecture Series, University of Kentucky, Lexington, 1990).

57. Jacques Derrida, "Signature Event Context," trans. Samuel Weber and Jeffrey Mehlman, *Glyph* 1 (1977): 172–197.

58. Jacques Derrida, *Of Grammatology*, trans. Gayatri C. Spivak (Baltimore: Johns Hopkins University Press, 1976).

59. Jacques Derrida, "Limited Inc a b c . . . ," trans. Samuel Weber, in *Limited Inc*, 29–110.

60. Mark Poster, *The Mode of Information* (Chicago: University of Chicago Press, 1990).

61. Jacques Derrida, "Afterword," *Limited Inc*, 136.

62. Ibid.

63. Soja, *Postmodern Geographies*, 122.

64. Quoted in Soja, *Postmodern Geographies*, 80.

65. Quoted in Soja, *Postmodern Geographies*, 81.

66. See Michel Foucault, "Panopticism," in *The Foucault Reader*, ed. Paul Rabinow (New York: Pantheon Books, 1984), 206–213, and David Harvey, *The Limits to Capital* (Chicago: University of Chicago Press, 1982).

67. Foucault, "Panopticism," 208.

68. Michel de Certeau, "Practices of Space," in *On Signs*, ed. Marshall Blonsky, 128.

69. These arguments are developed in Wolfgang Natter and John Paul Jones III, "Pets or Meat: Class, Ideology, and Space in *Roger and Me*," *Antipode*, 25 (1993), in press.

70. White, *Content of the Form*, xi.

71. White, "The Value of Narrativity in the Representation of Reality," in *Content of the Form*, 11.

72. Brian Harley, "Deconstructing the Map," *Cartographica* 26 (1989): 1–20.

73. Wolfgang Natter and John Paul Jones III, "Comments on Deconstructing the Map," *Cartographica* 26 (1989): 113–114.

74. See Michel Foucault, *The Order of Things* (London: Routledge, 1970) and *The Archaeology of Knowledge* (London: Routledge, 1972).

75. White, "The Fictions of Factual Representation," in *Tropics of Discourse*, 121–134.

76. For a hagiographic account, see Preston James, *All Possible Worlds* (Indianapolis, Ind.: Bobbs-Merrill, 1977); for a Kuhnian account, see Brian J. L. Berry, "Introduction: A Kuhnian Perspective," in *The Nature of Change in Geographical Ideas*, ed. Brian J. L. Berry (De Kalb: Northern Illinois University Press, 1978), 17–36.

77. See the earlier cited essays by Hart, Sauer, and Schaefer. The twin

impulses of anxiety and hegemony are stated in a particularly forthright manner in Nevin Feneman, "The Circumference of Geography," *Annals of the Association of American Geographers*, 9 (1919): 3–11.

78. Hartshorne, *Perspective on the Nature of Geography*, 169–170; and I. Hassan, "The Culture of Postmodernism," *Theory, Culture, and Society* 2 (1985): 123–124.

79. Weber, *Institution and Interpretation*, xi.

Index

Adorno, Theodor W., 17, 30–31, 101
Anthropology, postmodern, 14,
    139–145
    and feminism, 153–155
    reflexive analysis in, 142–145
    social contexts of, 145–153
Arendt, Hannah, 73, 109
Articulation, hegemonic, 87–89

B

Bakhtin, Mikhail, 173
Barbarism, manifestations of, 110–112
Barthes, Roland, 181
Baudrillard, Jean, 119–120
Benhabib, Seyla, 107
Benjamin, Walter, 30, 101, 133, 174
Bennett, Tony, 81–82
Berman, Marshall, 81, 114
Bernstein, Richard J., 83–84, 99–112
Bloch, Ernst, 80–81
Blumenberg, Hans, 18
Boggs, Carl, 74–82, 94
Braudel, Fernand, 132–133
Burgess, E. W., 173
Burton, Sir Richard, 150–151
Butler, Judith, 107

C

Capitalism
    cultural features of, 138, 145–146

hegemony of, 47
and modernism, 116, 117
and postmodern thought, 7–8
and transformation of space, 184
Capra, Fritjof, 70
Cartography, critique of, 193–195
Christaller, Walter, 180
Clifford, James, 150, 154, 155
Cohen, Colleen Ballerino, 153
Collective will, in social groups, 85
Colonialism, and response to postcolo-
    nial world, 150–153
Communication. *See* Language
Communitarianism, 67–73
Community, without unity, 67, 73
Conflict settlement, wrongs involved
    in, 46, 59
Connolly, William, 22–23, 24, 69, 72
Conservatism
    compared to rationalism, 104
    and postmodern thought, 2–3, 6
Consumer culture, postmodern, 138,
    145–146
Corlett, William, 66–74, 92, 94
Criticism, forms of, 27
Cultural analysis, postmodern,
    138–145
    and feminism, 153–155
    social contexts of, 145–153
Cushman, Dick, 148

205

D

Dallmayr, Fred, 83, 92
Davis, William M., 172
De Certeau, Michel, 189
Deconstruction, 66–74, 124
  and recontextualization of context,
    187
Deleuze, Gilles, 48
Democracy
  concepts of, 105–107
  diversity in, 57–58
  radical, issues in, 91–93
Democratic equivalence, concept of,
  89–91
Democratic socialism, failure of, 76
Derrida, Jacques, 20, 24, 25, 80,
  100–106, 186–188, 193
  and deconstruction of, 66–73
Differends, concept of, 45–46
Diversity
  in democracy, 57–58
  as justice, 53–54, 57, 59
Dorst, John, 143–144
Dreyfus, Hubert, 28

E

Eagleton, Terry, 144, 176
Ecological systems, and urban geography, 173–174
Enlightenment
  assessments of, 24–28
  heritage in Marxism, 80
  legacy of, 101
  and modernity, 115, 119
Ethical space, analysis of, 109–110
Ethnography, postmodern, 138–145
  and feminism, 153–155
  social contexts of, 145–153

F

Feminism
  and anthropology, 153–155
  and postmodernism, 9–10, 13, 14,

107–108
  and reflexive analysis, 144
Fischer, Michael, 148, 154
Fish, Stanley, 182
Flynn, Thomas, 51
Force relations, and local struggle,
  44–45
Formalism, Russian, 172–173
Foucault, Michel, 20, 24, 25, 26–28,
  31, 41–60, 69–70, 108, 125–126,
  129–130, 189, 194
Fragmentation, human, 87
Fraser, Nancy, 67, 107–108

G

Gadamer, Hans–Georg, 30, 56, 102,
  181, 182
Gallie, W. B., 17
Gender ideologies, and postmodernism, 156
Geography
  behavioral, 172
  and concepts of space, 170–171
  disciplinary history of, 168–185
  human intentionality in, 172
  humanistic, 183–184
  phenomenology in, 183–184
  poststructuralist, 188–191
  regional, 176–179
  and spatial science, 179, 180–181
  writing and mapping in, 191–195
Giddens, Anthony, 126, 184–185
Gramsci, Antonio, 65, 72–73, 83,
  85–86, 93
Green Party, 93
  assessment of, 78, 82
Gregory, Derek, 168

H

Habermas, Jürgen, 5, 21, 25–26, 28, 30,
  81, 100–106
Harley, Brian, 193–194
Hart, John Fraser, 177

resistance to, 45, 50
spatially organized, 189
Pratt, Mary, 150–151
Public space, analysis of, 109

R

Rabinow, Paul, 28
Radical democracy, issues in, 91–93
Radicalism, political, 75–76
Rationalism, compared to conservatism, 104
Reader response theory, 181–182
Reagan, Ronald, 122
Reality, social, concepts of, 42, 43
Reflexivity, in anthropology, 142–145
Reid, Herbert G., 74
Relph, Edward, 183
Representation, poststructuralist conception of, 186–187, 198
Resistance to power, 45, 50
Romanticism, 3–4
Rose, Dan, 153
Rosen, Stanley, 19–20, 24, 25
Rosenzweig, Franz, 101
Roszak, Theodore, 70
Rousseau, Jean–Jaques, 73
Russian formalism, 172–173

S

Sauer, Carl O., 172
Schaefer, Fred K., 180
Schlegel, Friedrich, 4, 5
Seamon, David, 183
Semple, Ellen Churchill, 172
Sharpe, Patricia, 153
Simulacra, postmodern, 120, 122–123
Social contestation
literature in, 173
spatial competition in, 173–174
Social contexts
and focus of postmodern anthropol-

ogy, 145–153
and literary work, 171–176
and regional geography, 176–179
Social life, spatiality of, 169, 170–171, 188–191
Social ontology, 41–42
Social physics, 180
Social reality, concepts of, 42, 43
Socialism, democratic, failure of, 76
Soja, Ed, 167
Space
ethical, 109–110
public, 109
reassertion in critical social theory, 125–130
social aspects of, 169, 170–171, 188–191
Space and time, culture of, 8, 13–14, 114, 125
Spatial science, 179, 180–181
Spatialization of historical narrative, 130–133
Speech, identification with politics, 73
Stewart, J. Q., 180
Stimmung, postmodern, 40–41, 56, 99–100
Stoller, Paul, 141
Strauss, Leo, 19, 25, 29
Structuralism, 179
and poststructuralist understanding, 185–188
Subjugation
and origins of domination, 69–70
of workers, 46

T

Taylor, Charles, 109–110
Theory, and political activity, 48–50, 53, 55–58
Theroux, Paul, 151
Traditionalism, 28–30
critique of, 81
Tuan, Yi–Fu, 183